IMAGES
*of Rail*

# STREET RAILWAYS OF EL PASO

**On the Cover:** In this pre-1910 view, Oregon Street stretches up the hill. No automobiles are seen yet, only three streetcars, buggies, and pedestrians. Those were the basic modes of transportation available in the pre-auto period. The first intersection visible is Main Street, which carried the mainline of the Southern Pacific Railroad, allowing trains to often block traffic as they passed through town. A little farther up the street, the El Paso and Southwestern Railway also crossed Oregon Street. Oregon Street carried streetcars for the Mesa, Sunset Heights, Arizona, Fort Bliss, Highland Park, and Government Hill lines. The middle car is passing the YMCA building. The Mills Building has not been built at the time of the photograph. (Otis Aultman photograph, courtesy of Border Heritage Center, El Paso Public Library.)

IMAGES
*of Rail*

# STREET RAILWAYS OF EL PASO

Ronald E. Dawson

ARCADIA PUBLISHING

ISBN 978-0-7385-7114-0

Published by Arcadia Publishing
Charleston, South Carolina

Printed in the United States of America

Library of Congress Control Number: 2009922895

For all general information contact Arcadia Publishing at:
Telephone 843-853-2070
Fax 843-853-0044
E-mail sales@arcadiapublishing.com
For customer service and orders:
Toll-Free 1-888-313-2665

Visit us on the Internet at www.arcadiapublishing.com

*This book is dedicated to Frank J. Mangan Jr. (1921–2009),*
*author, historian, and, more importantly, friend.*
*Frank loved El Paso, history, and streetcars.*

# Contents

# ACKNOWLEDGMENTS

The author is indebted to all the historians and photographers who have shared their insight and materials in the preparation of this work. He gratefully acknowledges and appreciates the assistance of the Paso del Norte Streetcar Preservation Society, the Southwest Chapter of the Railroad and Locomotive Historical Society, the Railroad and Transportation Museum of El Paso, the El Paso County Historical Society, and the Border Heritage Center of the El Paso Public Library. This work also would not be possible without the assistance of streetcar archivist/historian R. L. Thomas.

Unless otherwise indicated, photographs are courtesy of the collection of the Paso del Norte Streetcar Preservation Society (PDNSPS). Images credited with EPPL are courtesy of the Aultman Collection of the Border Heritage Center, El Paso Public Library.

Journal No. 4 of the Railroad and Transportation Museum of El Paso.

# INTRODUCTION

From mule cars to streamliners, El Paso has a rich history of street railways. Rail transit existed in the largest city on the Mexican border from 1882 to 1974 and in a very real way was responsible for the growth of El Paso neighborhoods.

The population of El Paso grew exponentially after the coming of the railroads in 1881. In 1880, there were only 3,845 citizens, but by 1920, El Paso had passed the 100,000 mark. The growth of Fort Bliss and the presence of the military in El Paso became a significant factor in the early 1900s, particularly after Pancho Villa's raid on Columbus, New Mexico, in 1916. All of these ingredients—the farming, the manufacturing, the mining, the commerce, and the military—stimulated the growth of the city and made mass transit a necessity.

A mule car system was established in 1882 by a group of progressive businessmen, including Solomon Schutz, J. F. Crosby, Joseph Magoffin (the mayor), A. Krakauer, and Noyes Rand. By October 1882, a bridge was constructed at the foot of Stanton Street, and mule car service began to Ciudad Juarez. El Paso would continue to plod along behind the slow and cantankerous mules until public sentiment demanded an electric car system in 1902. Built around 1865, Mule Car No. 1 survives to this day and is still considered "very original," which means it contains 80 to 90 percent unrestored and not refurbished components and materials.

A completely new system was planned and a new company established. It became the El Paso Electric Railway, a subsidiary of the Stone and Webster Corporation headquartered in Boston. Stone and Webster had a number of electric railway properties around the country and used its own construction supervisors and engineers supplemented by local laborers. After much sidewalk supervising and constant newspaper coverage, the new line was put in place on January 11, 1902, with great local pride and fanfare.

The first line was built to Juarez but was quickly followed by the Depot, Smelter, and Park lines. The streetcar company started out with eight open-air, single-truck cars, then added four more. But by the end of 1902, all 12 cars were in daily usage, and orders were placed for more cars. The system grew rapidly as more homes and businesses began to be built in the outlying areas.

There was great interest in an interurban line to Ysleta, east of El Paso. The line opened in 1913 as the Rio Grande Valley Traction Company, also a Stone and Webster company. Although the interurban was organized as a separate company, it operated under the auspices of the El Paso Electric Railway using their crews and carbarn facilities.

Another interesting line developed in the far northeast part of El Paso. Builder and developer Frank R. Tobin built the El Paso Suburban Railway. The intent was for the line to be electrified, but in the end, it used a steam dummy (a trolley body built around a steam engine) capable of pulling one or two passenger cars. The line was built to carry prospective buyers to a real estate development 5 miles beyond Fort Bliss called Tobin Place. The line began at the end of the Fort Bliss streetcar line and ran on the east side of the El Paso and Southwestern Railroad out to the Tobin development. However, real estate sales were poor, water was scarce, and the development never gained a foothold. The line existed for seven years from 1907 to 1914.

Streetcar lines continued to be built to neighborhoods. The Arizona Street line climbed around Golden Hill Terrace and ended close to the home of legendary politician A. B. Fall. Although the Arizona line was single tracked, it had passing tracks every few blocks. The Highland Park line was said to be the "crookedest streetcar line in America" since it took many turns climbing up into Highland Park in an effort to avoid steep grades. A line was built up to Madeline Park in Kern Place and was called the Mesa line although it never ran on Mesa Street, only crossing it. This line crossed a trestle near the old Dudley School on what is now Campbell Street. By 1906, Fort Bliss had grown, and a streetcar line was constructed to the post. At 6 miles, it was the electric company's longest line, not counting the days of the interurban to Ysleta. Manhattan Heights had its own line up Piedras Street to Mobile. The Smelter line passed through Sunset Heights before crossing the railroad on an overpass and dropping down to the side of Paisano Drive. A line was built out to Government Hill, ending on Roosevelt and Dover Streets. There was a shuttle to Richmond Terrace off the Government Hill line, leaving Hueco Street on Houston Street, going north to Cambridge Street, then turning back west.

Yandell Street, originally Boulevard Avenue, was double tracked and was the primary east-west route for a number of the car lines. That track was removed in 1937, and thereafter east-west lines went out Myrtle and Alameda Streets. The Fort Bliss line turned north on Piedras Street at Alameda. The Fort Bliss and Government Hill lines followed the same route up to the Alta Vista neighborhood at Hueco and Copia Streets, where they diverged. One old-timer motorman recalls splitting a switch there, the front truck of the car going on the Government Hill line and the rear truck trying to go on the Fort Bliss route.

There was a resurgence of traffic during World War II, and the company was able to pick up 10 used cars from the Houston system. At the end of 1943, the El Paso Electric Company sold its Transportation Division (streetcars and buses) to El Paso City Lines, a subsidiary of the National City Lines, a corporation owned by bus interests and notorious for converting streetcar lines to buses. City Lines then was able to discontinue streetcars on the Fort Bliss and Park lines in August 1947, leaving only the Juarez line using streetcars. The Juarez route was able to remain in streetcars because the treaty with Mexico specified street railway, and it continued to be a profitable line in any case. City Lines realized in 1950 that they were using streetcars dating as far back as 1912 and decided it was necessary to upgrade the fleet. That led the company to purchase 25 PCC-type streetcars (named after the Presidents Conference Committee).

Over the years, the El Paso PCCs carried literally millions of passengers back and forth across the border. With the realignment of the border following the Chamizal agreement between the United States and Mexico, the existing international bridges were torn down in the 1960s and new ones planned. It was expected that the streetcars would end. Surprisingly, tracks were installed in the new bridges, and the cars continued running. Problems with labor, however, caused the Mexican government to cancel the streetcar franchise and block the tracks in 1973. It has been postulated that the line was opposed by Juarez merchants as it made it too convenient for Mexican citizens to travel to El Paso to shop. If so, that would make it the only streetcar line to fail because it was too successful.

El Paso streetcars are the vehicles that, in essence, helped build a city.

# *One*

# The Mule Cars 1882–1902

Railroads came to El Paso in 1881, bringing entrepreneurs, businessmen, gunslingers, salesmen, miners, and some assorted undesirables. In any case, the population of the city burgeoned from a few hundred to several thousand in short order. City fathers soon realized the need for some type of public transit—for in those days, if people did not own a horse or buggy, they walked to wherever they needed to go. Although it is widely reported that Anson Mills was the founder and architect of the first mule car system, it was, in fact, a group of other civic leaders, including Joseph Magoffin and Noyes Rand. The most pressing need was for a bridge across the Rio Grande to Ciudad Juarez. In 1881, the river could only be crossed by ferry attached to a rope or a footbridge farther away from the town center. Although there eventually were four different companies with 13 cars and more than 40 mules, the first mule car belonged to the El Paso and Juarez Street Railway, later the El Paso and Juarez Traction Company. This was Mule Car No. 1 pulled by Mandy the mule, the town pet. Gen. Anson Mills was to come into the picture later in the early 1890s, at which time he headed a consolidation of the four companies, forcing out Zack White, who had organized the Santa Fe Street Railway. The first line was south on El Paso Street, east on Seventh Street, then crossing the river on the newly built Stanton Street Bridge. Later the Santa Fe Street Bridge was built, and a loop was established south on Stanton Street, through Juarez, and back north over the Santa Fe Street bridge to El Paso Street and San Antonio Street. The mule cars ran for 20 years from 1882 to 1902. After some infighting over whether a new electric system would be inaugurated or whether the mule car system could be electrified, it became obvious to civil engineers that mule car tracks were much too light and rickety to handle the much heavier electric cars.

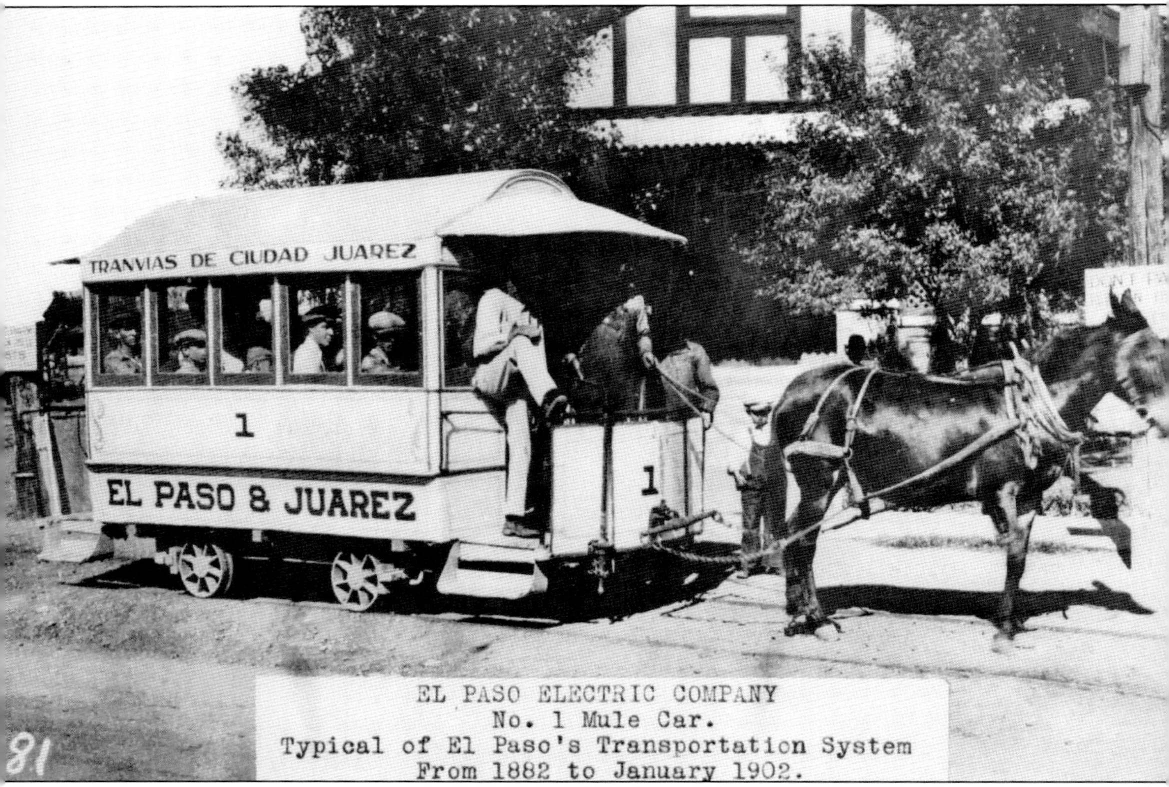


**CLASSIC MULE CAR PHOTOGRAPH.** One of the clearest images of Mule Car No. 1 is shown here on Cotton Street near the carbarn and in front of the building used as the crewmen's lounge. No. 1, built by the John Stephenson Company of New York about 1865, survives today and is in storage pending restoration. After the first electric cars were introduced in 1902, the mule car was given to W. Floyd Payne in recognition of his efforts on behalf of the street railway in securing street franchises. For a time, it was mounted on blocks in his backyard as a playhouse for his daughter. It was then returned to the El Paso Electric Railway in the 1930s and was kept on its property. J. B. Binckley, who had been a young conductor on the car before the start of the 20th century, was dismayed to find it in a dilapidated condition in 1953. He enlisted the help of the El Paso County Historical Society, and it was restored and placed on display in 1955 in San Jacinto Plaza. (Courtesy of EPPL.)

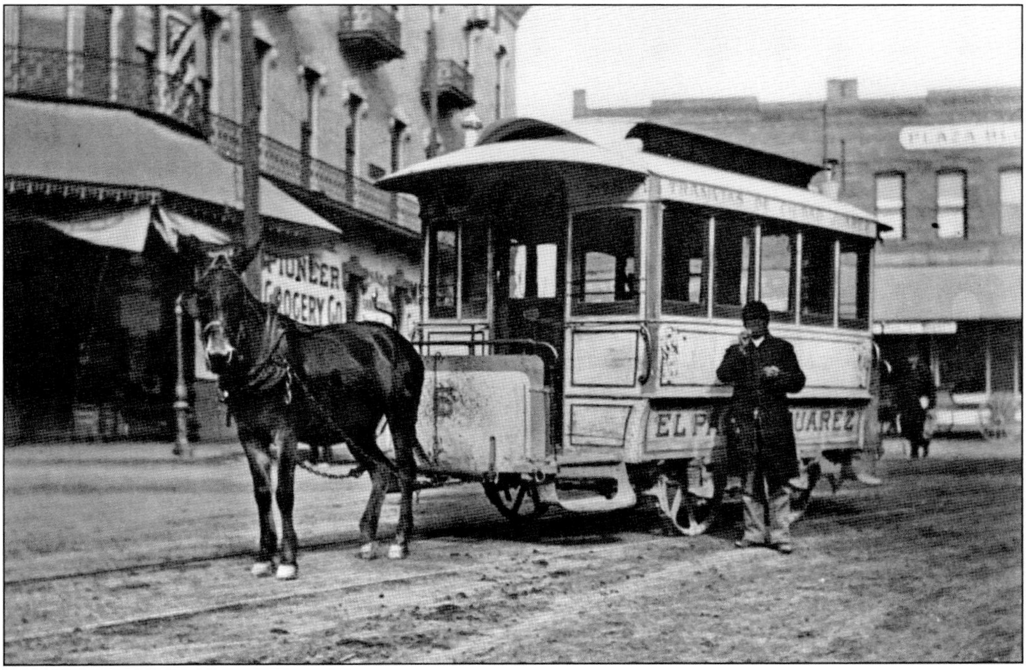


**MULE CAR NO. 5.** The driver, dressed for winter weather with an overcoat, takes a smoke break as Mule Car No. 5 pauses at the head of El Paso Street. Visible in the background is the Plaza Block in the location the Plaza Theater would eventually occupy. The mule car has just turned south from St. Louis Street (now Mills Street) and is destined for Ciudad Juarez.

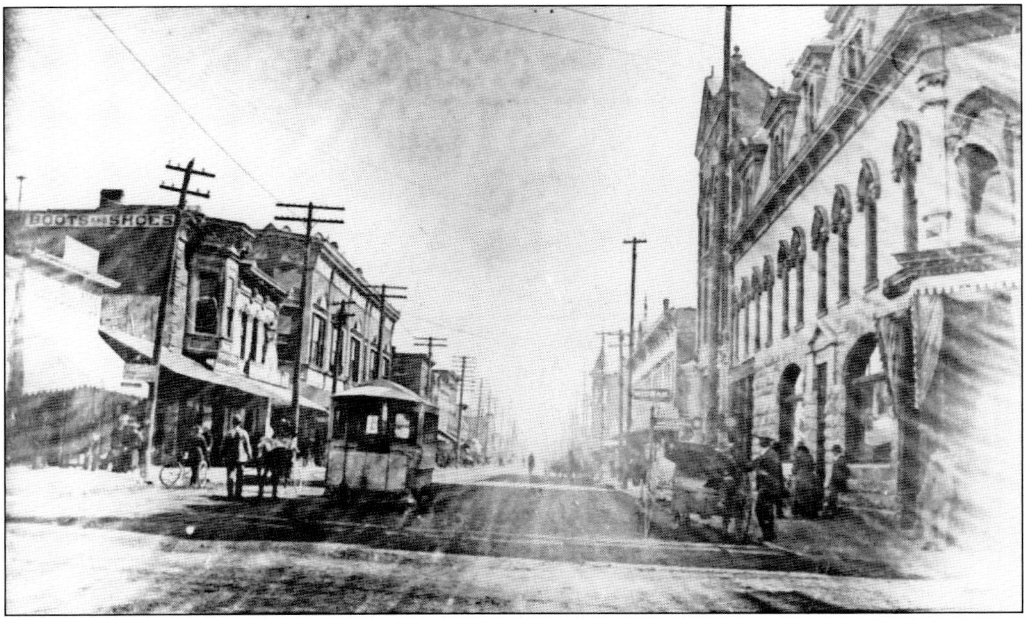


**MULE CHANGES ENDS.** In this overexposed but historically significant photograph of Mule Car No. 1, the driver is walking the mule around to the other end of the car to reattach the rigging and proceed back eastward on the San Antonio Street line. The original First National Bank Building is on the right, which once housed the law office of gunslinger John Wesley Hardin. (Courtesy of EPPL.)

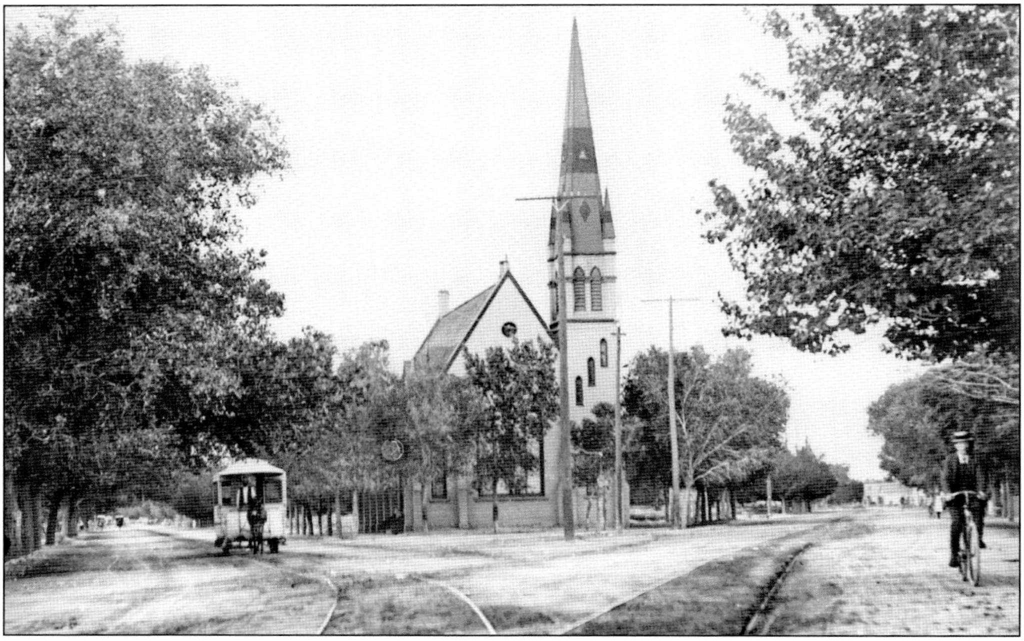

**BICYCLE-RIDING EDITOR.** The bicycle rider is believed to be S. H. Newman, editor of the *Lone Star* newspaper, riding to work in a suit and vest. He is at the intersection of Magoffin Avenue and San Antonio Street. The original First Baptist Church is in the background. A mule car, possibly No. 1 judging from the roofline, is approaching the intersection. The rickety condition of the light rail is evident. (Courtesy of EPPL.)

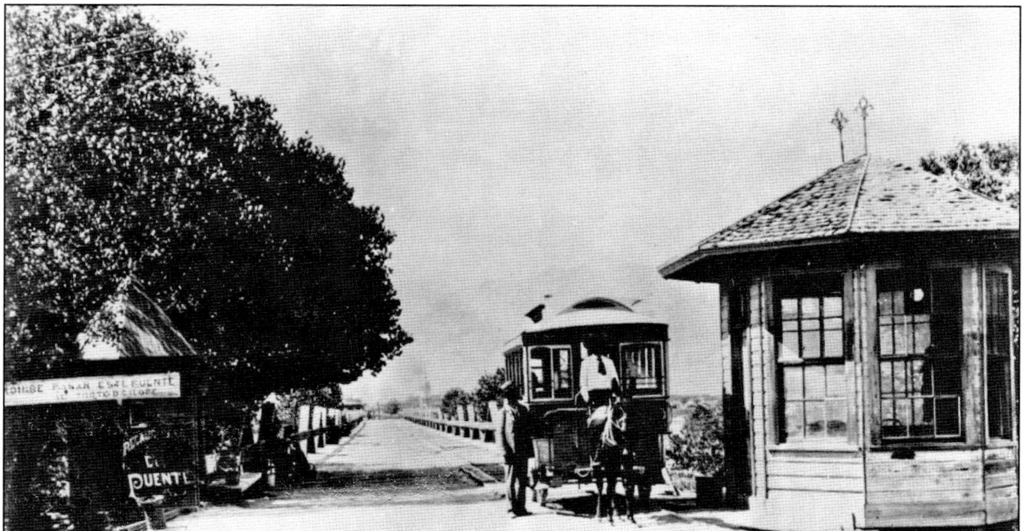

**INTERNATIONAL MULE CAR.** This is an 1880s or 1890s photograph of a mule car from El Paso passing over the Stanton Street international bridge and arriving at the Mexican customs checkpoint. The uniformed customs official visits with the driver in the summer heat. The leisurely pace of the round-trip to Mexico took more than an hour.

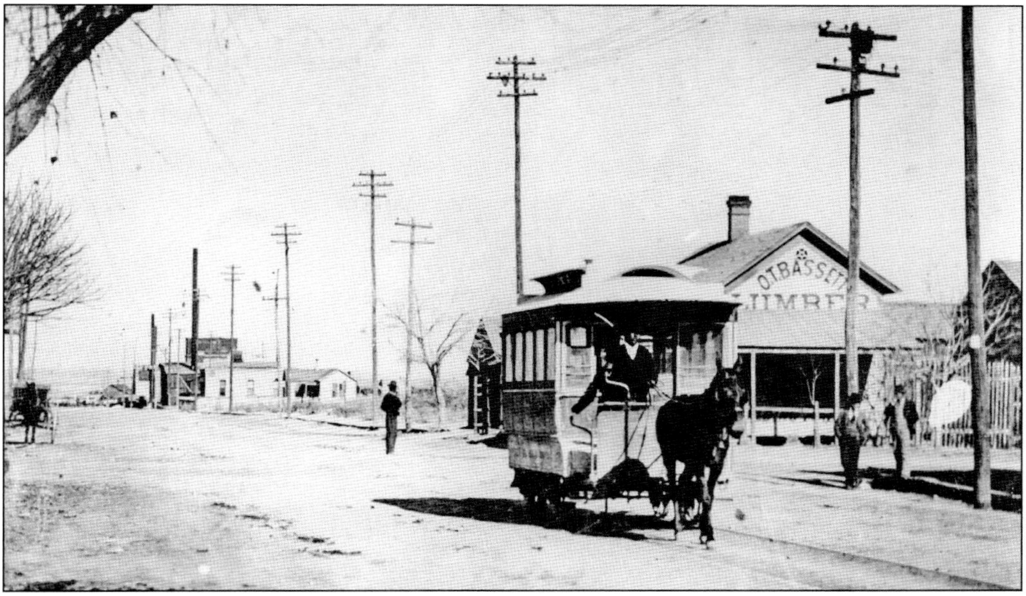

**O. T. Bassett Lumber.** This mule car is shown in what later would become the middle of downtown, passing the O. T. Bassett Lumber Company on Mills Street. Bassett would later build El Paso's first skyscraper in 1930, the Bassett Tower on Texas Avenue, designed by famed architect Henry Trost. This mule car is likely coming from the Southern Pacific train station on Kansas Street before the Union Depot was built. (Courtesy of EPPL.)

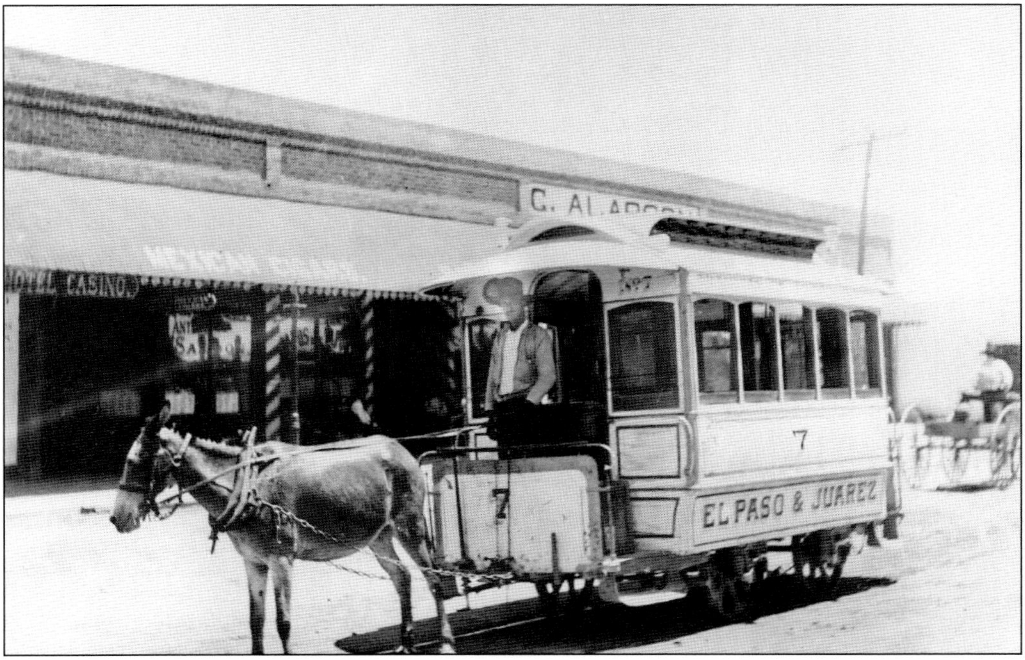


**Mule Car No. 7.** Here an unidentified driver pauses No. 7 on Avenida Constitucion in Ciudad Juarez around 1900, two years before the advent of electric car service. Note the "Bombay" type roof, indicating it was built after 1870. By the beginning of the 20th century, the mule car track and rolling stock were in relatively dilapidated condition, occasioning frequent rider complaints and newspaper editorials calling for electric cars.

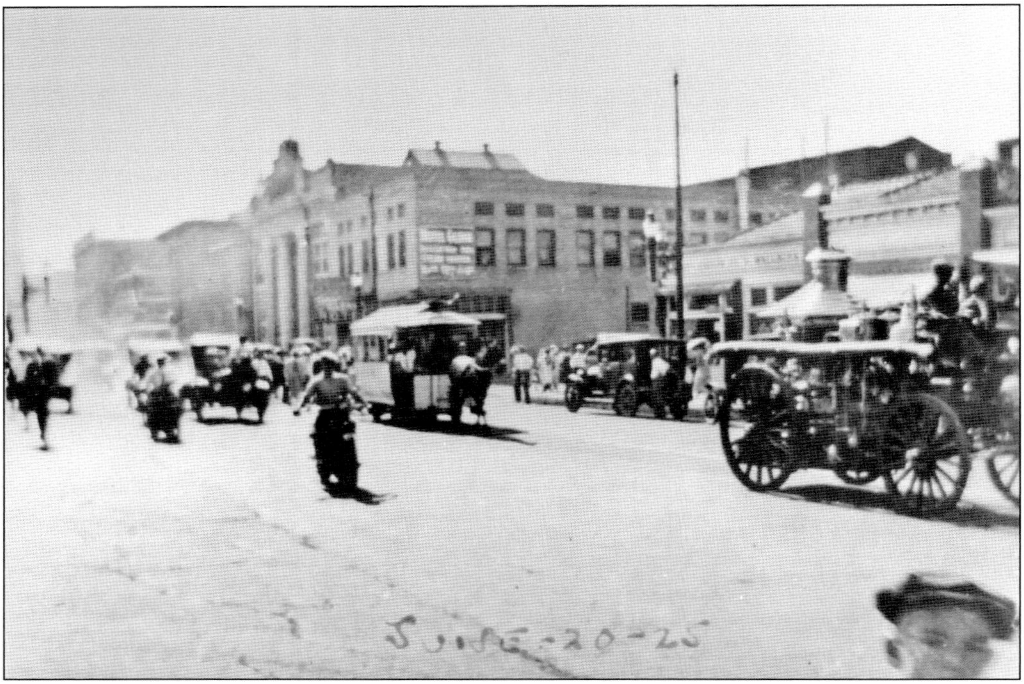

**A 1925 Parade.** In 1925, when Alves Dixon of the El Paso Electric Railway was promoted to another position in the Stone and Webster group of electric railways, old Mule Car No. 1 was taken out of retirement to be in the parade to carry Dixon to the Union Passenger Depot for his departure. In this view (above), the parade is making its way down San Francisco Street with the horse-drawn fire wagon in the lead. Following is the mule car, a variety of autos, and a streetcar. Another view (below) shows the assembled dignitaries in front of Union Passenger Station, more commonly known as Union Depot. From left to right are unidentified, Lee Newman, unidentified driver, Alves Dixon, Will Burges, and two unidentified. (Both, courtesy of EPPL.)

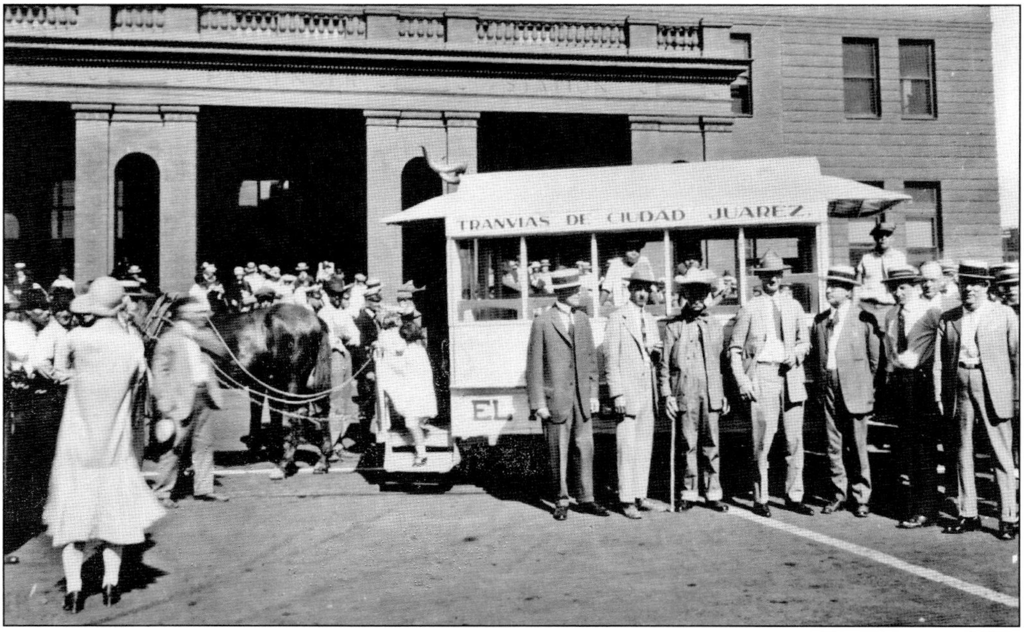

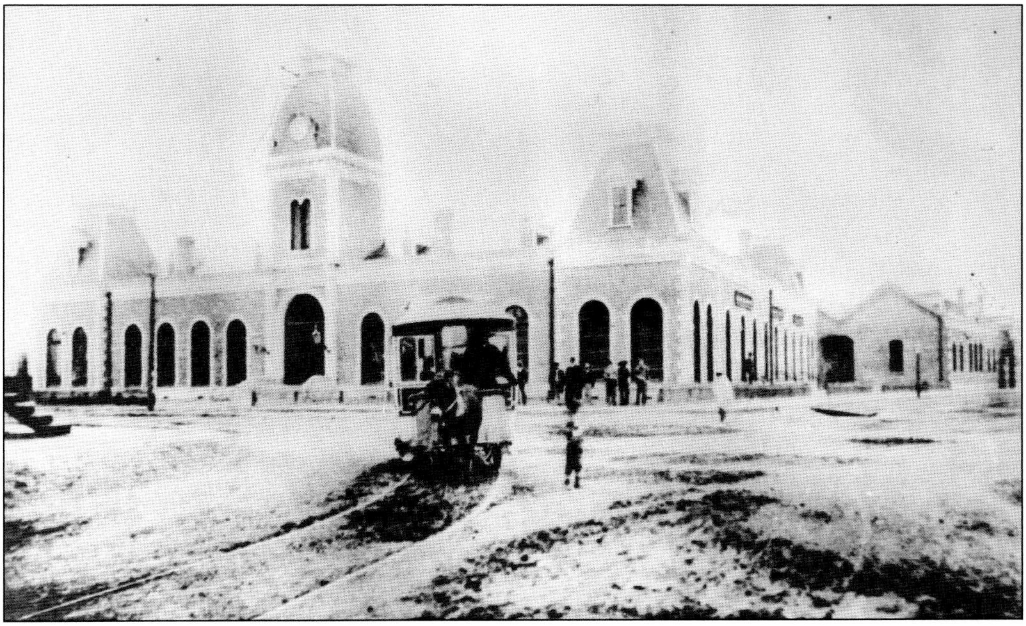

**Customs House in Mule Car Days.** This 1880s view shows a mule car rounding the corner near the Juarez Customs House on Avenida 16 de Septiembre at Avenida Juarez. After moving south on Juarez Avenue, the car will cross the Santa Fe Street Bridge, angle over to El Paso Street, and continue down to the El Paso town center.

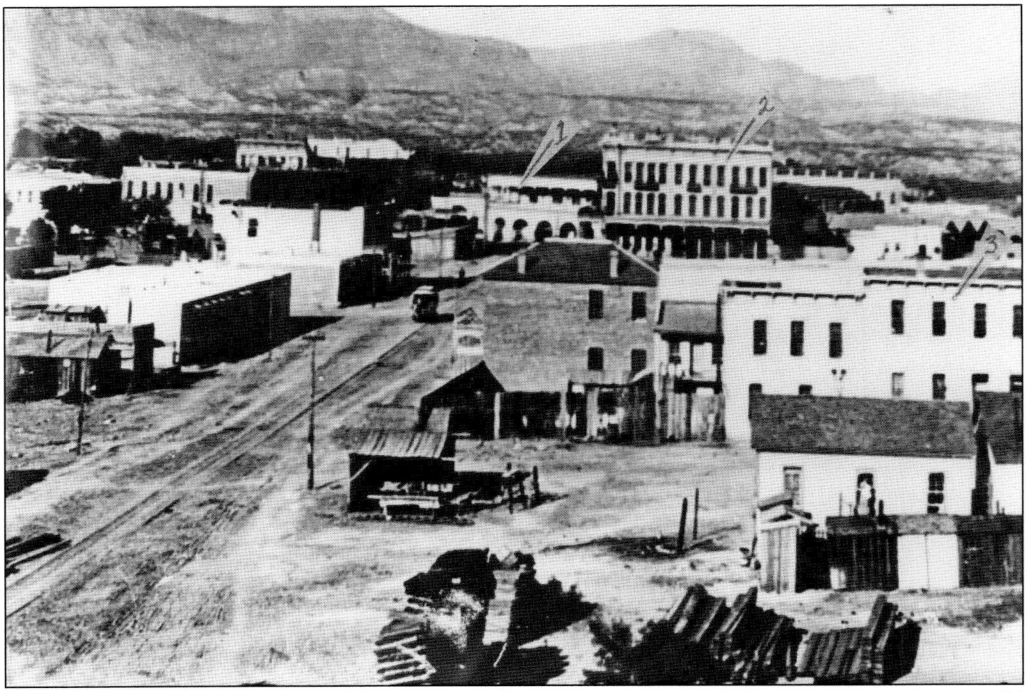


**El Paso in 1884.** This early view shows a mule car coming toward the camera on what would become Mills Street. In the background are hotels: (1) the Central, (2) the Grand Central, and (3) the Pacific. The thin mule car tracks were often covered with dirt and debris on the unpaved streets.

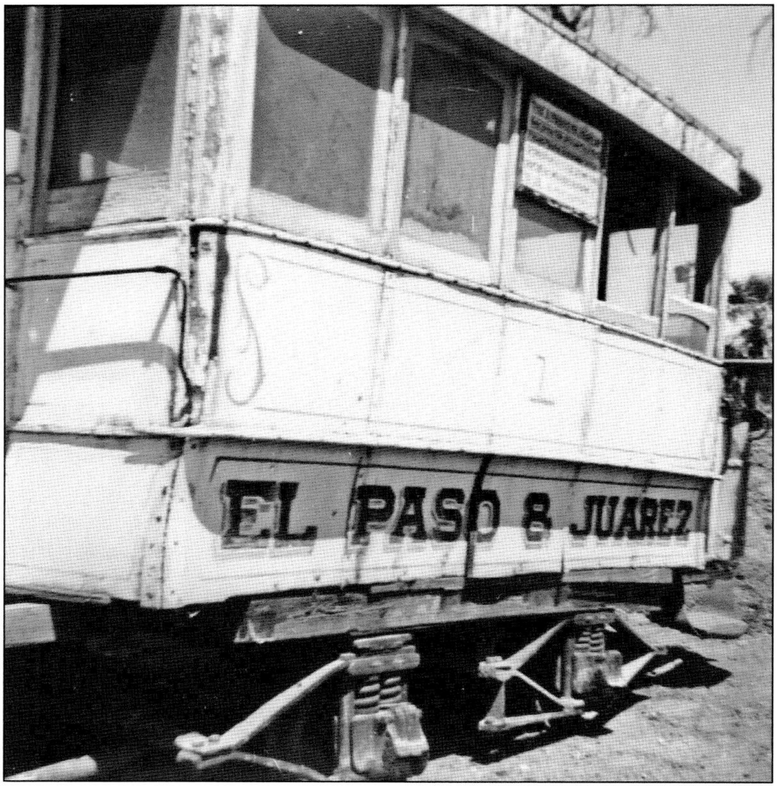


**No. 1's Running Gear.** The trucks under No. 1 in this 1950s photograph are not original. In fact, it appears that Mule Car No. 1 had at least three wheel sets over the years. This is apparently the wheel set fabricated for the mule car sometime after the 1925 parade. To fit, one side of the springs of one wheel set had to be truncated and the body shimmed up.

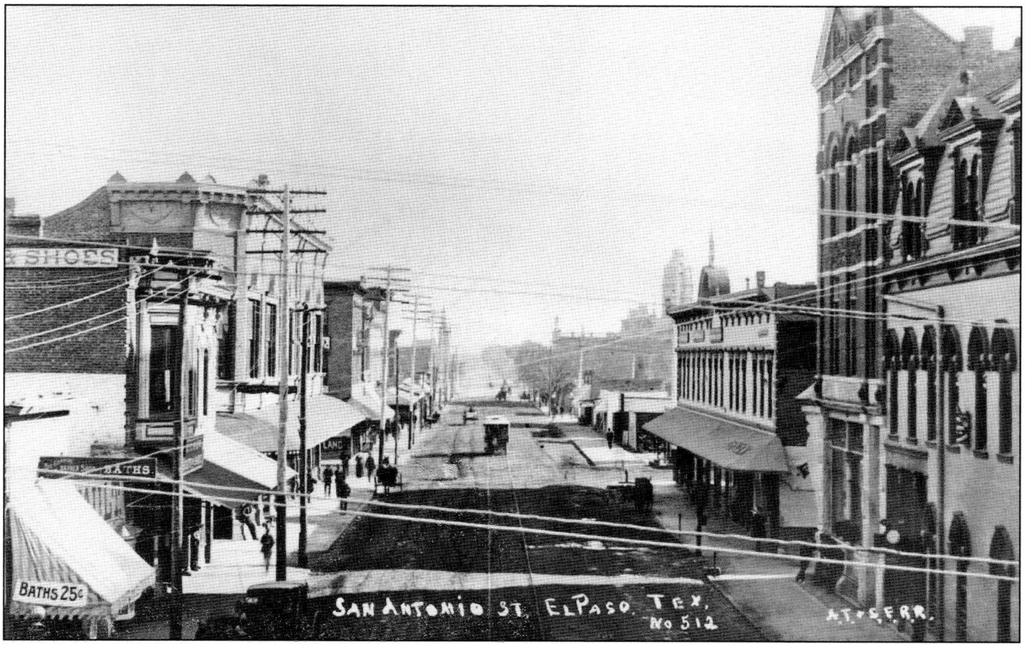


**A Dusty San Antonio Street.** Only horses, wagons, and a mule car are visible in this 1880s or 1890s view of San Antonio Street. In the distance (right) is the Victorian El Paso County Courthouse. The barbershop (left) is offering baths for a quarter, and the Santa Fe Railroad has a ticket office in the building in the right foreground. (Courtesy of EPPL.)

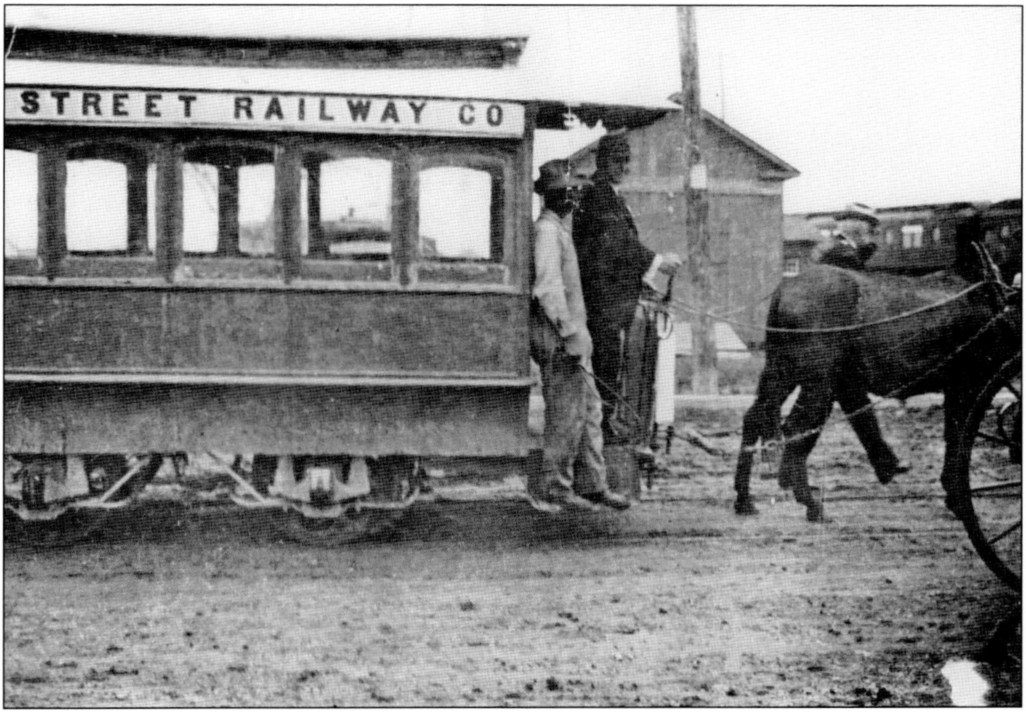


**City Street Railway.** In the only known image of the City Street Railway, a car is seen traveling on what appears to be Santa Fe Street near the Santa Fe Railway depot. The four mule car companies were consolidated in the early 1890s under the auspices of Anson Mills.

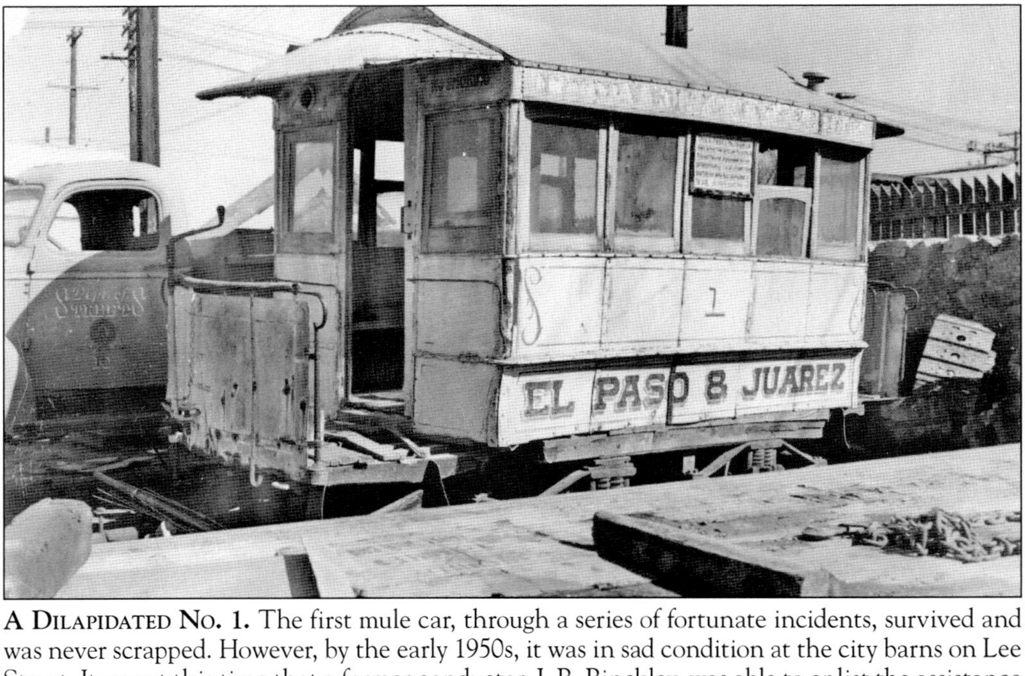


**A Dilapidated No. 1.** The first mule car, through a series of fortunate incidents, survived and was never scrapped. However, by the early 1950s, it was in sad condition at the city barns on Lee Street. It was at this time that a former conductor, J. B. Binckley, was able to enlist the assistance of the El Paso County Historical Society to restore the old mule car.

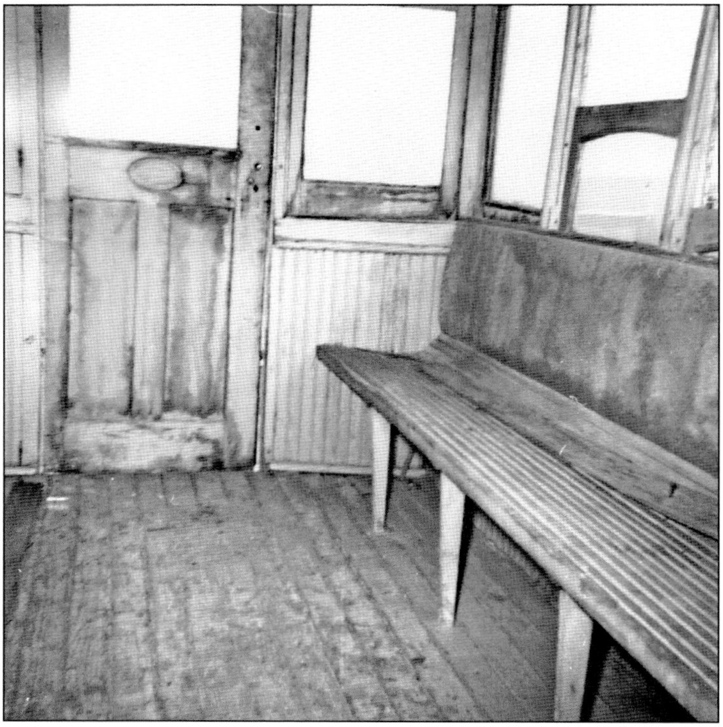

**Mule Car Interior.** This photograph, taken in the 1950s before the restoration of the mule car, shows the spartan wood bench interior and the remarkable state of preservation of the components of the car. The car was heated in the winter by an iron stove at one end with a chimney that protruded through the roof.

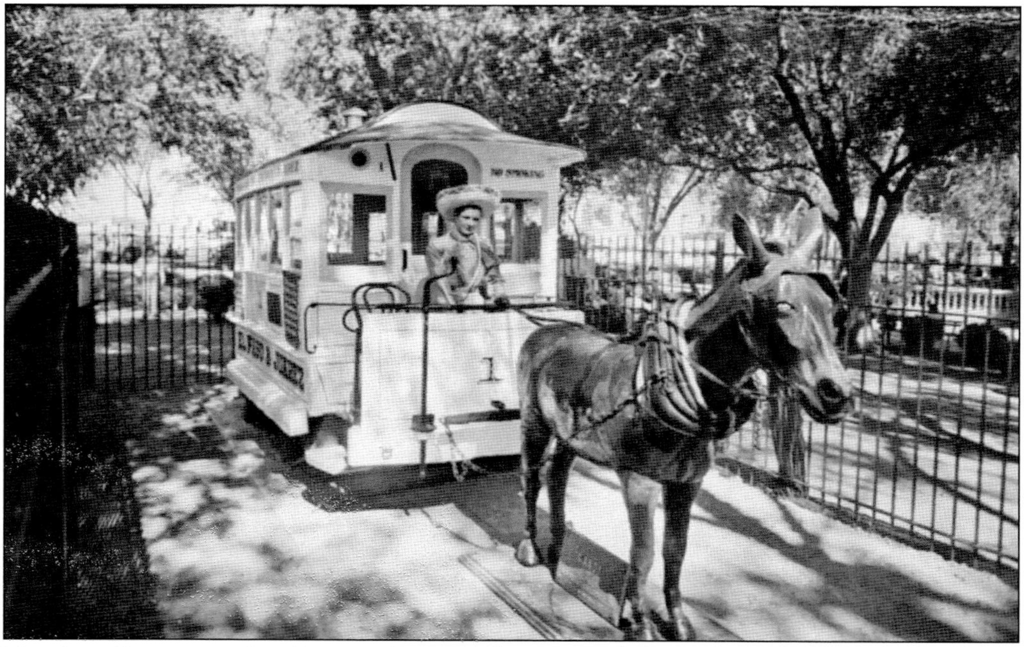


**No. 1 on Display in San Jacinto Plaza.** This postcard shows Mule Car No. 1 on display in the city's central plaza after the 1955 restoration by the El Paso County Historical Society. The society raised the funds for the restoration and the casting of the mule sculpture. The mold for the bronze sculpture of the mule was done by two Texas Western College students at the time, James Goodman and Howard Hoffman. Other local businesses contributed the mule rigging and clothing for the mannequin of the driver.

# *Two*

# Interurban to Ysleta and the Tobin Railway

Ysleta, 9 miles east of El Paso, had once been the county seat and was the next largest settlement to the east. Local business leaders began to agitate for an electric interurban to connect the city to Lower Valley settlements and to Ysleta. Stone and Webster, after much hesitation, finally agreed to construct the line if citizens of El Paso could raise $60,000 in capital and secure a 50-foot right-of-way on the proposed route. The right-of-way was obtained with the exception of a few hold-outs, but only $12,000 in capital was raised. Stone and Webster reduced the amount required to $15,000, and local businessmen pledged the remaining amount, allowing construction to begin.

The interurban to Ysleta allowed El Pasoans not only to commute to Ysleta, but also the opportunity to get out of the city. Four large and fast 44-passenger interurban cars were bought from the St. Louis Car Company in 1913 and operated hourly from Union Depot in El Paso to the center of Ysleta. The cars entered and left El Paso on the Park line. Farther east, the line often followed the banks of the Franklin Canal. Since the cars were single enders, they made a loop at Union Depot and probably used a loop at Ysleta to turn for the return trip. Unfortunately, the areas it served were too sparsely populated, and enough traffic was never generated to make the line profitable. Thirty-two passenger single-truck Birneys were substituted on the line, and in 1925, it was cut back to Ascarate. In 1929, the line to Ysleta was abandoned altogether, and the streetcar route then terminated on Alameda Street across from the well-known Del Camino Courts, with its famous Bullfighter Café.

Frank Tobin's El Paso Suburban Railway was short-lived and only operated a steam dummy from the end of the Fort Bliss streetcar line 5 miles out to Tobin Place, where he had created a real estate development. After 1914 and Tobin's death, the line folded.

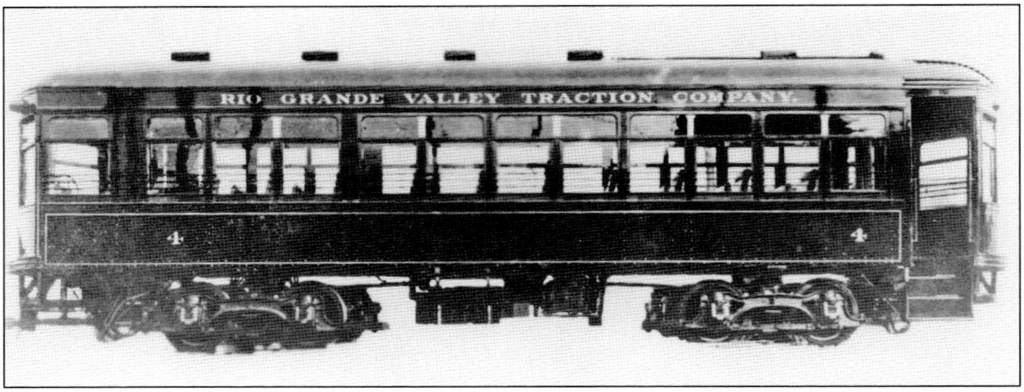


**INTERURBAN NO. 4.** This photograph of Rio Grande Valley Traction Company No. 4 is likely a builder's photograph as no trolley pole has yet been installed on the interurban. In the early years of the El Paso–to–Ysleta interurban, the cars operated hourly from each end of the line, one leaving from the center of Ysleta and another from Union Depot in El Paso.

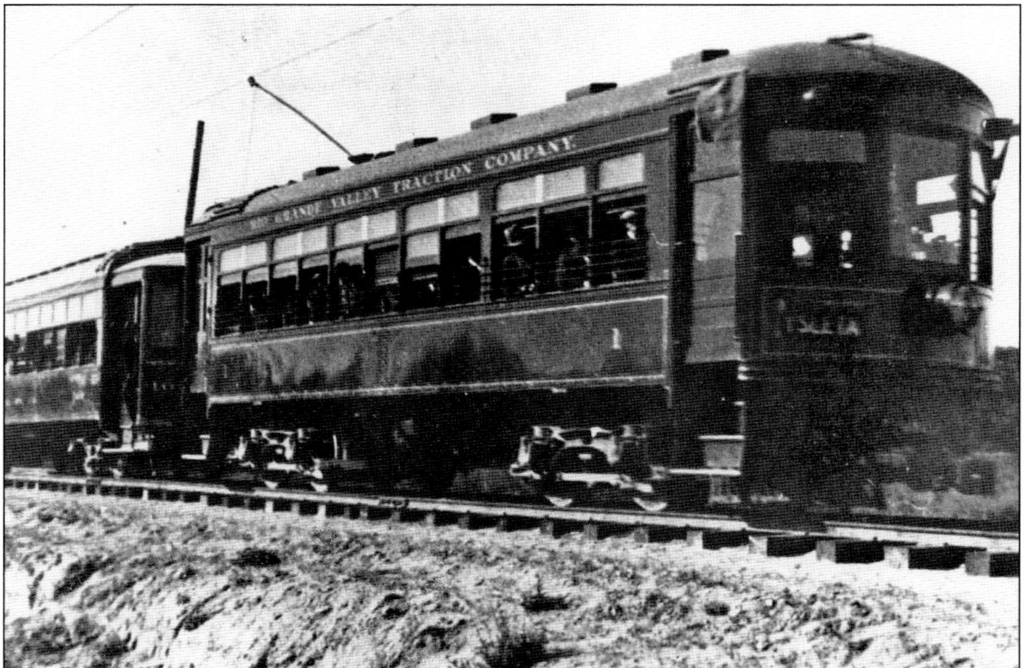


**NO. 1 AT SPEED IN THE COUNTRYSIDE.** Initially there were four of the large new interurbans operating on the line. Here is No. 1 at speed. It was able to attain 60 miles per hour easily with its 200-horsepower motors. The interurban is pulling an unpowered trailer similar to the Stone and Webster roof types received in 1912 and 1914.

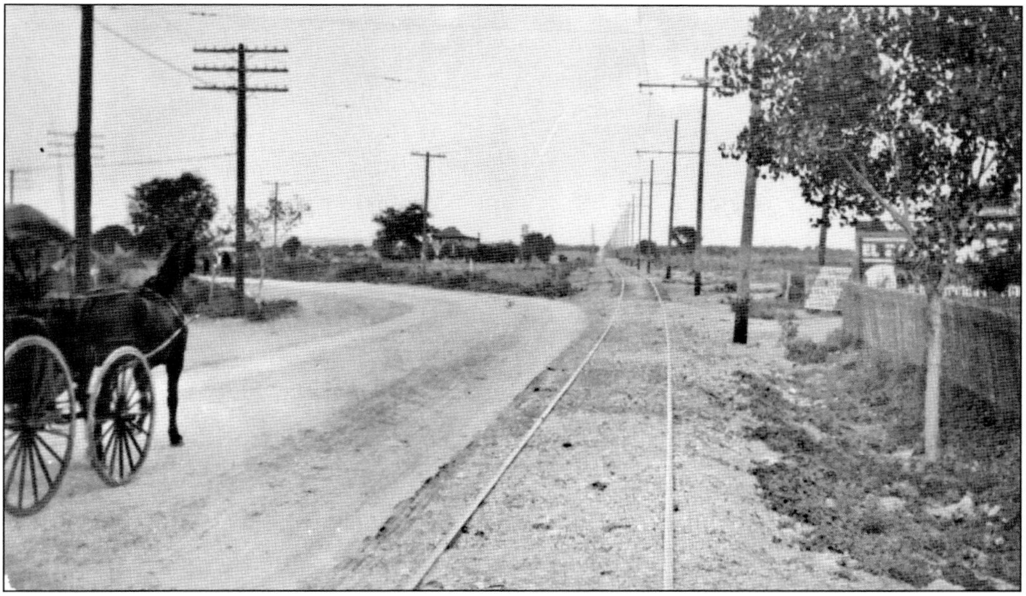

**Interurban Right-of-Way.** In this scene, the interurban leaves the side of the road and heads off into the countryside. Notice the lightly ballasted track, unlike that of a Class 1 railroad. The horse and buggy at the left is still the transportation of choice for many families. Electricity had come to many rural areas by this time.

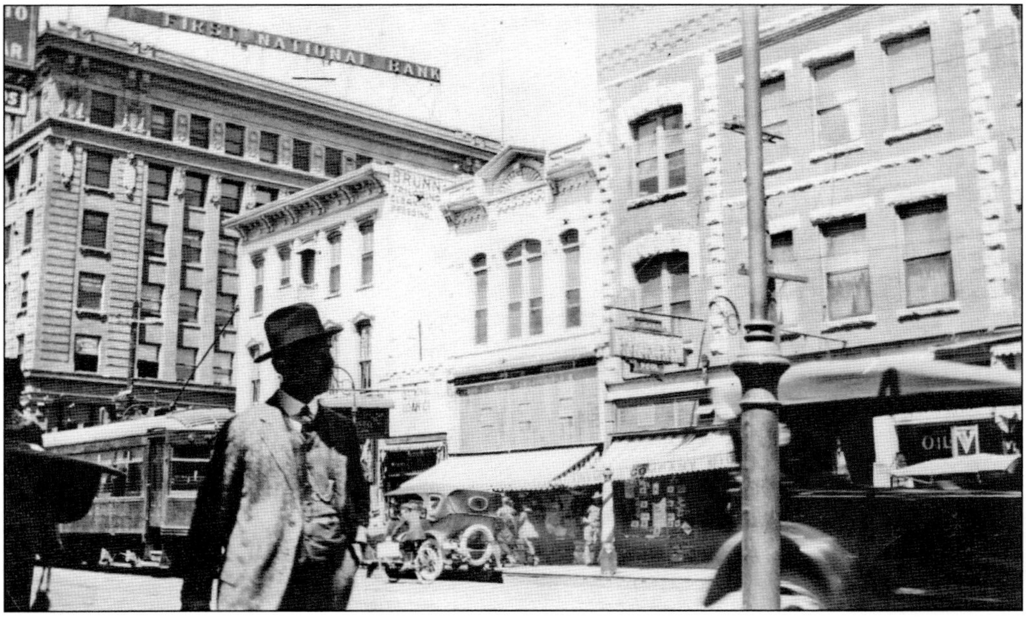


**Interurban on a Downtown Street.** This scene, believed to be taken in the early 1920s, features the Curry Building, built about 1884, in the foreground, and the First National Bank Building, built in 1916, in the background. This building later became American Furniture. The interurban car is passing behind the gentleman thought to be a Dr. Higgins and is on its way to the Union Depot.

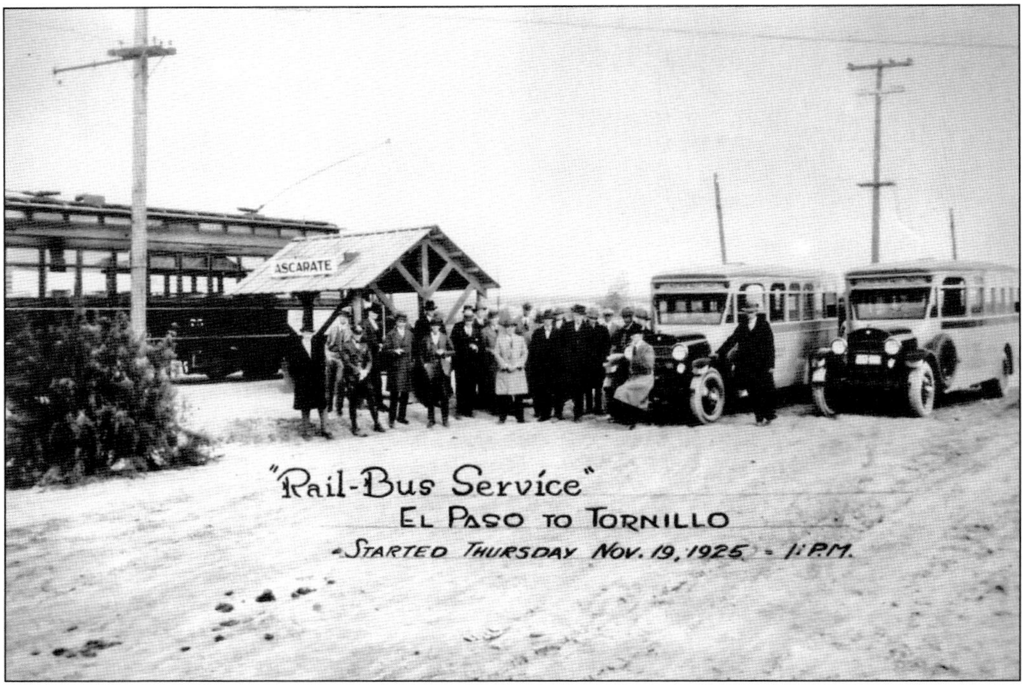


**RAIL-BUS SERVICE.** In 1925, the interurban line was cut back to Ascarate, and thereafter, buses covered the remainder of the route to Ysleta, Clint, Fabens, and Tornillo. Car No. 75 is covering the service on this November 21, 1925, date. By this time, two of the original interurbans have already been sent down to another Stone and Webster property, the Galveston-Houston Interurban Railway. (Courtesy of EPPL.)

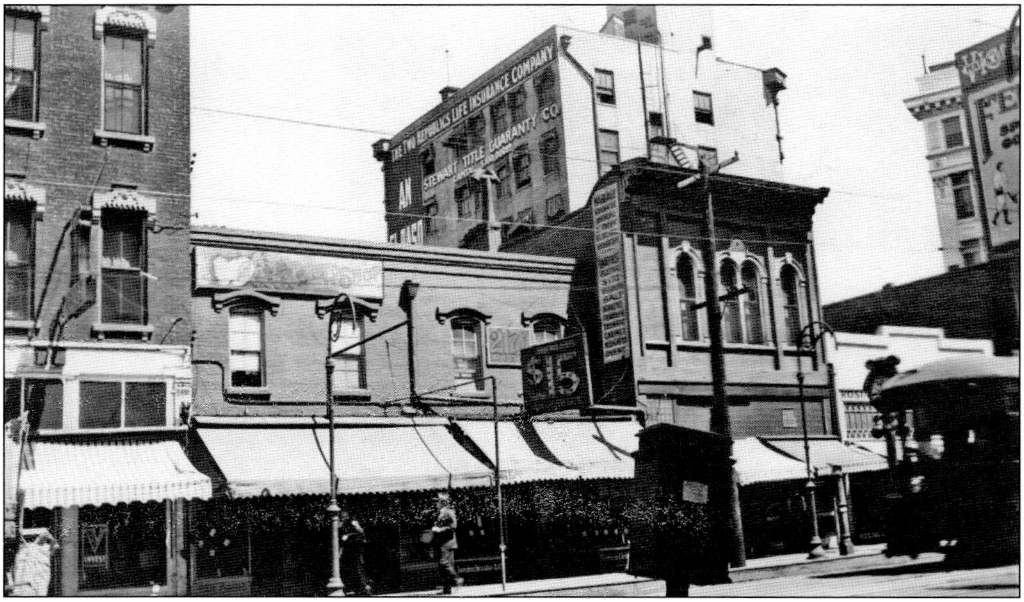


**THE 200 BLOCK OF EAST SAN ANTONIO STREET.** Here is a view of an interurban just entering the photograph frame on the right. The building in front of the interurban is the Hills Building, said to be the first two-story brick building built in El Paso. The tall building at the back is the Rio Grande Valley National Bank, fronting on Mesa Street.

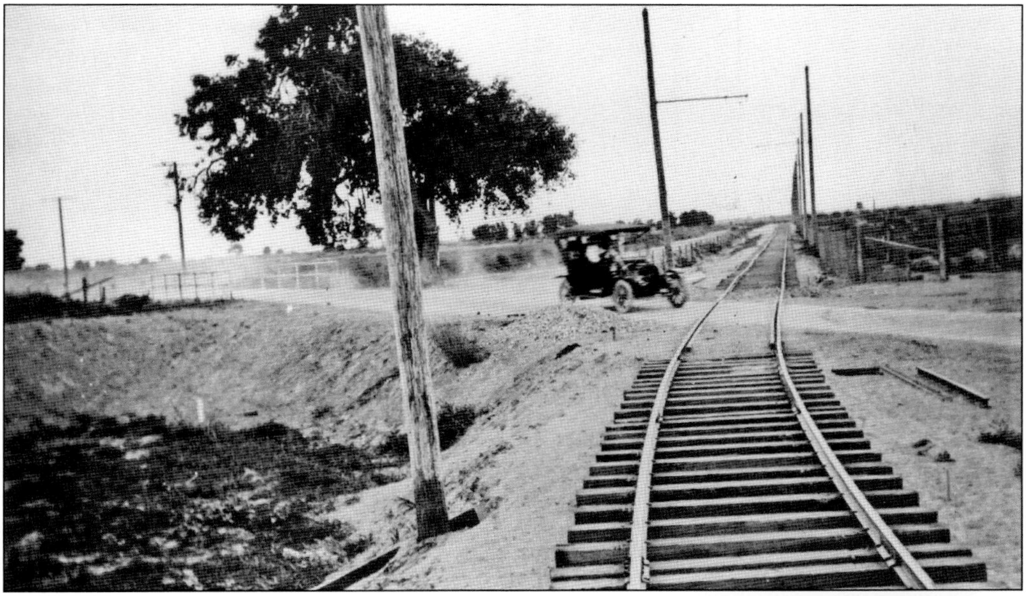

**INTERURBAN GRADE CROSSING.** Motorists in the 1920s were as careless about safety then as drivers are now. Witness this roadster racing to cross the tracks before the arrival of the interurban car. At this point, the rails follow the banks of the Franklin Canal for much of the way to Ysleta.

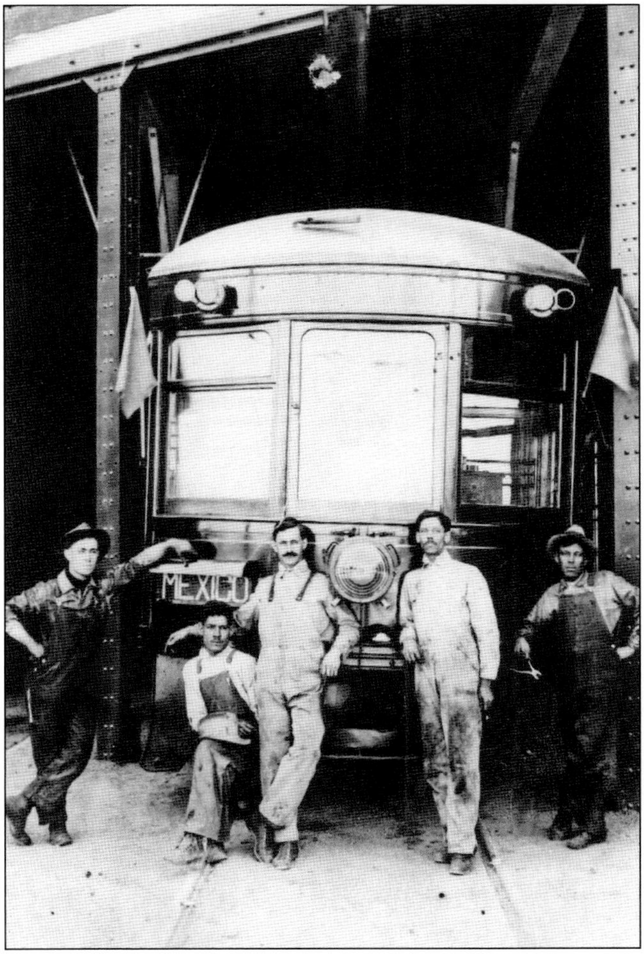


**AN INTERURBAN CAR IN THE BARN.** Four carbarn maintenance workers pose for the camera in front of one of the four big interurban cars. It is signed for Mexico and carries white flags, indicating it is an extra movement. After the closure of the line to Ysleta, this car might have been used on the Juarez line; however, it was built for high speeds, not just for city streets.

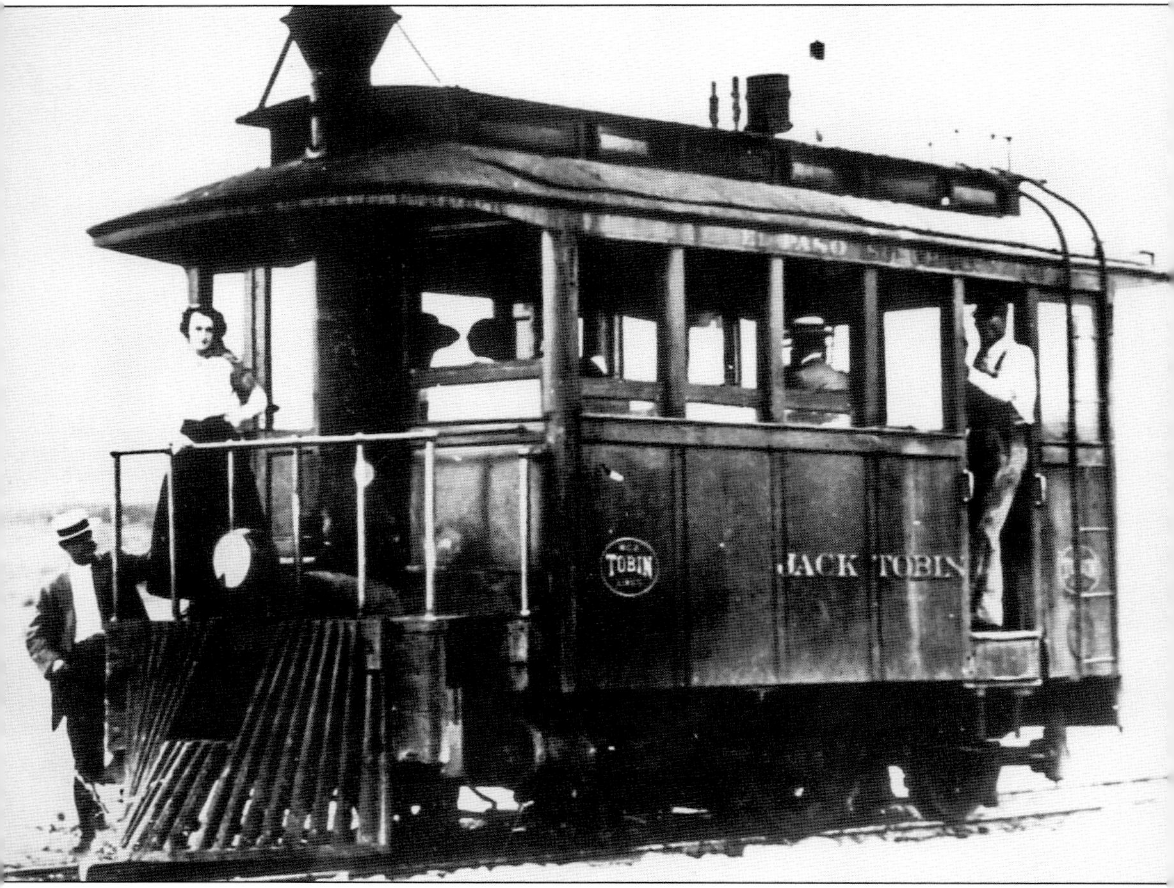


**The El Paso Suburban Railway.** This steam dummy trolley is named *Jack Tobin* for the son of the railway owner and real estate developer Frank R. Tobin. Steam dummies had trolley-like bodies to carry passengers and were propelled by a steam engine, obviating the need for building overhead catenary. Being that close to the boiler must have been uncomfortable for riders in the summer months. (Courtesy of EPPL.)

# *Three*

# Early Electric and Open Cars

Everything changed in El Paso on January 11, 1902. That was the day of the institution of the new electric railway system. After all the infighting over which company would build the system and where, it was finally ready to go. On that day there was a grand celebration and parade. Two new single-truck open streetcars pushed a flatcar carrying Mandy the mule. Along the side of the flat was a banner announcing "A Reward for 35 Years of Faithful Service." Since Mandy had only worked 20 years in El Paso, it was reported she had worked in San Antonio 15 years prior to coming to El Paso. On the new cars were the mayor and council plus invited dignitaries. The trip across to Juarez was made without incident, and the system was dubbed a success. The public was unaware that company officials had made a test run the night before to ascertain that everything was in order for the big day. The early cars were almost entirely open nine-bench cars with canvas curtains, which could be lowered in inclement weather. The cars provided a much quicker and smoother ride than did the mule cars. By 1907, closed double-truck cars were being ordered to handle the increasing traffic demands. In its first years, the system was an unqualified success.

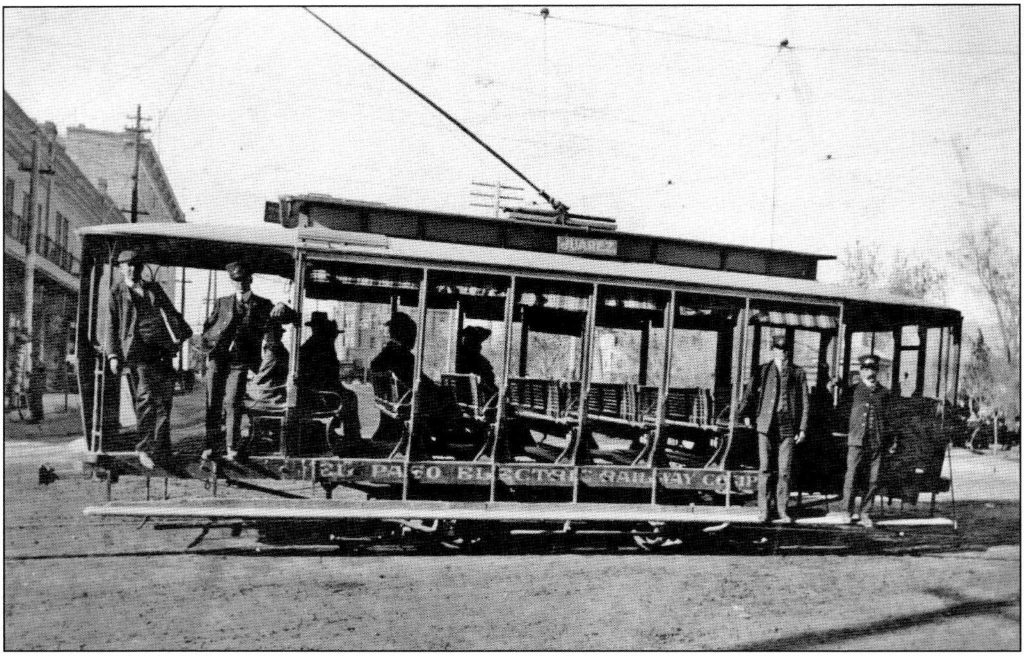


**First Electric Car.** This open car, built by the American Car Company in St. Louis, is one of an order of eight such cars arriving in January 1902 to inaugurate electric car service in El Paso. This car is posed at the intersection of St. Louis Avenue (later Mills Street) and Oregon Street with San Jacinto Plaza on the right.

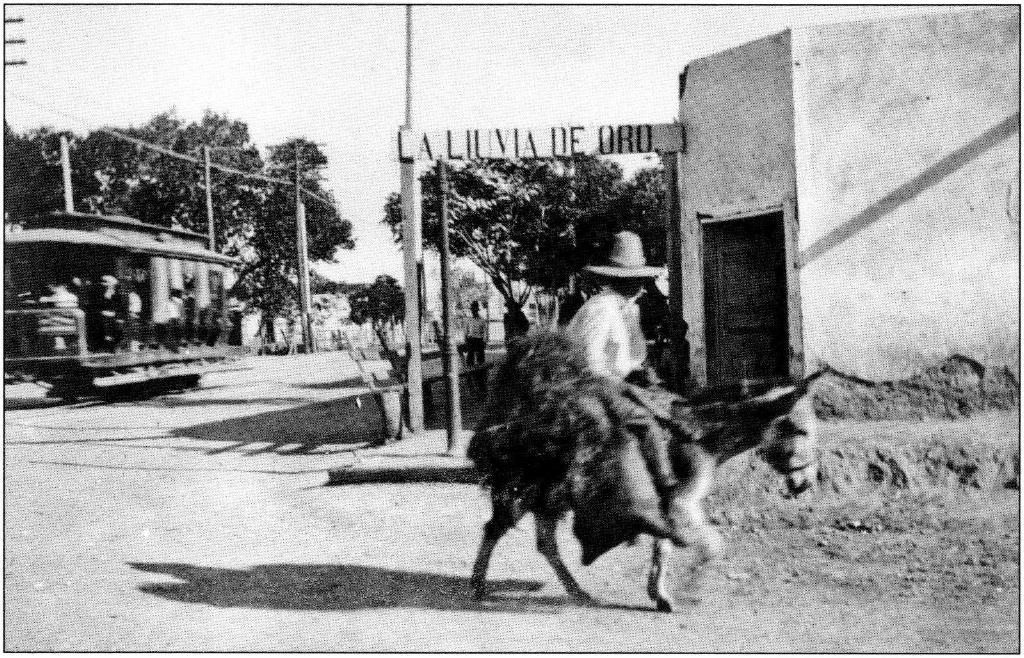


**No. 1 and a Mule.** Old and new modes of transportation are contrasted here in this 1902 view taken in Ciudad Juarez. No. 1, the first electric car, whizzes by in a blur as a Mexican citizen plods along with his load of hay or grain. The translation of the establishment La Lluvia de Oro is "The Golden Rain."

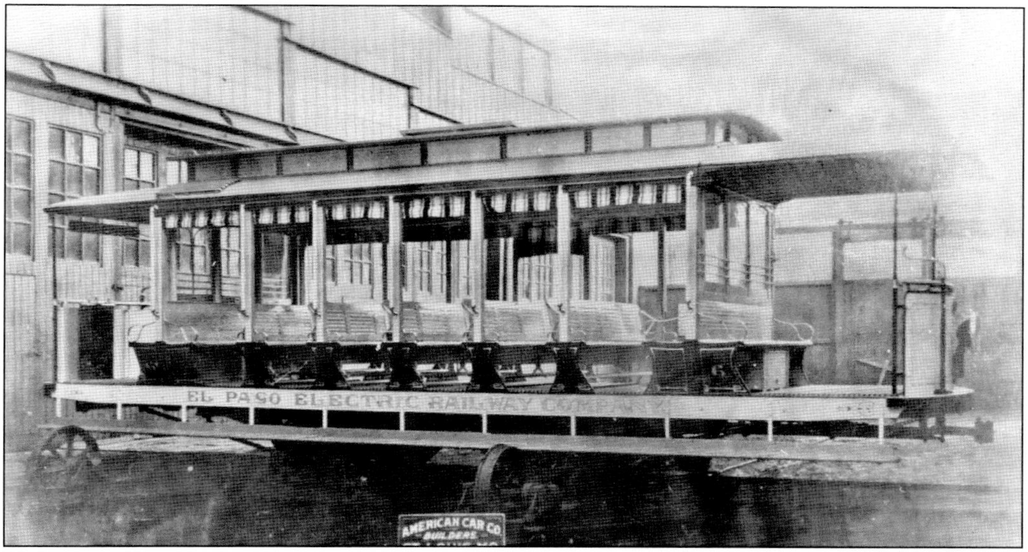


**First Open Cars.** This early open, nine-bench electric car is shown here in a builder's photograph from the American Car Company in St. Louis. Cars were typically shipped without trolley poles installed to avoid clearance problems. The cars were shipped on railroad flatcars, and the poles were then installed at the company shop in El Paso.

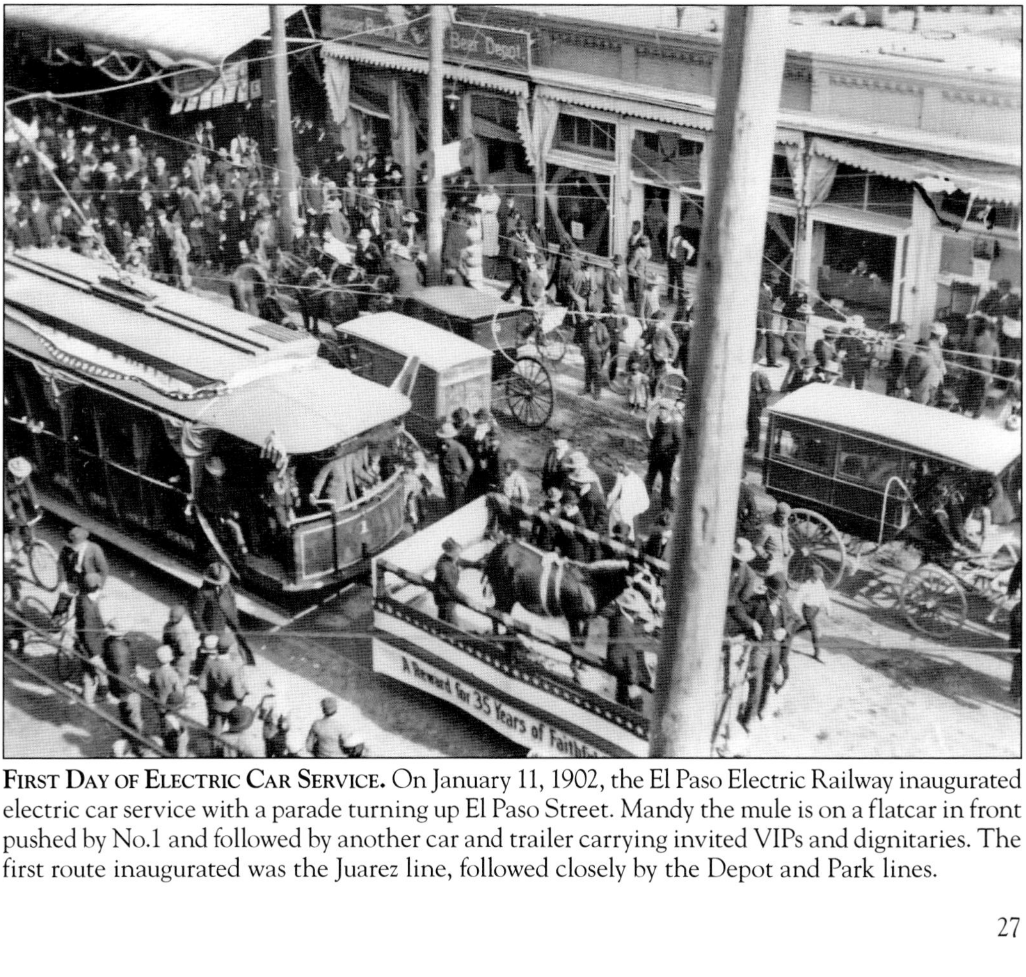


**First Day of Electric Car Service.** On January 11, 1902, the El Paso Electric Railway inaugurated electric car service with a parade turning up El Paso Street. Mandy the mule is on a flatcar in front pushed by No.1 and followed by another car and trailer carrying invited VIPs and dignitaries. The first route inaugurated was the Juarez line, followed closely by the Depot and Park lines.

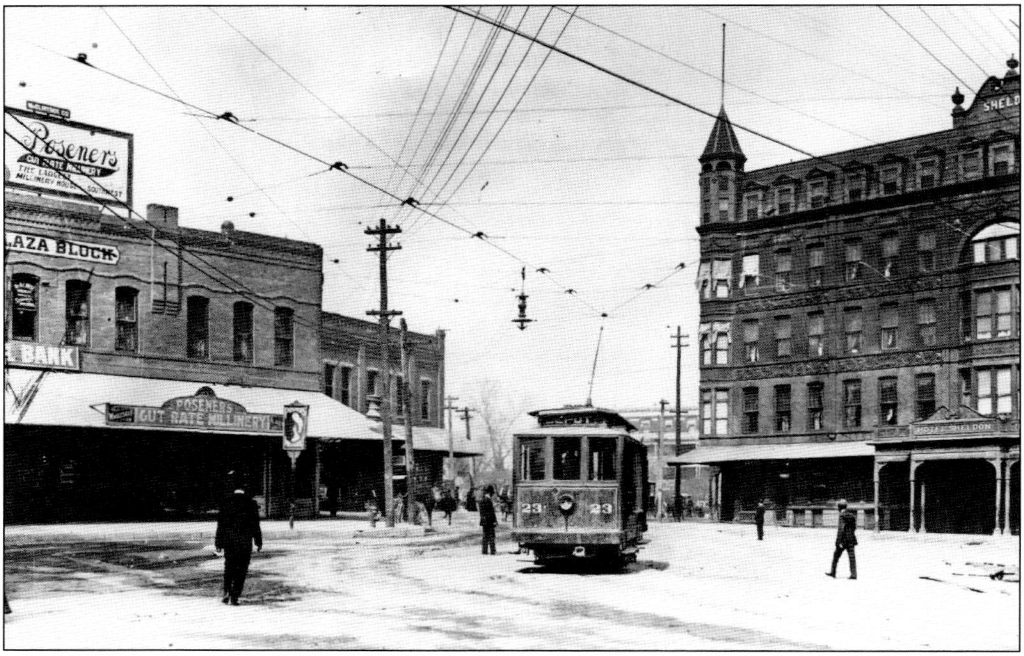


**DEPOT CAR NO. 23.** Open car 23 passes through Pioneer Plaza, also known as Little Plaza, on the Depot line with the Sheldon Hotel in the background. Note that the trolley pole is at the junction of the overhead wire for San Francisco and El Paso Streets. If properly engineered, the front part of the car will swing right, causing the pole to take the right wire. (Courtesy of EPPL.)

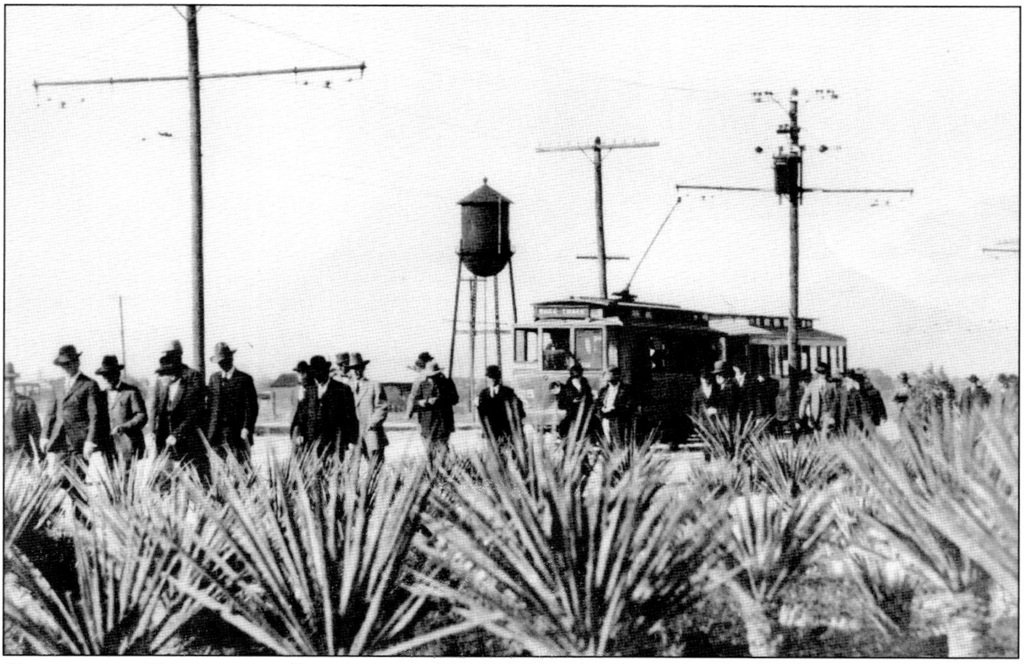

**CARS TO THE RACETRACK.** Semi-convertible car No. 25 unloads patrons at the Juarez Hipodromo racetrack. The second car is a trailer as it has no trolley pole or motor. The El Paso Electric Railway constructed a branch line off its Juarez line to serve the racetrack about 1910. The line lasted until 1945. (Courtesy of EPPL.)

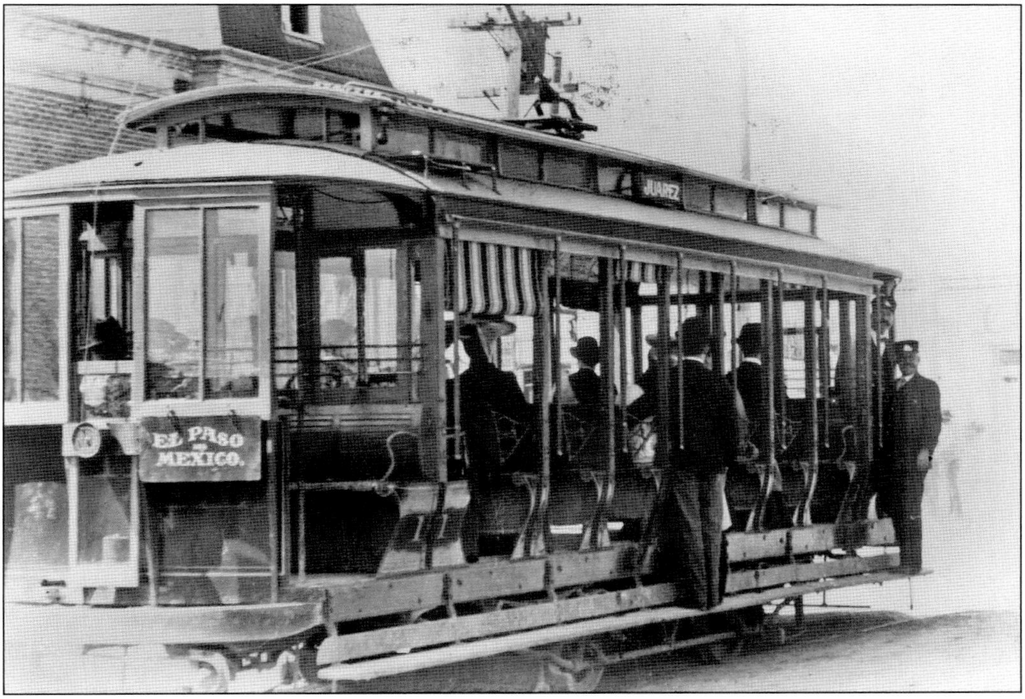


**CAR NO. 1 AT THE JUAREZ CUSTOMS HOUSE.** Car No. 1, an open, nine-bench car, is shown in the early 1900s on the Juarez line. Patrons in those days seemed to wear heavy clothing even in warm weather. By the end of the first year, crowds had necessitated the purchase of additional cars. The conductor stands on the running board. (Courtesy of EPPL.)

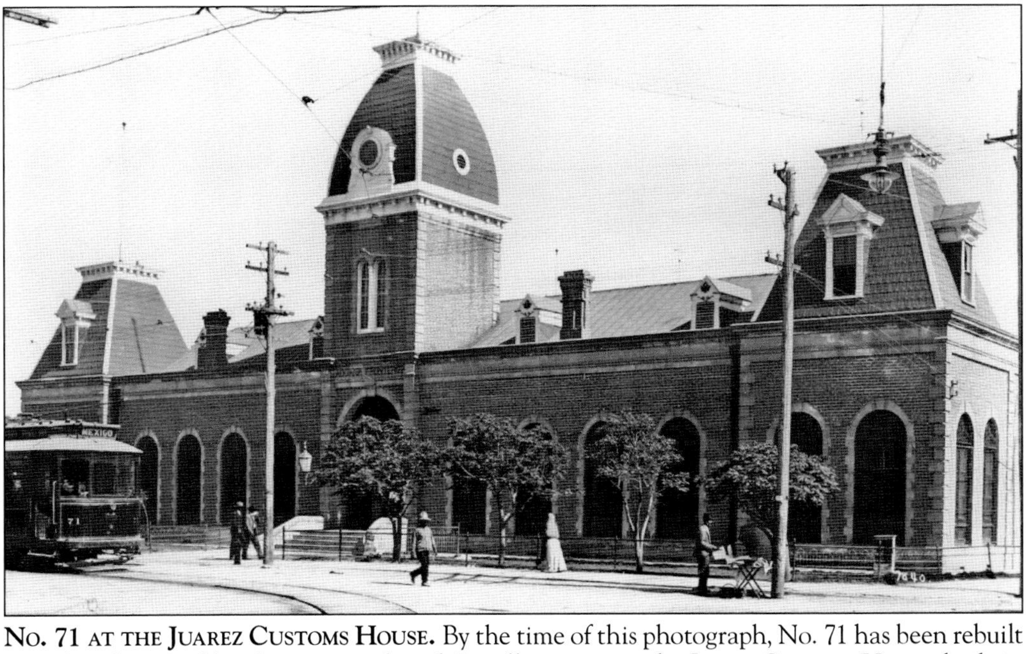

**NO. 71 AT THE JUAREZ CUSTOMS HOUSE.** By the time of this photograph, No. 71 has been rebuilt to a closed car and has been renumbered. It will swing past the Juarez Customs House, built in the 1880s. Avenida 16 de Septiembre is still unpaved at this time. Through the years, the Juarez line was always the most heavily patronized of the system. (Courtesy of EPPL.)

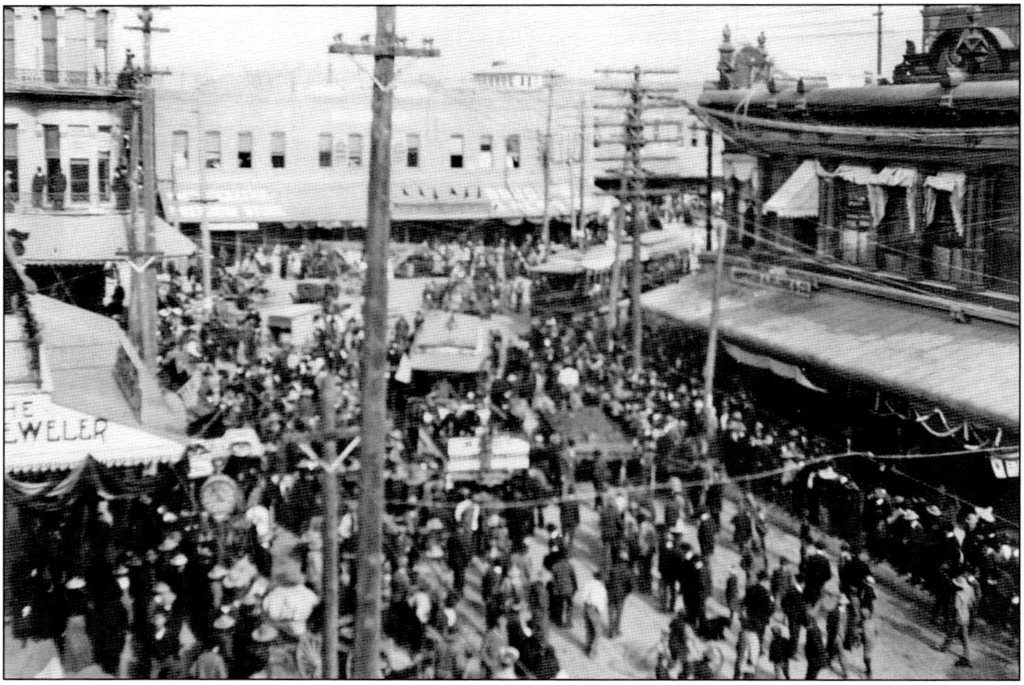

**ANOTHER VIEW OF JANUARY 11, 1902.** In this view of the first day of electric car service, one can see that more streetcars have joined the procession. Large crowds are watching the cars pass through Little Plaza near the Sheldon Hotel (left). Mandy seems to be the primary attraction at this time. The McGinty Band is riding in the third car.

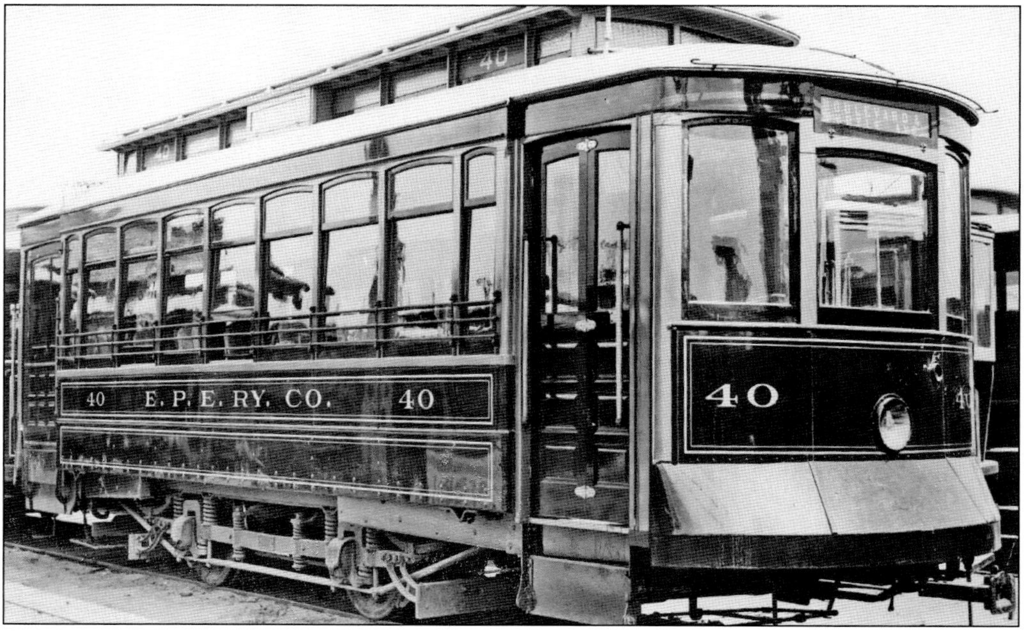


**CINCINNATI CAR COMPANY.** No. 40, the first of a group of 10 cars from the Cincinnati Car Company in 1910, is shown at the carbarn. These large single-truck cars were the only Cincinnati cars in the system. By 1912, the State of Texas had outlawed open cars and semi-open cars because of accidents with patrons jumping on and off. Thereafter orders were made for closed cars such as this.

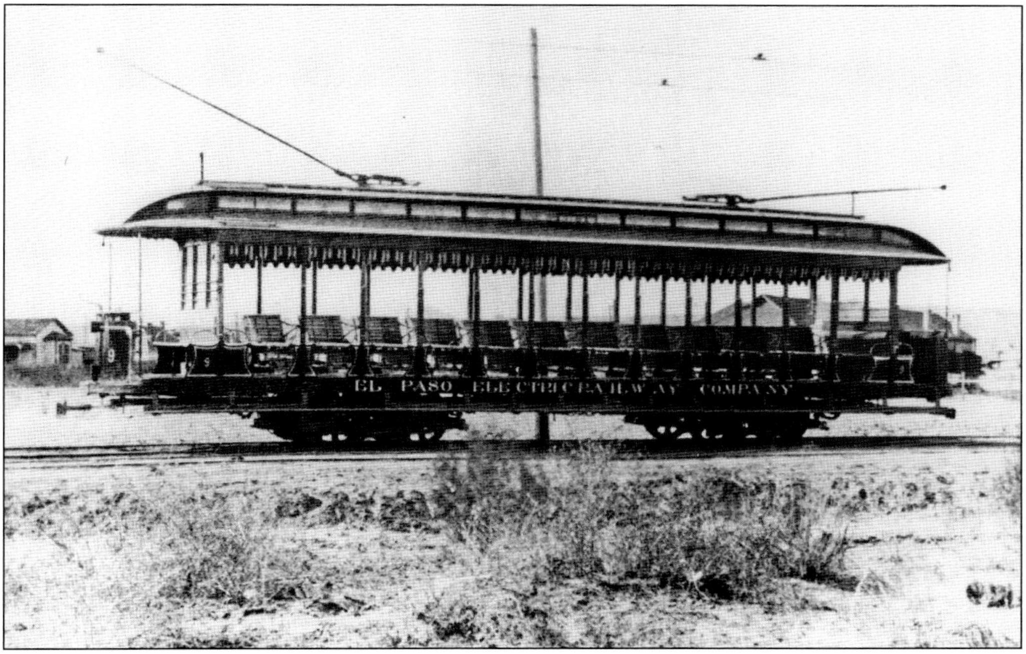


**A DOUBLE-TRUCK OPEN CAR.** Two "orphan" cars came from the Laconia Car Company in New Hampshire, Nos. 9 and 11. They were large double-truck open cars with 13 benches. These railroad roof cars were the only Laconia cars on the property and, in later years, were rebuilt to closed cars and renumbered 81 and 83.

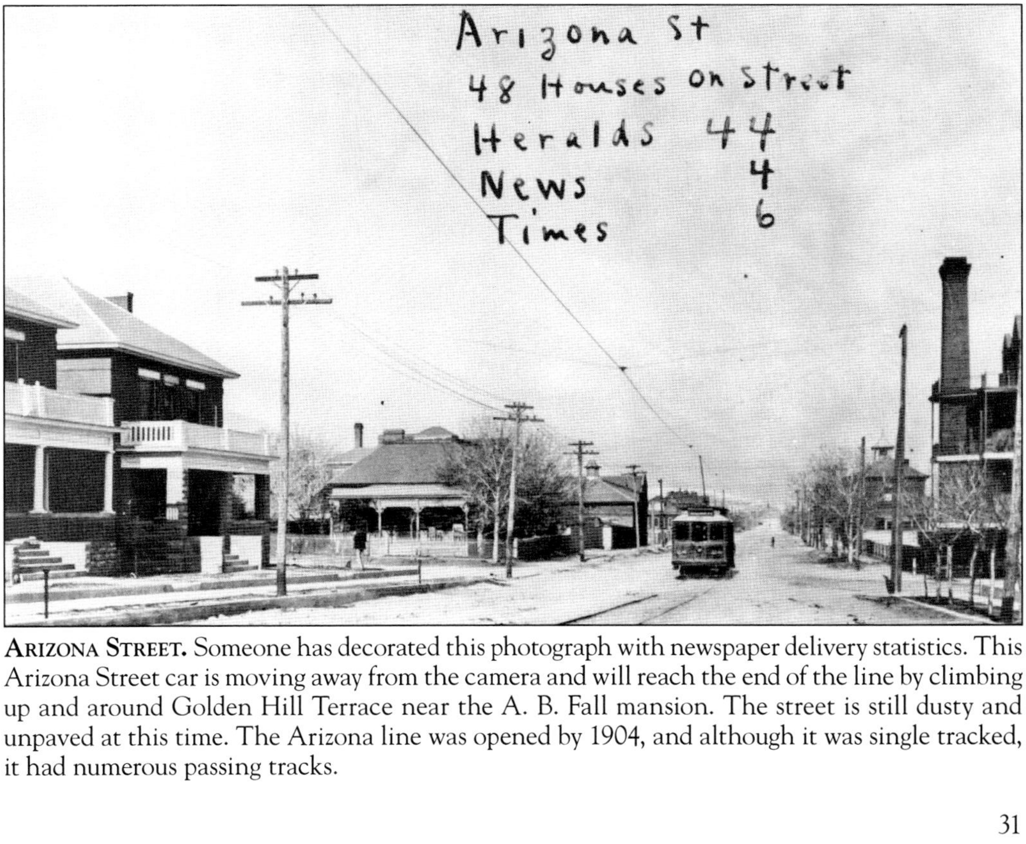


**ARIZONA STREET.** Someone has decorated this photograph with newspaper delivery statistics. This Arizona Street car is moving away from the camera and will reach the end of the line by climbing up and around Golden Hill Terrace near the A. B. Fall mansion. The street is still dusty and unpaved at this time. The Arizona line was opened by 1904, and although it was single tracked, it had numerous passing tracks.

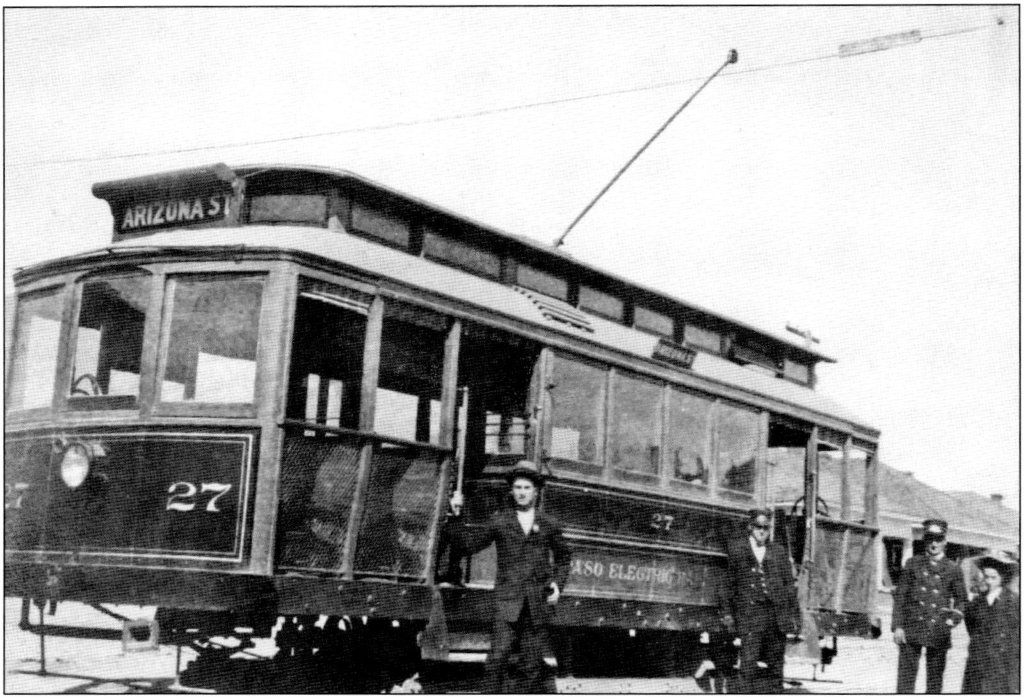


**No. 27 on the Arizona Street Line.** At this point in time, No. 27, originally an open car, has been rebuilt into a semi-convertible. The open areas at the end were protected with a fence-like structure. The electric railway was concerned about the number of injury claims and took steps to improve safety. Not much later this car was converted to a closed car.

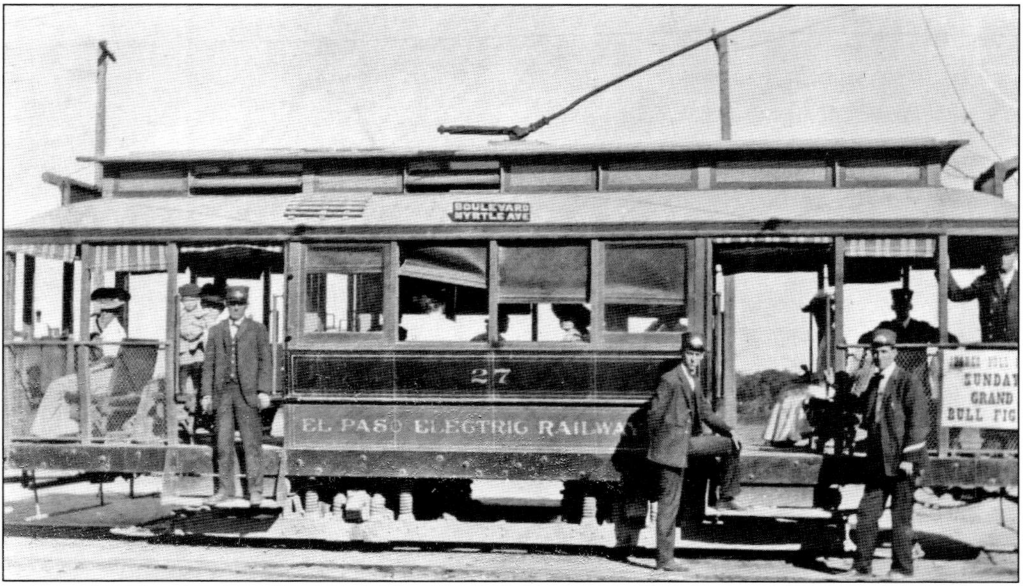


**No. 27 on the Boulevard-Myrtle Line.** Here is a nice side view of No. 27 on the Boulevard Avenue and Myrtle Avenue line. A Sunday bullfight at the Juarez Bull Ring is advertised on the safety fence. Customers could reach the Juarez Bull Ring from any part of town simply by transferring to the Juarez car downtown. There are no less than five EL Paso Electric Railway employees in this photograph.

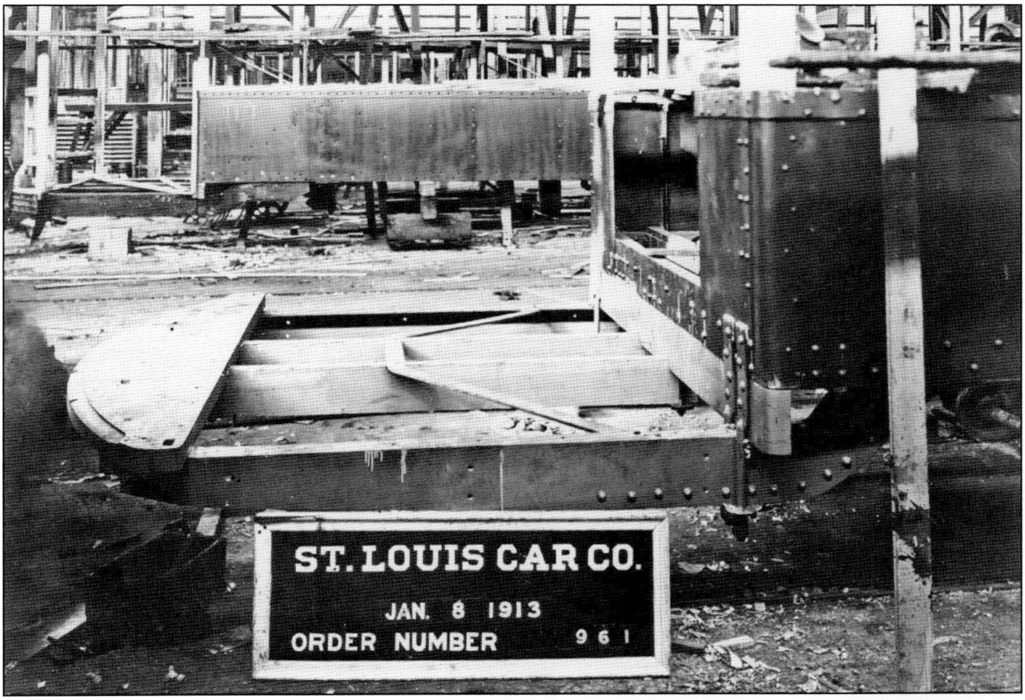


**BUILDER'S PHOTOGRAPH FROM THE ST. LOUIS CAR COMPANY.** This image is a builder's photograph of one of the first order of six Stone and Webster roof cars still under construction, which were ordered in 1912 and delivered in 1913. These were four motor cars with St. Louis 47B trucks and were numbered 85 to 90.

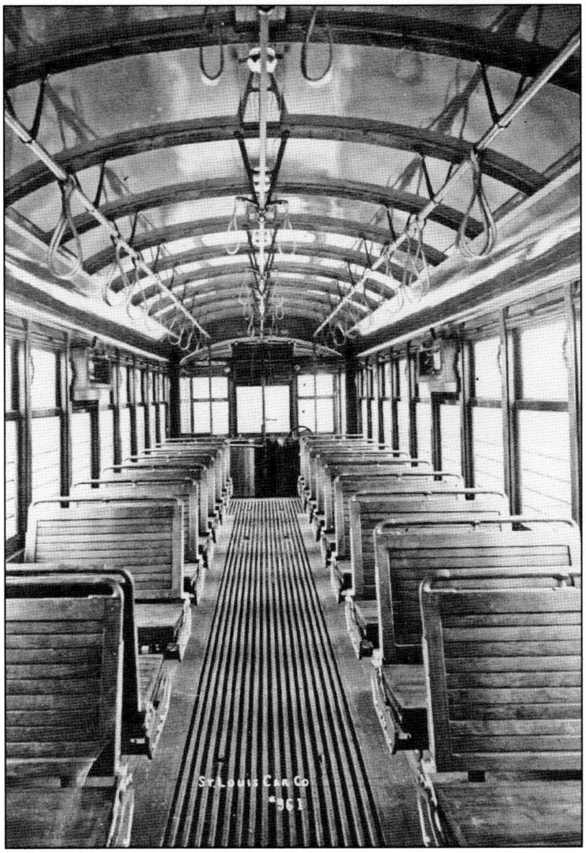


**BUILDER'S PHOTOGRAPH OF A CAR INTERIOR.** This is a St. Louis Car Company photograph of the interior of one of the six cars on order—No. 961. These cars, numbered 85 to 90, originally had wooden slatted seats before the 1931 rebuild. The back of the seats could be flipped over to face either direction. It was a double-ended car.

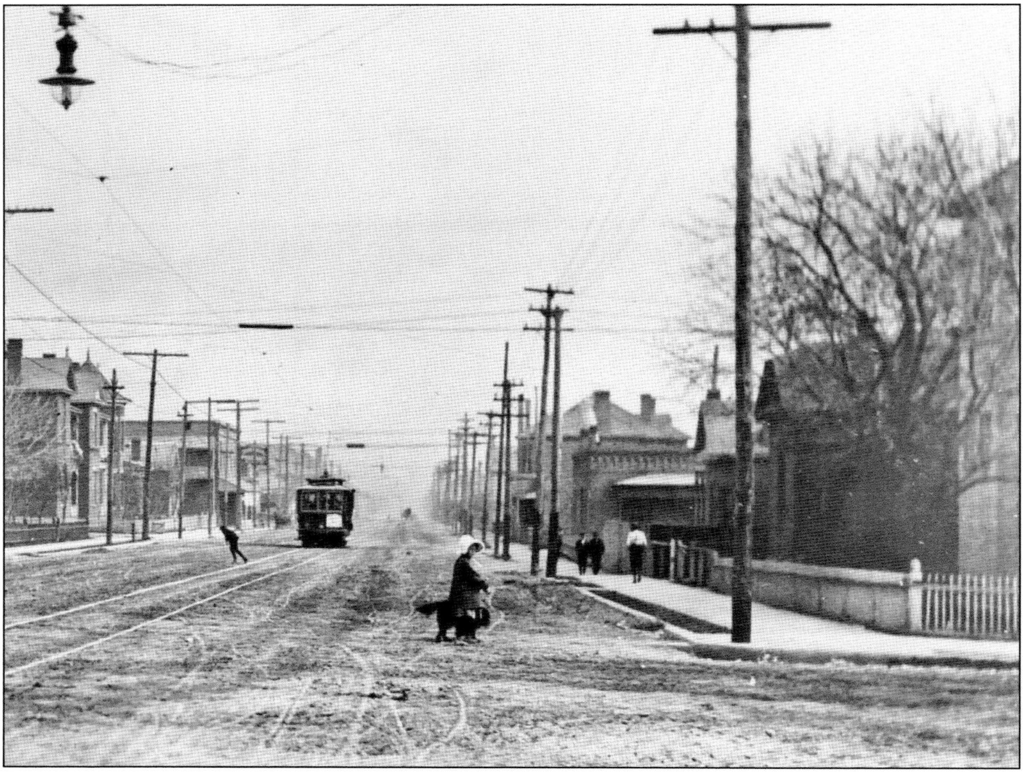

**BOULEVARD AVENUE.** The above photograph, probably taken between 1910 and 1918, looks eastward as a trolley navigates the 500 block of Boulevard Avenue, later Yandell Street. It may have been a windy day: witness the dust in the distance and the little boy crossing the track and leaning into the wind. The little girl in the bonnet shepherds her dog safely across the street. Boulevard is unpaved and single tracked at the time of the photograph. The photograph below shows the same block in the 1920s. Automobiles are present; the street, now named Yandell, is paved, and there is a double track for the streetcars to handle the traffic more efficiently.

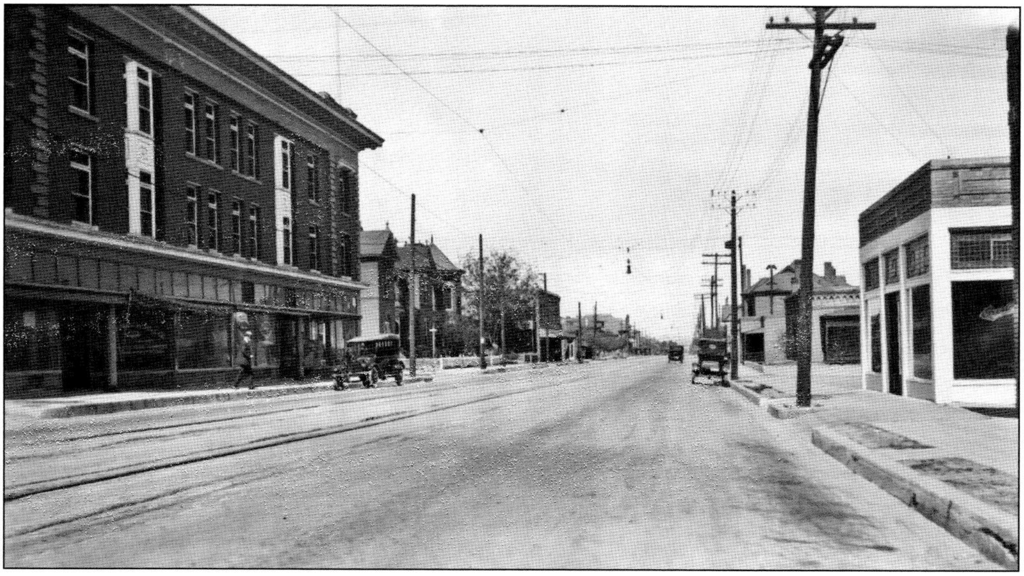

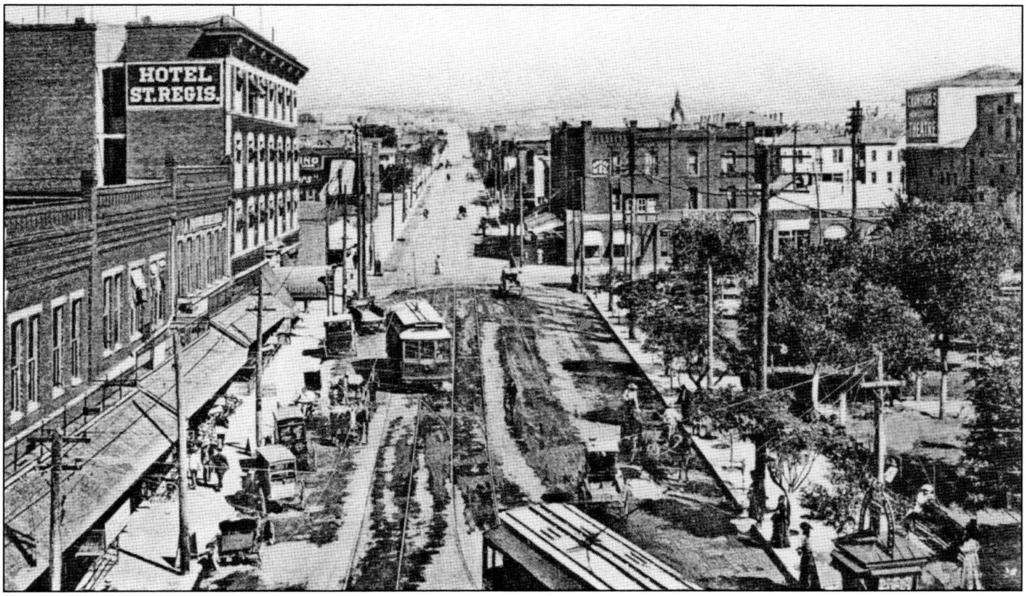


**OREGON STREET LOOKING NORTH.** This 1907 postcard view shows streetcars on Oregon Street with the San Jacinto Plaza on the right. The street is still unpaved, and this is still a horse-and-buggy era. The small booth at the lower right-hand corner was a ticket and information booth for the El Paso Electric Railway.

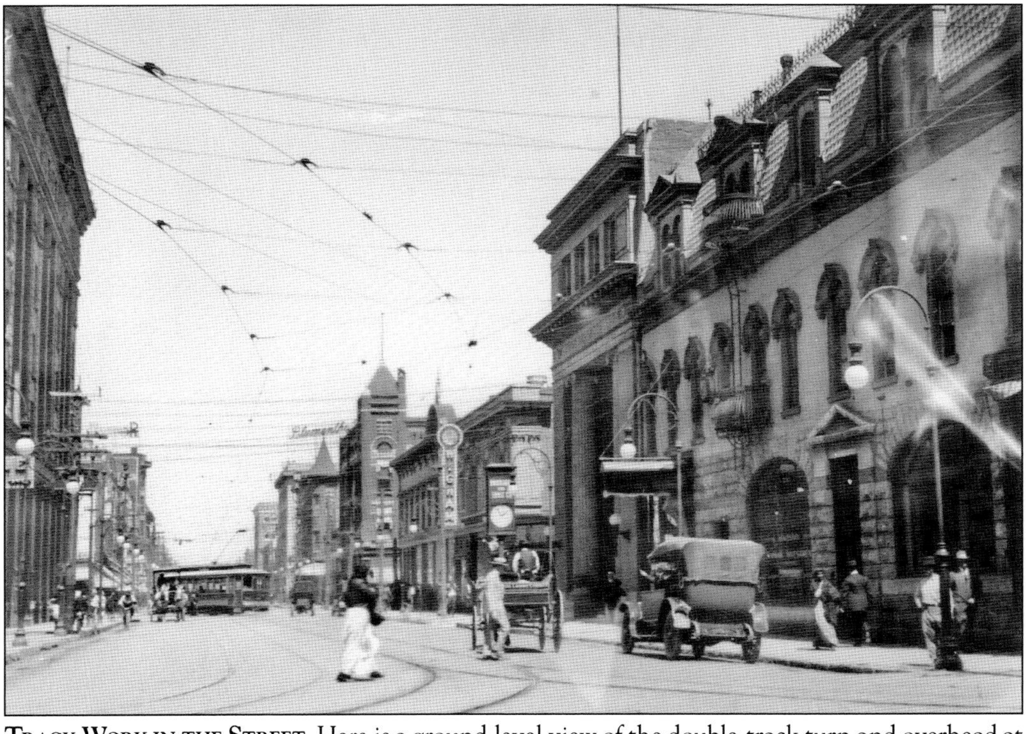

**TRACK WORK IN THE STREET.** Here is a ground-level view of the double-track turn and overhead at the corner of El Paso and San Antonio Streets. A streetcar in the distance is turning onto Oregon Street. Juarez cars would enter the picture on the right, make a left turn where the car is, then reenter the picture from the left, making a short loop within a larger loop. (Courtesy of EPPL.)

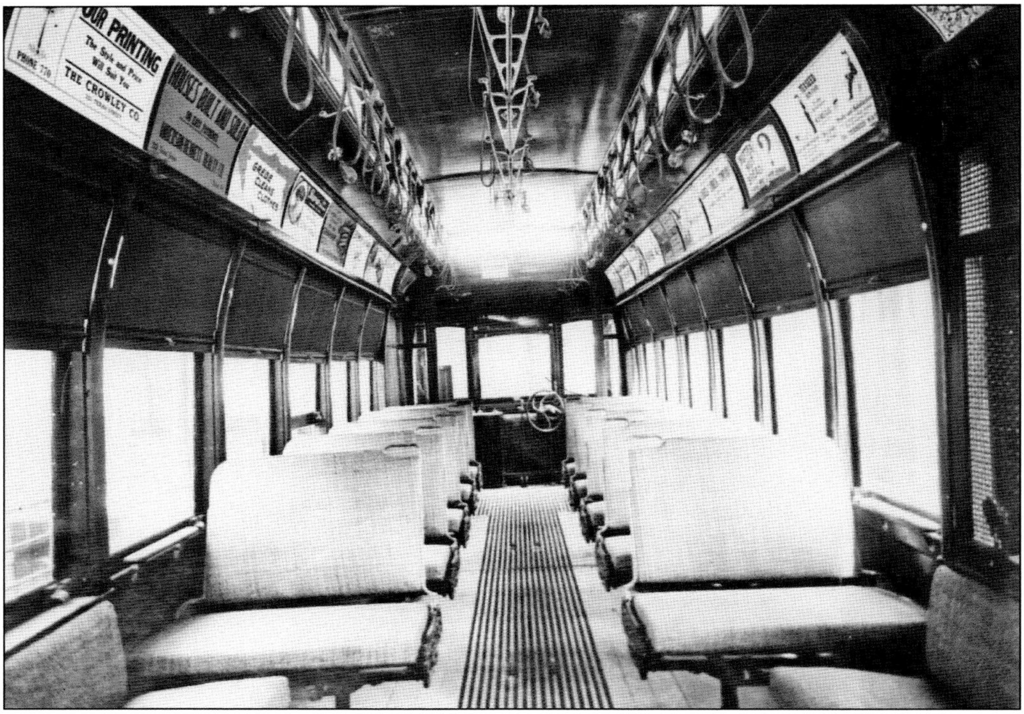


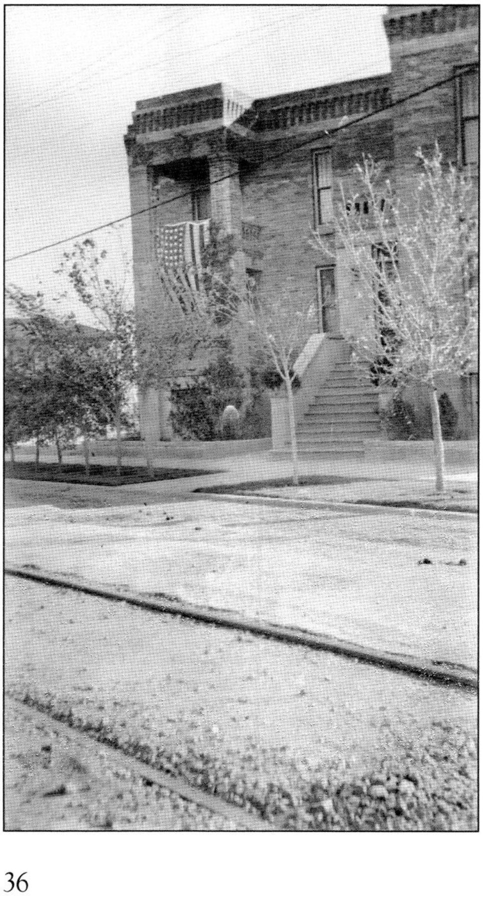

**EARLY CAR INTERIOR.** This photograph of the interior of an early car appears to be a series-40 Cincinnati car, making the date sometime after 1910. By this time, wooden slatted seats were not attractive to patrons, and the streetcar company from then on ordered cars with upholstered seats. Advertising cards placed above the windows added to the revenue of the operating company.

**ON THE SUNSET HEIGHTS LINE.** This early photograph of an apartment building at 1106 Mundy Street in the Sunset Heights neighborhood shows the streetcar track in the street on Mundy. The street appears to be paved but not the area between tracks, which would be the responsibility of the El Paso Electric Railway. This scene is near Vilas School.

# *Four*

# DOWNTOWN

El Paso is situated in a somewhat unique geography. Its very name, in fact, is derived from El Paso del Norte, or the Pass of the North. This pass is located between the southern tip of the Franklin Mountains and the Rio Grande River, which constitutes the United States–Mexico border at this point. In this narrow pass lies downtown El Paso. In the late 1880s, El Paso became not only an agricultural center, but a mining, commercial, and railroad center as well. First with mule cars, and later with electric cars, citizens were able to come downtown easily to do their shopping. Streetcar lines radiated in all directions to neighborhoods and even to Ysleta, but downtown was the center of all things El Paso in those days. A 6¢ ticket and a penny transfer, for example, could get you from Fort Bliss to downtown, where you could transfer to a car to Mexico, a total distance of 9 miles. San Jacinto Plaza, with its alligator pond, was at the center of town, and all carlines passed by either on the south side or the west side of the plaza. From the east came the Highland Park, Government Hill, Manhattan Heights, Fort Bliss, and Washington Park lines. Prior to 1929, the Ysleta interurban came into town on Alameda Street over the Park line. From the north, down Oregon Street, came the Mesa, High School, Arizona, Sunset Heights, and Smelter lines. From the west came the Depot line, and of course, from the south, the Juarez, Second Ward, and Hipodromo lines. In 1943, to relieve congestion on the loop, the Park and Fort Bliss lines turned back at Myrtle and San Antonio Streets, about a six-block walk from San Jacinto Plaza. Downtown was a place people could shop, pay their bills, and see a movie, then take an electric car home, all in an easy afternoon.

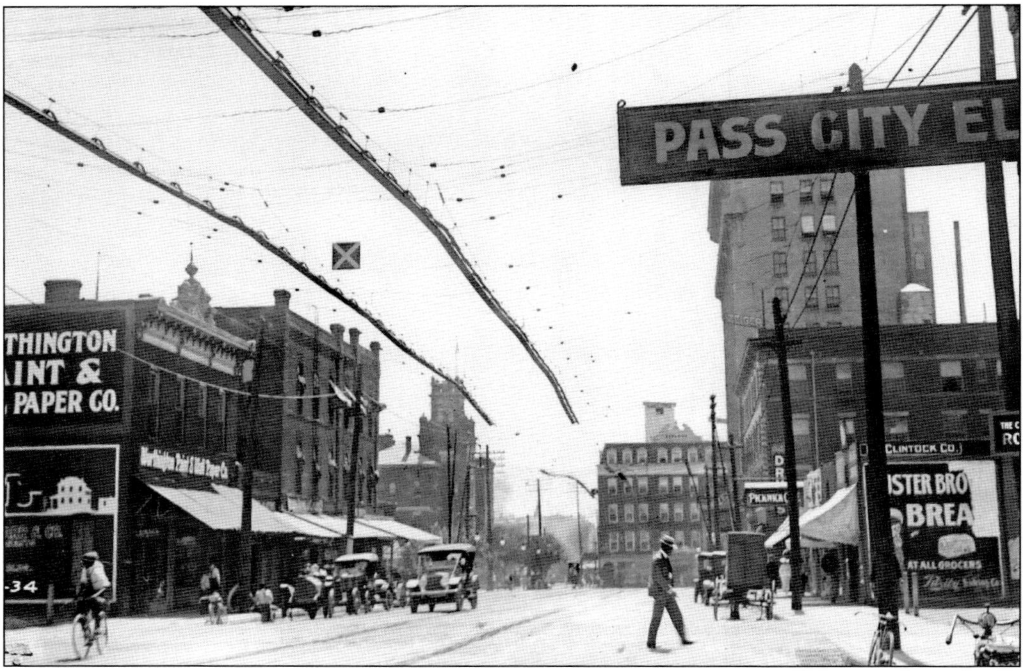


**Crossing the Railroad.** The first image (above) shows a 1920s view looking south on Oregon Street to the Sheldon Hotel in the background. The heavy construction of the streetcar overhead catenary, which powers the electric cars, is necessary since the streetcar line crosses over the El Paso and Southwestern Railway at this juncture. The reinforced overhead protects the line from steam locomotive heat and smoke. The image below is a different view of the same junction, now looking east to the El Paso and Southwestern headquarters building in the distance. The railroad crosses Oregon Street and the car line in the foreground. The Crawford Theater is visible to the right, and a billboard worker is pasting a new advertising sign in the foreground. (Both, courtesy of EPPL.)

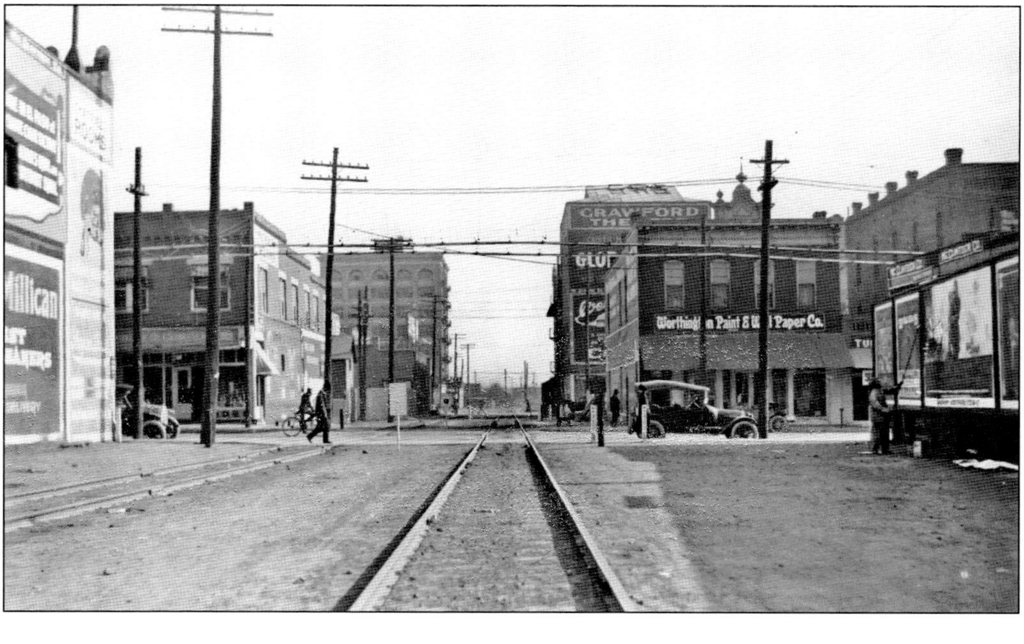

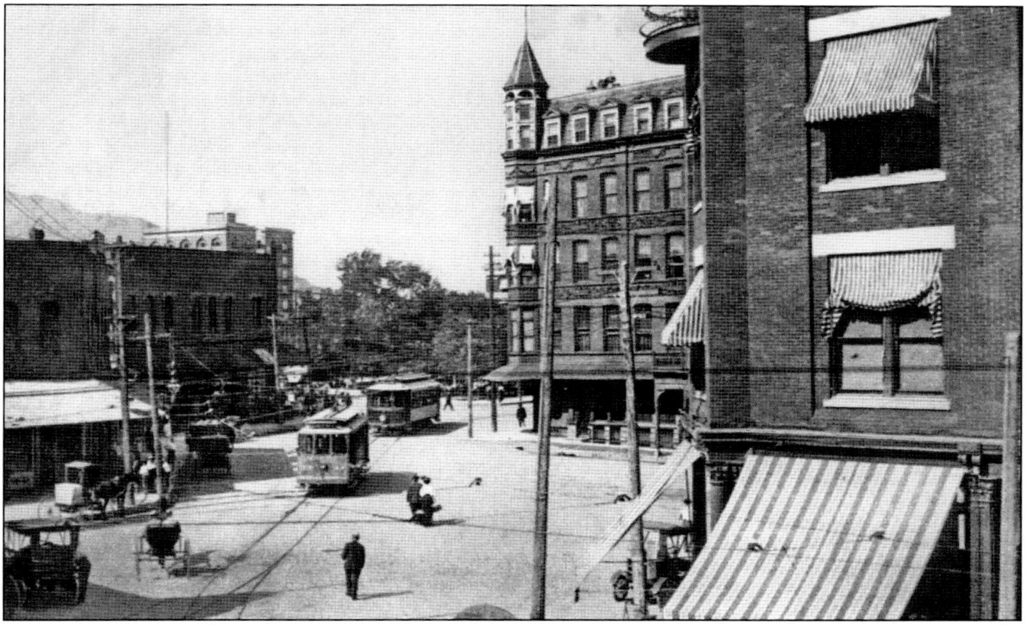

**PIONEER PLAZA.** The above image shows the main city plaza, San Jacinto, in the background with trees as these two monitor-roofed streetcars enter Pioneer or Little Plaza with the five-story Sheldon Hotel as a backdrop. This scene is devoid of automobiles and can be dated between 1906 and 1910 because the El Paso and Southwestern Railroad building is present in the distance but the huge Mills Building has not yet been built on the left. The image below is from 1910, as the 12-story Mills Building is under construction on the left. The streetcar in the center of the photograph could turn right on San Francisco Street for Union Depot or left onto El Paso Street, then left again on San Antonio Street for the Juarez line.

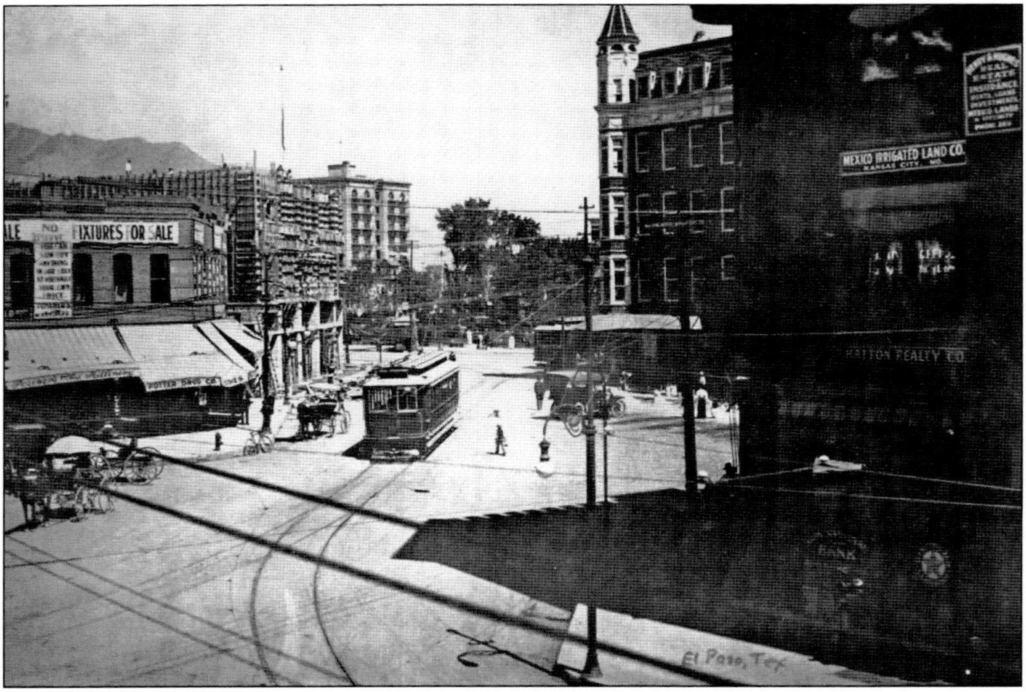

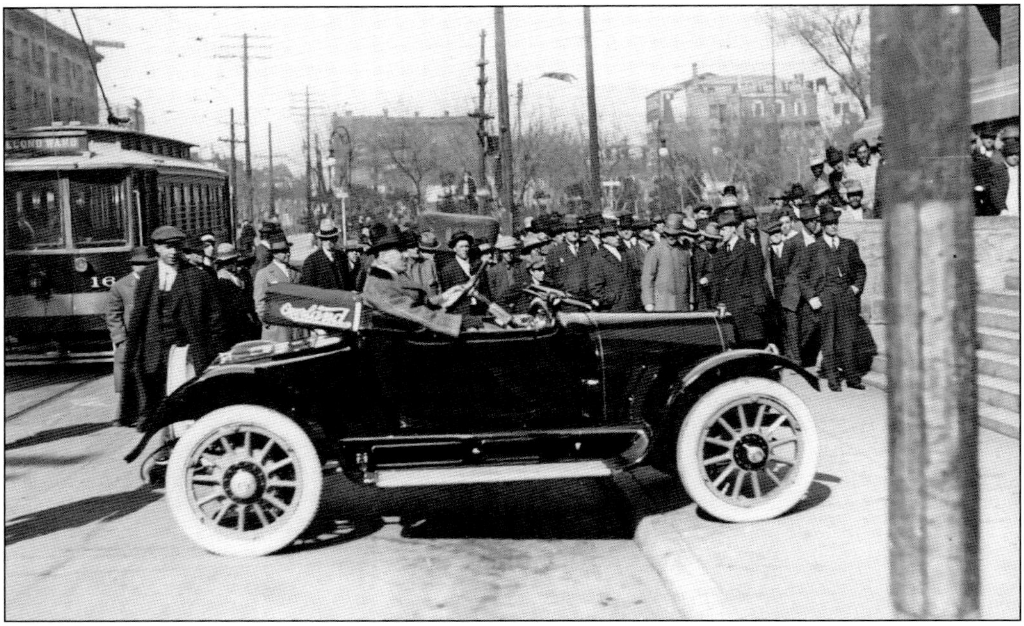


**No. 16 Passes a Demonstration.** Car 16, on the Second Ward line, passes northbound on Oregon Street in front of the U.S. Federal Courthouse. Apparently, a large crowd has gathered to watch the stair-climbing ability of a new Overland roadster. In 1935, a new federal courthouse was built on San Antonio Street across from the county courthouse. (EPPL.)

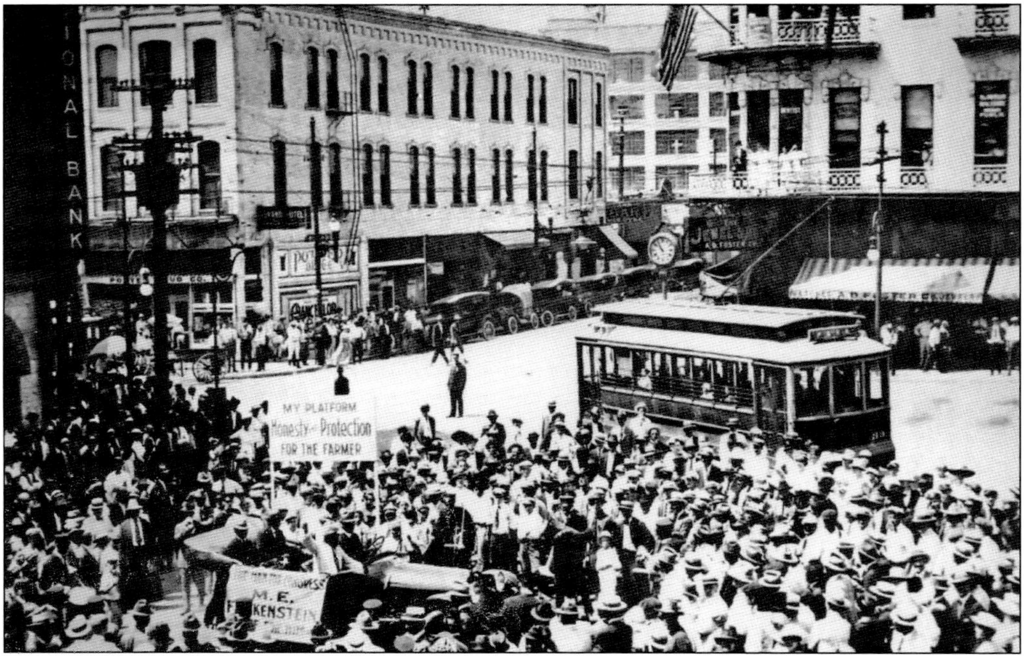


**A Political Rally.** A Park line single-truck streetcar in Pioneer Plaza eases past a crowd listening to a politician stumping from his open roadster. The streetcar is approaching the three-way intersection of Mills, San Francisco, and El Paso Streets. The orator, M. E. Frankenstein, promises "Honesty and Protection for the Farmer." He shares a famous name with the character in Mary Shelley's early-1800s novel.

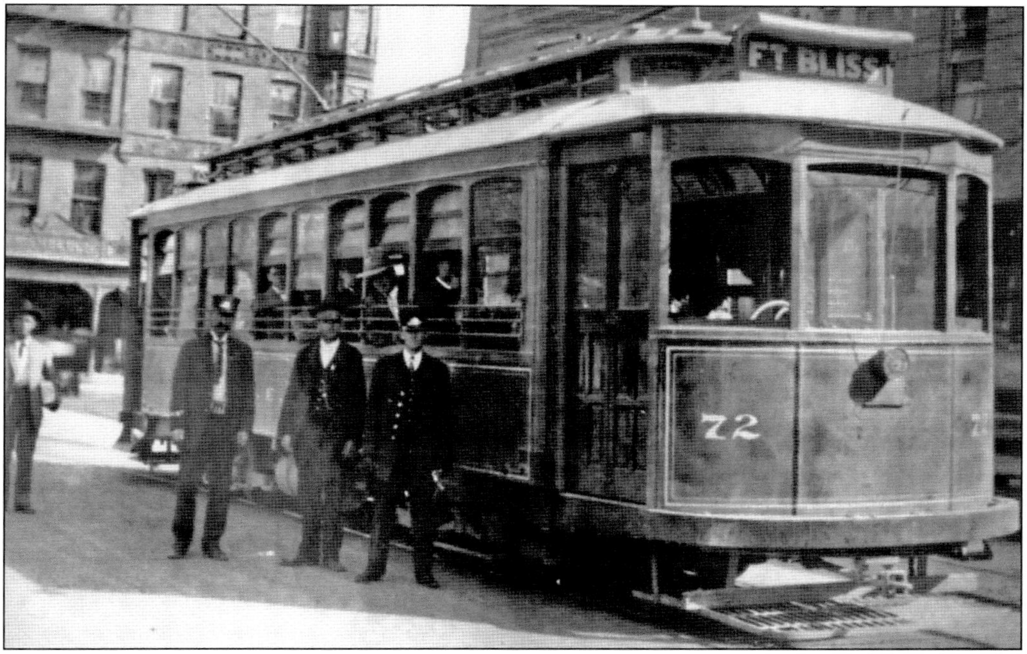


**FORT BLISS CAR.** Car 72 waits for departure from San Jacinto Plaza in the center of town. Originally cars on the Fort Bliss line went north to Yandell, then east to Five Points. In 1937, however, the Yandell Street trackage was removed, and from then on, Fort Bliss cars went out Myrtle and Alameda Streets. The Fort Bliss line was completed in 1906. (James E. Agan.)

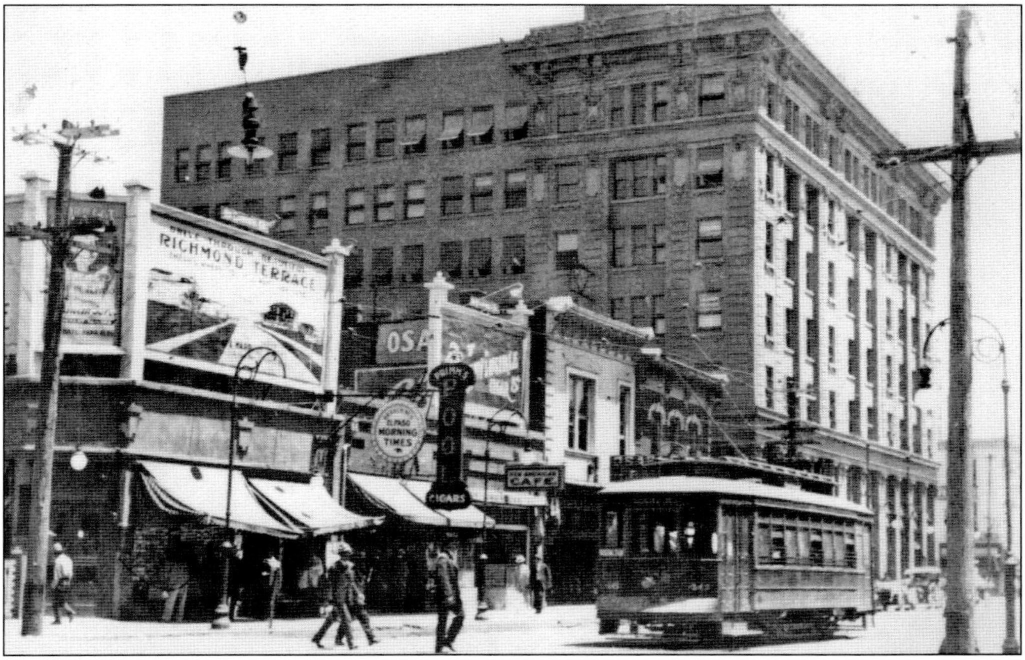


**A 40-SERIES CAR ON SAN ANTONIO.** One of the 40-series cars passes the imposing El Paso National Bank Building. The billboard on the real estate office (left) advertises lots in Richmond Terrace, which was served by a shuttle car off the Government Hill line. (Charles Smallwood photograph, courtesy of PDNSPS.)

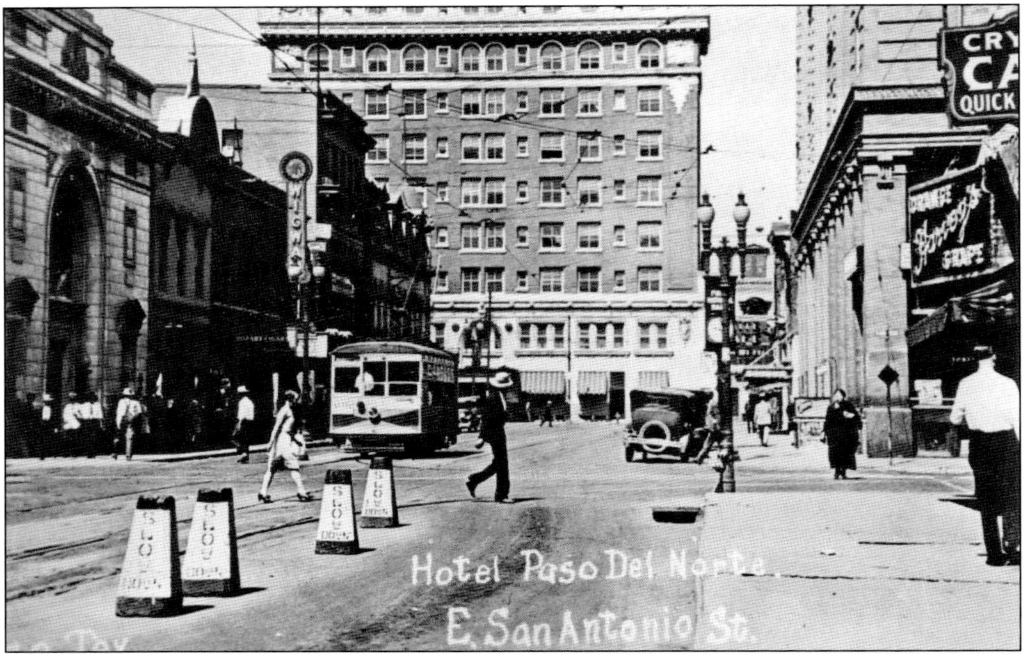


**The Bow Tie Paint.** The El Paso Electric Railway was well aware of sales promotion schemes, one of which, according to the *Electric Railway Journal*, was to paint Depot line cars in distinctive paint to attract arriving visitors. This single-truck Birney sports the "bow tie" motif in the 1930s as it makes its way down San Antonio Street. The motorman can be seen standing at the controls. (Courtesy of Allen Berner Collection.)

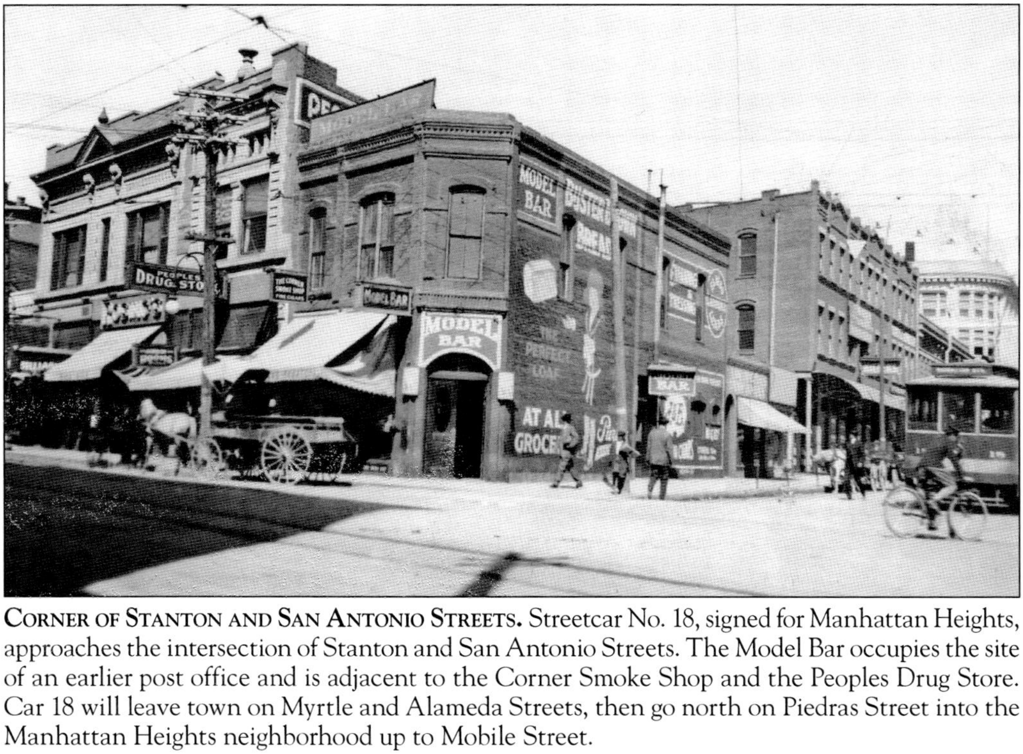


**Corner of Stanton and San Antonio Streets.** Streetcar No. 18, signed for Manhattan Heights, approaches the intersection of Stanton and San Antonio Streets. The Model Bar occupies the site of an earlier post office and is adjacent to the Corner Smoke Shop and the Peoples Drug Store. Car 18 will leave town on Myrtle and Alameda Streets, then go north on Piedras Street into the Manhattan Heights neighborhood up to Mobile Street.

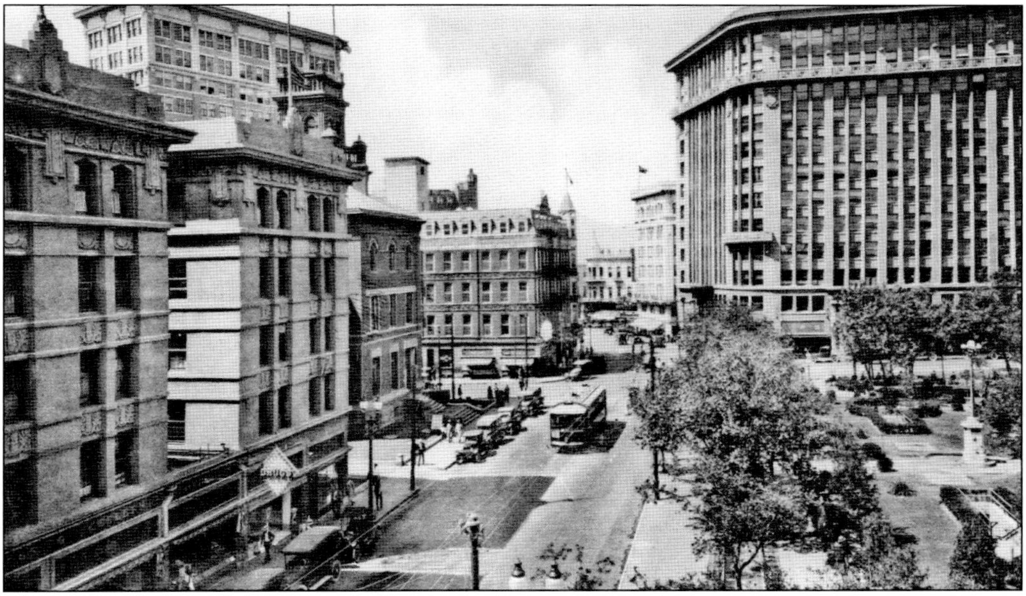

**MILLS STREET AT SAN JACINTO PLAZA.** In this view looking west on Mills Street, San Jacinto Plaza is on the right and the Roberts-Banner Building is on the left. The streetcar on Mills Street is referred to as a Stone and Webster, or "turtle-roof," type because of its unusual roof design. El Paso bought six of these in 1912 and six more in 1914 from the St. Louis Car Company.

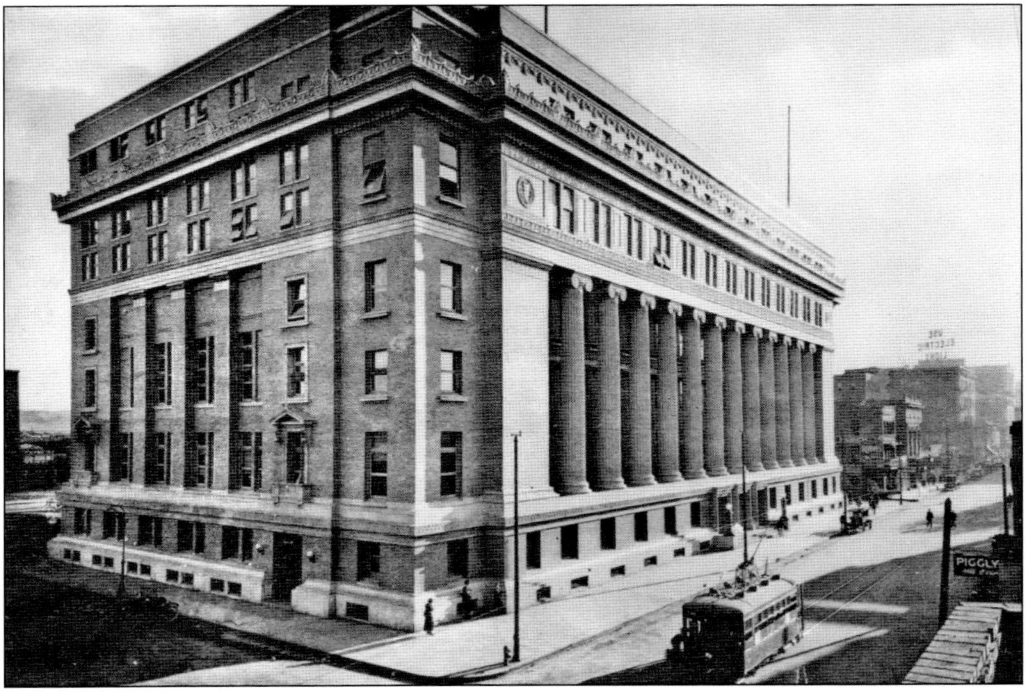


**PASSING THE COUNTY COURTHOUSE.** Birney Safety Cars, designed by Charles O. Birney, whose brother lived in El Paso, came to El Paso in 1918. Over the years, the system would have 40 of these small 32-passenger cars, which were useful on less traveled lines. This Birney passes the El Paso County Courthouse, built in 1917 in the Classical Revival style. The stately columns were covered by a facade in a 1950s remodeling.

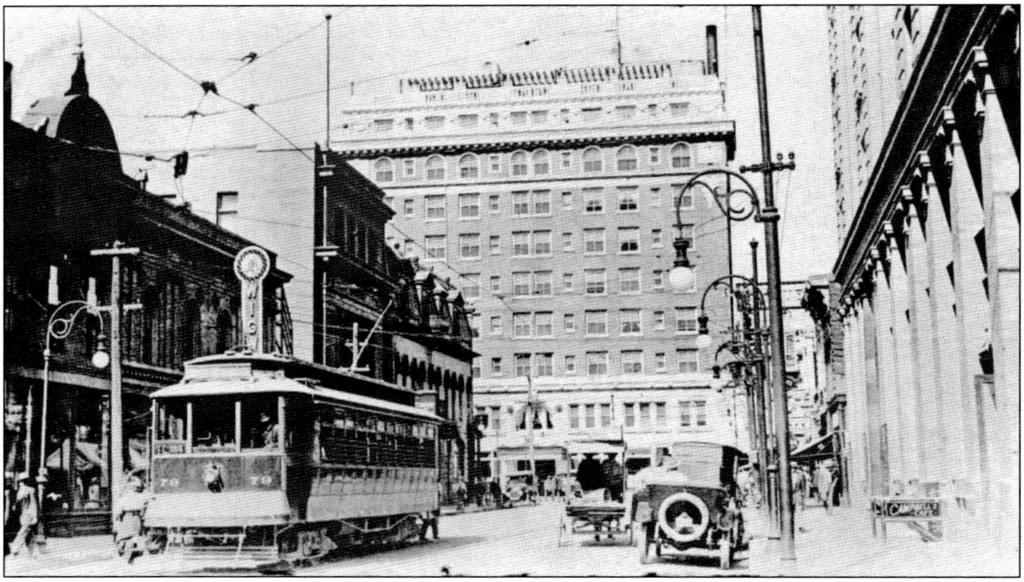

**CAR NO. 79.** No. 79 was, in fact, rebuilt from an open car in the 15–19 series in the El Paso shops. This W. H. Horne postcard shows the curved side design for increased strength. No. 79 is traveling east on San Antonio Street with the Wigwam Theater on the left. The Wigwam later became the State Theater. The No. 79, built about 1907, lasted until the late 1930s.

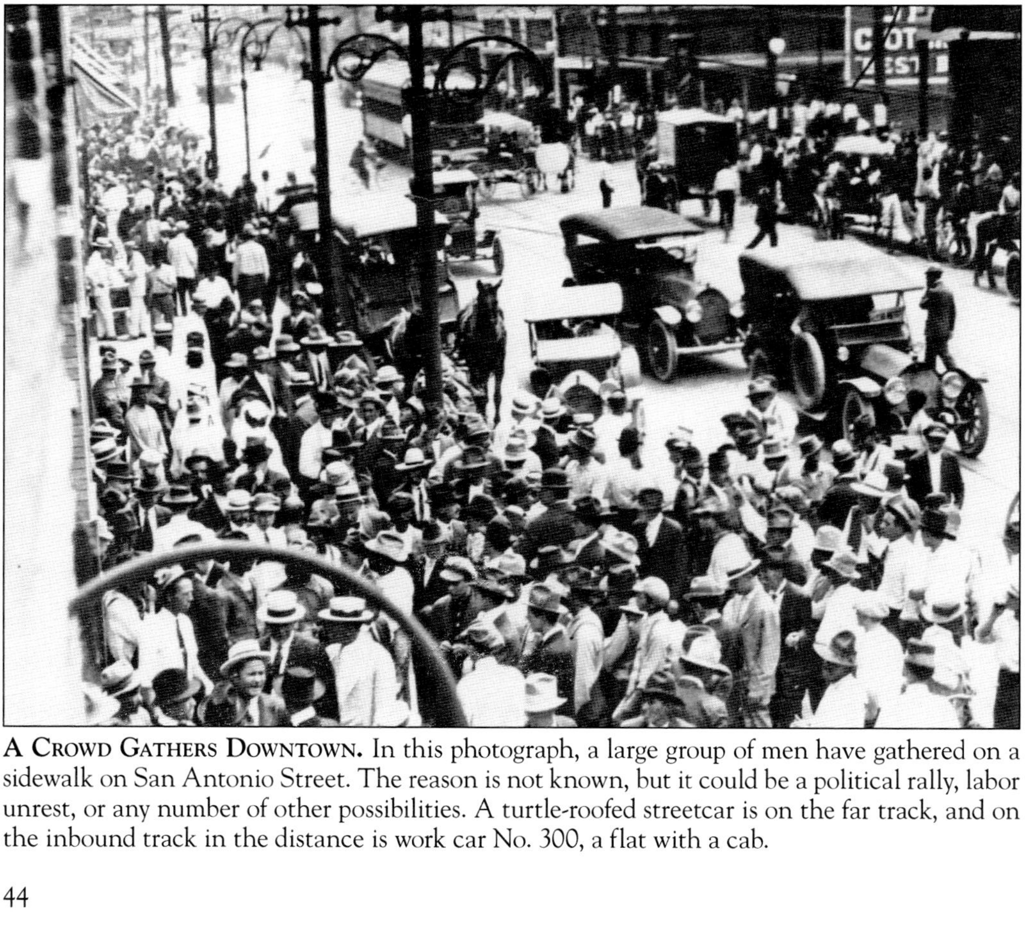

**A CROWD GATHERS DOWNTOWN.** In this photograph, a large group of men have gathered on a sidewalk on San Antonio Street. The reason is not known, but it could be a political rally, labor unrest, or any number of other possibilities. A turtle-roofed streetcar is on the far track, and on the inbound track in the distance is work car No. 300, a flat with a cab.

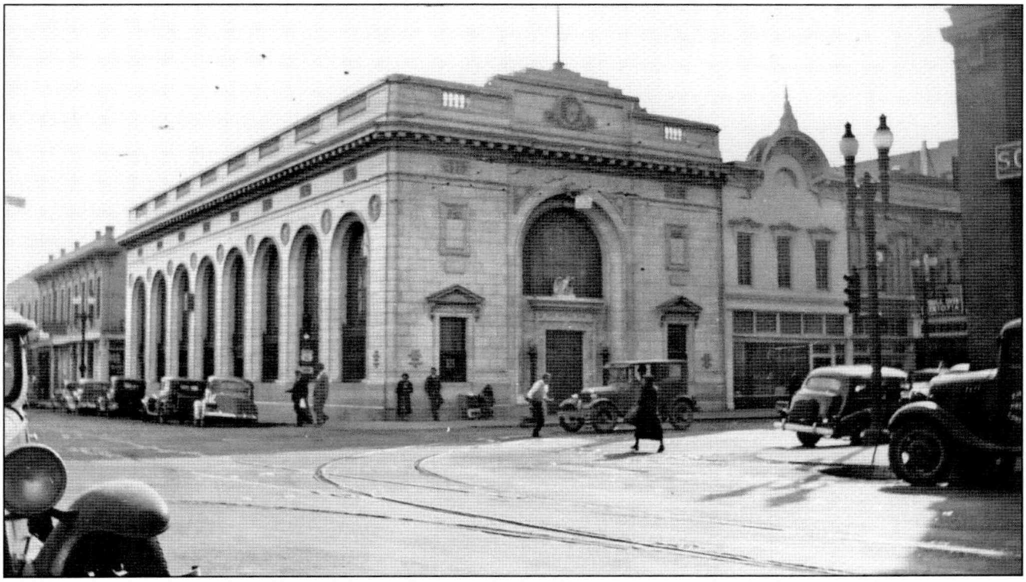

**State National Bank.** This 1930s view looks across the intersection of Oregon and San Antonio Streets to the State National Bank building with a front entrance on San Antonio. This was also a streetcar intersection as the Second Ward streetcars came into downtown from South Oregon Street (left center) and crossed busy San Antonio Street. The Second Ward was the area south of downtown to the international border.

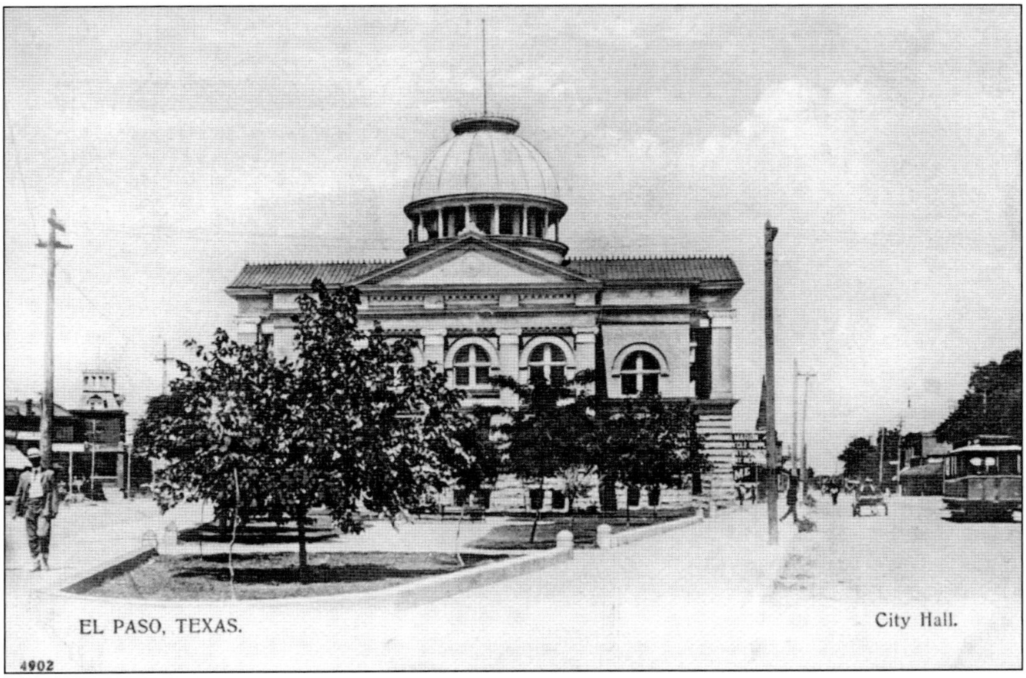


**El Paso City Hall.** This handsome brick-and-stone building with a dome housed the El Paso City Hall for many years. Streetcar lines straddled the city hall, with cars coming in on Myrtle Avenue on the left and leaving the town center on San Antonio Street on the right. In this pre-automobile photograph, streets are not yet paved, and the electric trolley is still the fastest way to travel.

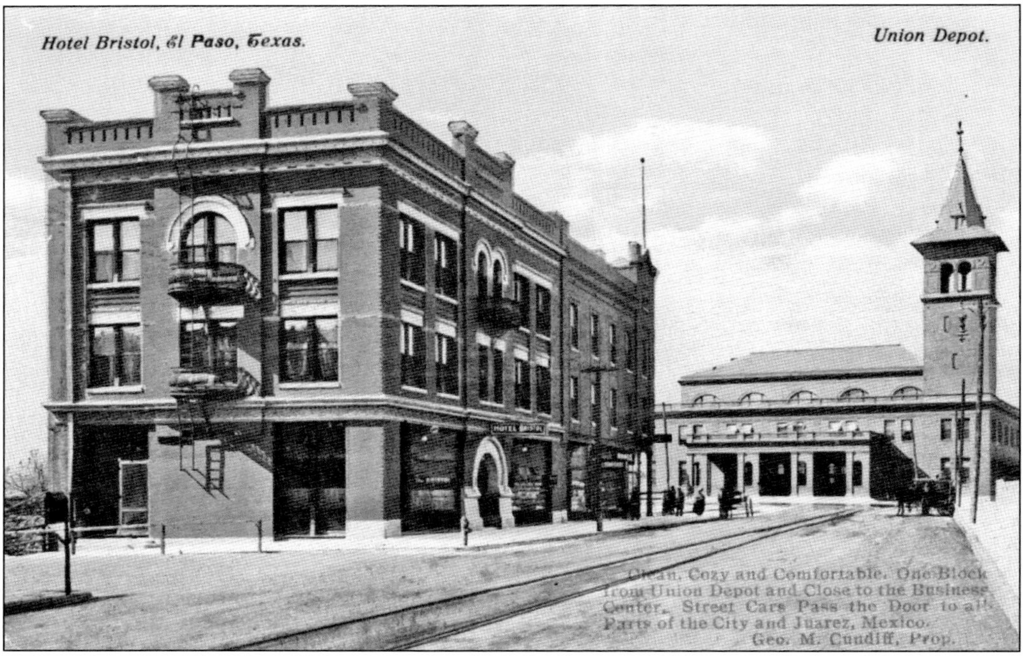


**UNION PASSENGER DEPOT.** El Paso's Union Passenger Station at the foot of San Francisco Street once served five railroads. Built in 1906, it had a streetcar line until 1930. On the left are the "railroad hotels," the Bristol and the Greentree. Both hotels catered to railroad travelers and workers who needed a place to stay within walking distance of the depot and also on a carline.

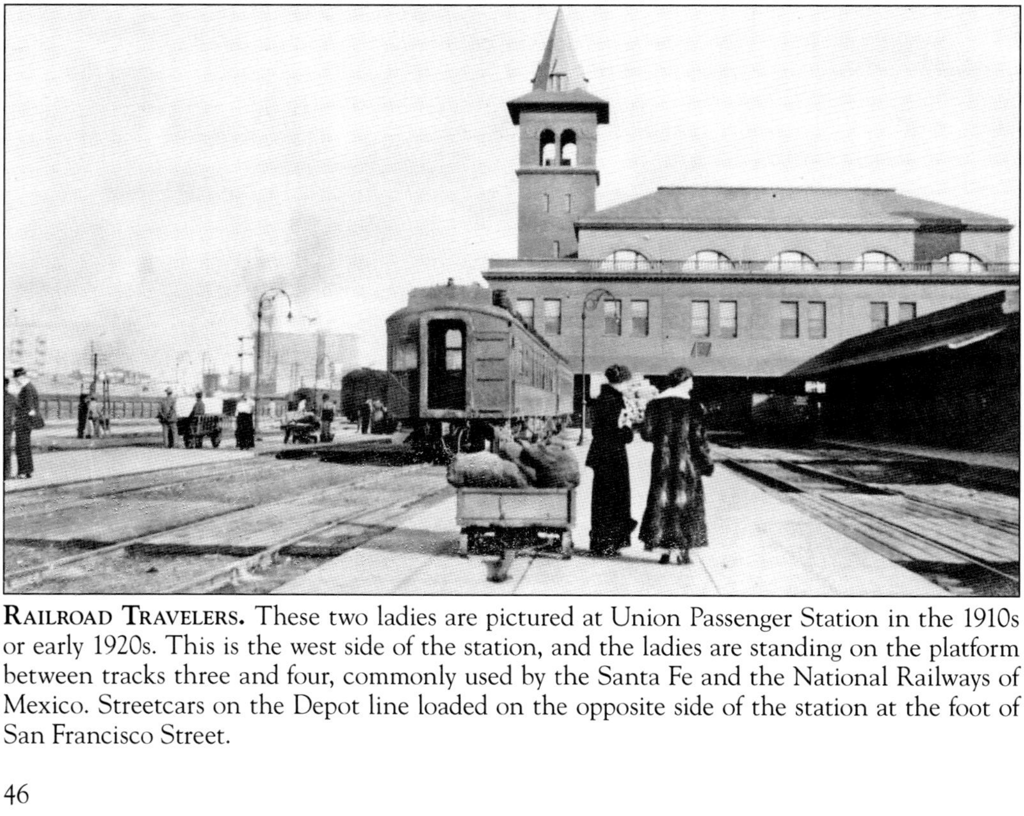

**RAILROAD TRAVELERS.** These two ladies are pictured at Union Passenger Station in the 1910s or early 1920s. This is the west side of the station, and the ladies are standing on the platform between tracks three and four, commonly used by the Santa Fe and the National Railways of Mexico. Streetcars on the Depot line loaded on the opposite side of the station at the foot of San Francisco Street.

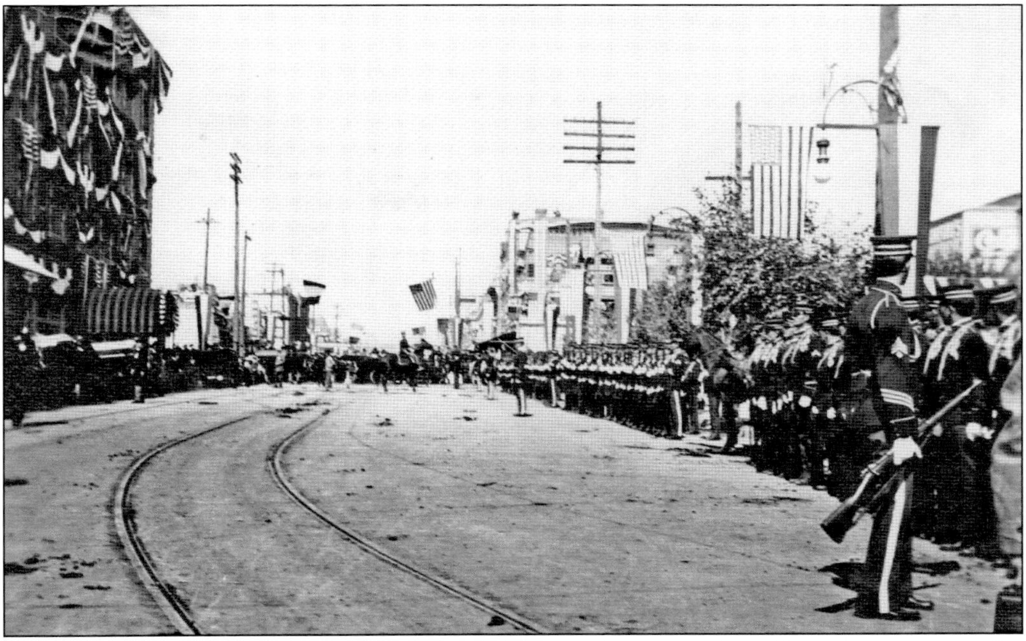

**Awaiting President Taft.** This large crowd and the military guards and bands are awaiting the special train of Pres. Howard Taft, coming to El Paso to meet with Mexican president Porfirio Diaz. San Jacinto Plaza on the right is a backdrop for the train, which will traverse the middle of Main Street before coming to a stop. The streetcar tracks in the foreground are on Oregon Street. (Courtesy of EPPL.)

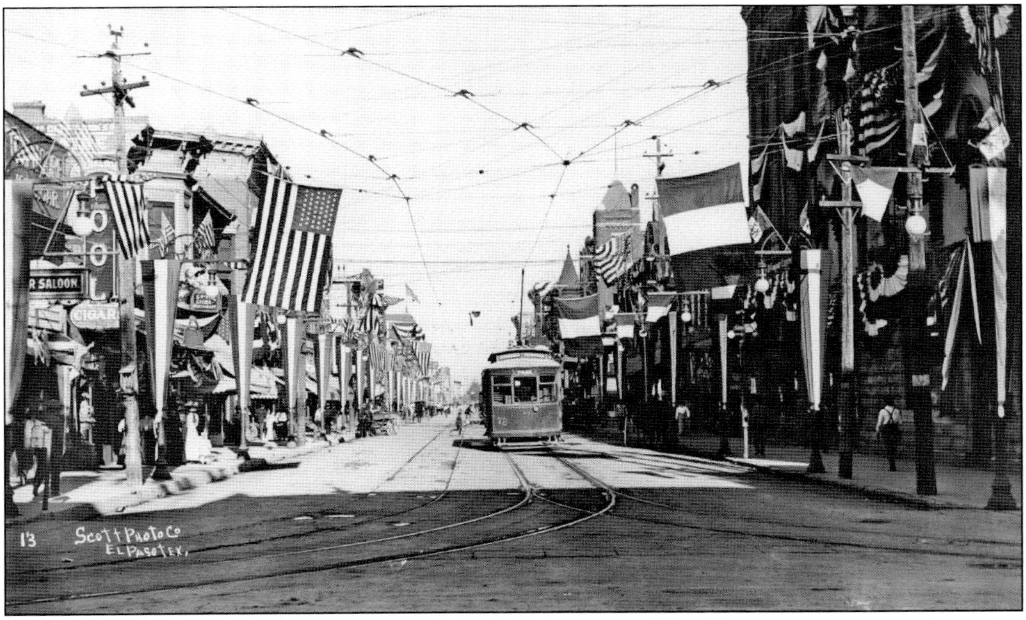


**American and Mexican Flag Displays.** Park streetcar No. 78 is moving away from the intersection of San Antonio and El Paso Streets as San Antonio Street is heavily decorated with American and Mexican flag colors, celebrating the historic meeting in El Paso of Presidents Taft and Diaz in October 1909. Car 78 is a car shops rebuild of an earlier semi-convertible car. (Courtesy of EPPL.)

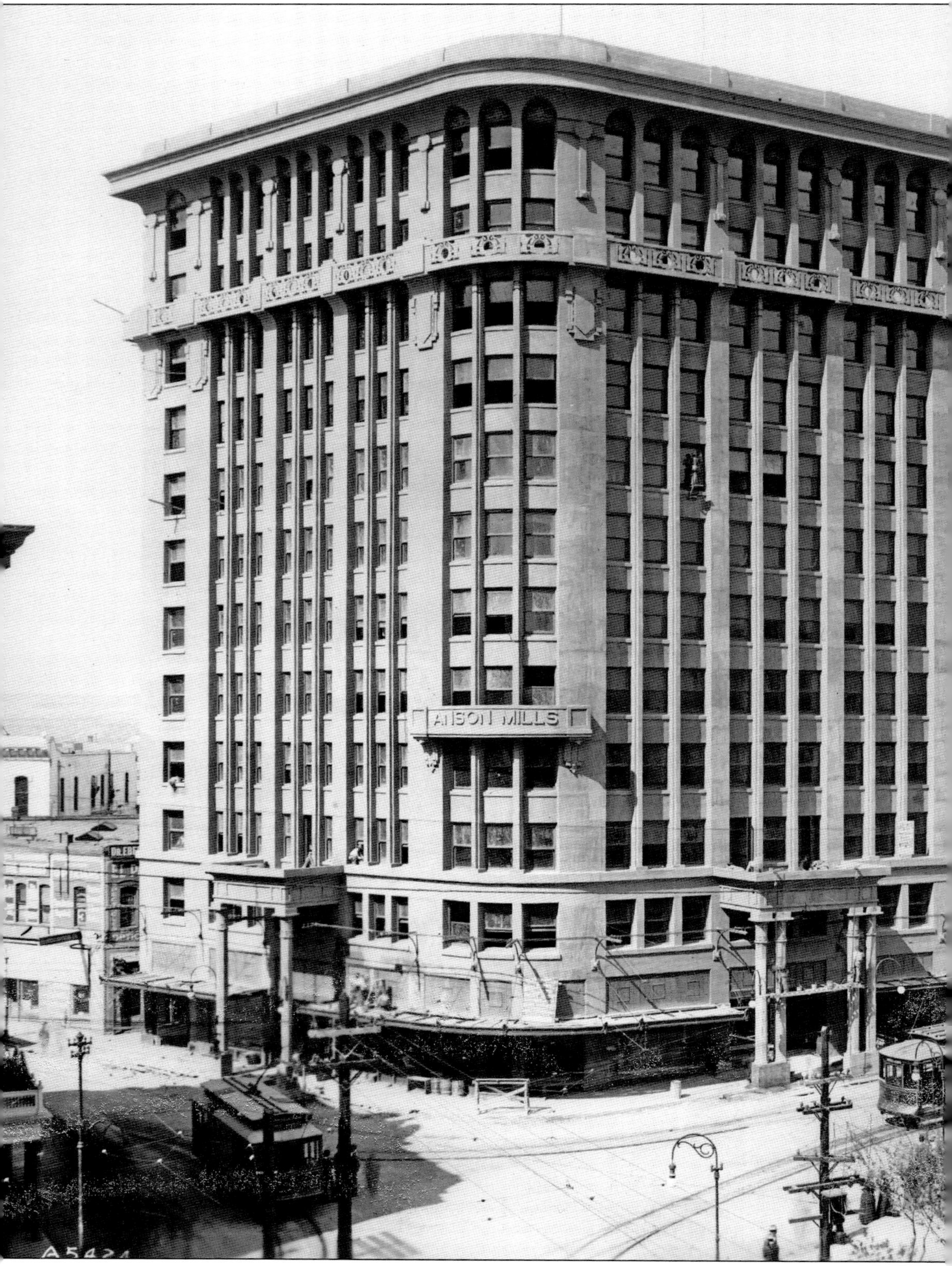
ANSON MILLS

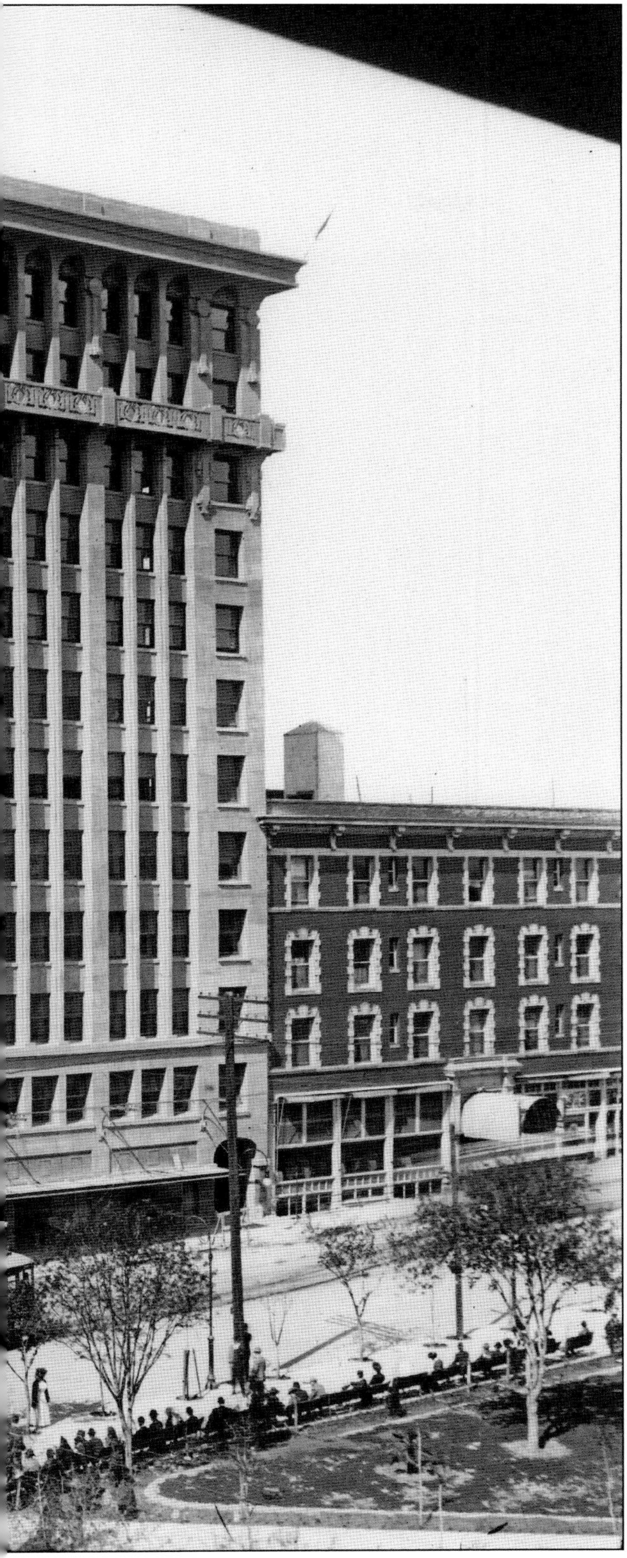

**Streetcars by the Plaza.** In this 1911 photograph, the Mills Building is getting its finishing touches. Named for El Paso icon and pioneer Anson Mills, it was, at the time, only the second concrete-frame skyscraper in the country. It stands on the site of the 1832 Ponce de Leon Ranch, later also the site of the Grand Central Hotel, which burned. Two monitor-roof streetcars are visible pausing near the El Paso Electric Railway's ticket booth. Judging from the gentlemen lining the benches, there is adequate sidewalk supervision of the construction project. (Courtesy of EPPL.)

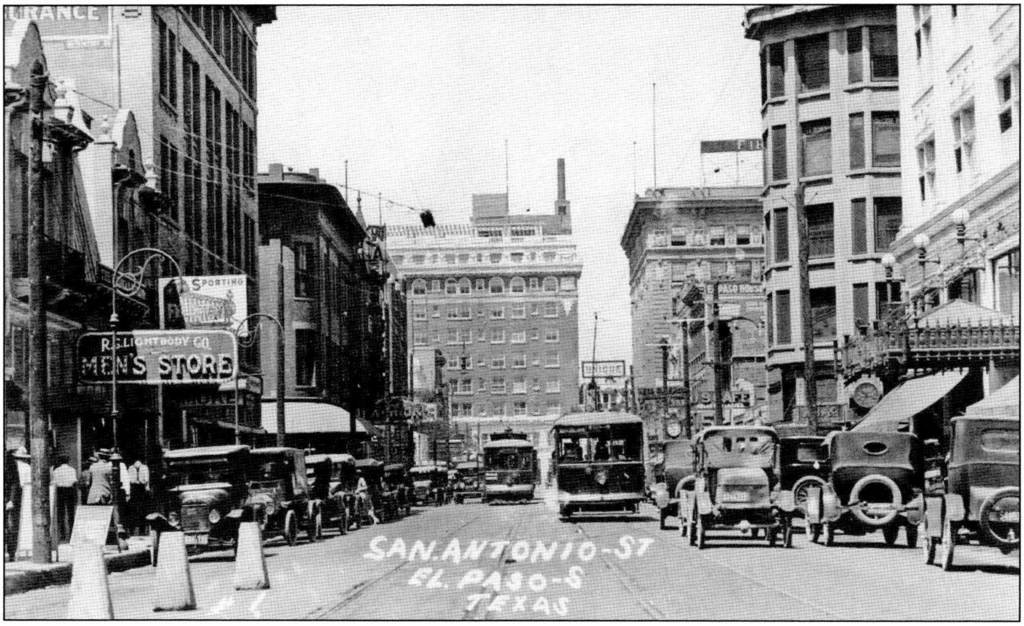


**DOUBLE TRACKS ON SAN ANTONIO STREET.** In the earlier streetcar days, San Antonio Street was double tracked, allowing both east and west movement of streetcars. In this postcard view, a single-truck Birney (right) is moving away from the camera and a monitor-roof trolley (left) is approaching the camera. After 1950, one track was removed, and streetcar traffic was eastbound only.

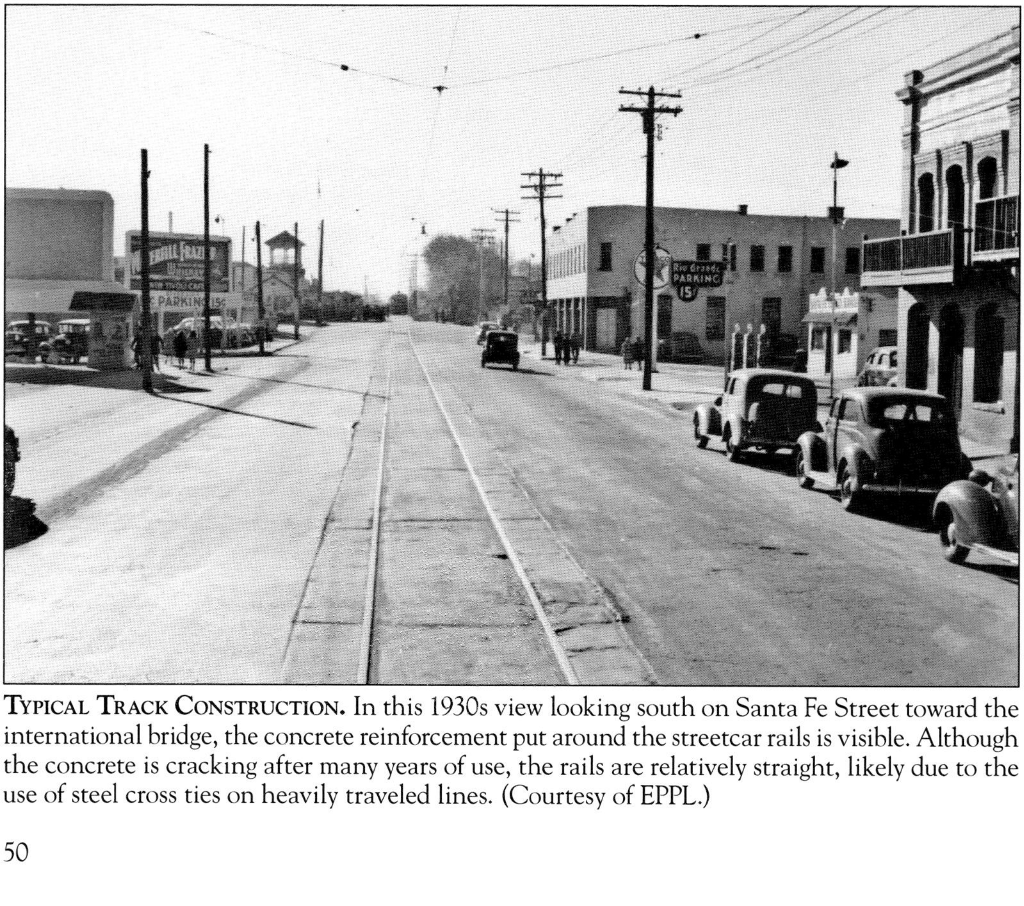


**TYPICAL TRACK CONSTRUCTION.** In this 1930s view looking south on Santa Fe Street toward the international bridge, the concrete reinforcement put around the streetcar rails is visible. Although the concrete is cracking after many years of use, the rails are relatively straight, likely due to the use of steel cross ties on heavily traveled lines. (Courtesy of EPPL.)

## *Five*

# Fort Bliss, the Mexican Revolution, and the World Wars

Fort Bliss moved to its present location on La Noria Mesa in 1893, putting it 5 miles from the center of downtown. A streetcar line was built out to the post in 1906, which had the effect of stimulating real estate sales for properties along the route to the post. The Fort Bliss line separated from the Government Hill line at the corner of Hueco and Copia Streets in a small neighborhood shopping center called Alta Vista. It then went under the railroad on Copia Street, passing Memorial Park on its way up the hill. After crossing Altura Street, it veered off to the left following a canal on what is now Justus Street (then Copia Street). What is now Copia Street was originally Henderson Street at this point. The track then made a wide swing to the right and traveled down the median of Fort Boulevard. In 1922, a shuttle line was built east on Stevens Street out to the William Beaumont Army Hospital. The Beaumont shuttle was short-lived, lasting only 15 years until 1938. Angling left on Tompkins Street, the Fort Bliss line crossed Dyer Street, then the railroad at grade, and made its way up to a loop around a little rock building next to Club Road. During the Mexican Revolution in the 1910s, then during World War I and later World War II, the Fort Bliss line enjoyed heavy patronage. After Gen. John J. "Black Jack" Pershing arrived to take command of the expedition into Mexico to pursue Pancho Villa, there were troops stationed in various parts of town, not only on Fort Bliss proper. Camp Cotton was an example, and most of these encampments were served by streetcars. The end to the Fort Bliss line came in 1947 when the El Paso City Lines sought to convert all lines to buses, with the exception of the Juarez line.

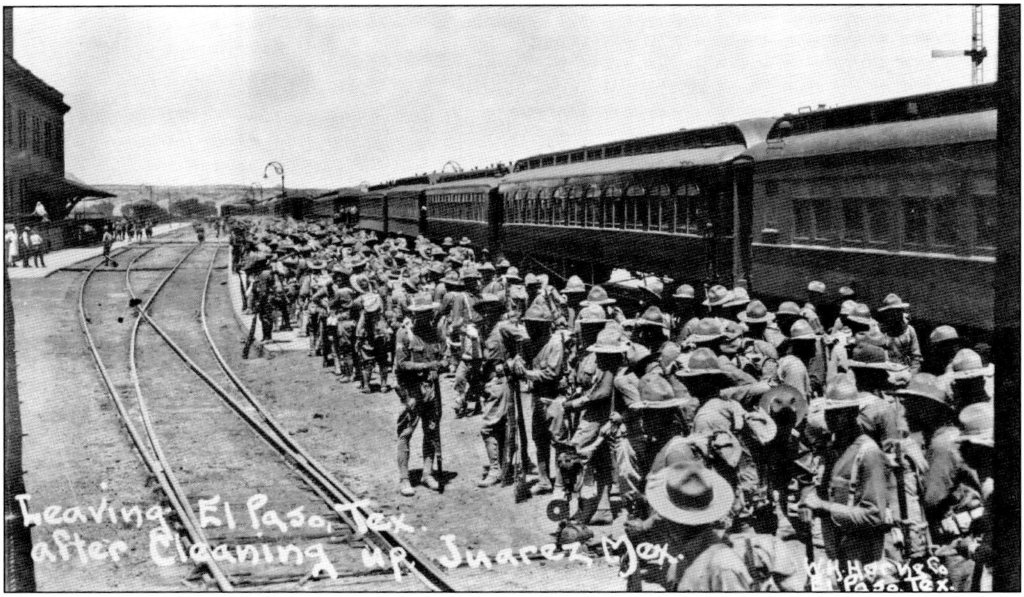


**Troops Leaving El Paso.** In this W. H. Horne postcard, a large contingent of troops is at Union Depot preparing to depart after securing the United States side of the border against skirmishes in Juarez between the revolutionaries and the Federals, which, at times, threatened to spill across the border. The Depot line looped at the San Francisco Street entrance of the depot.

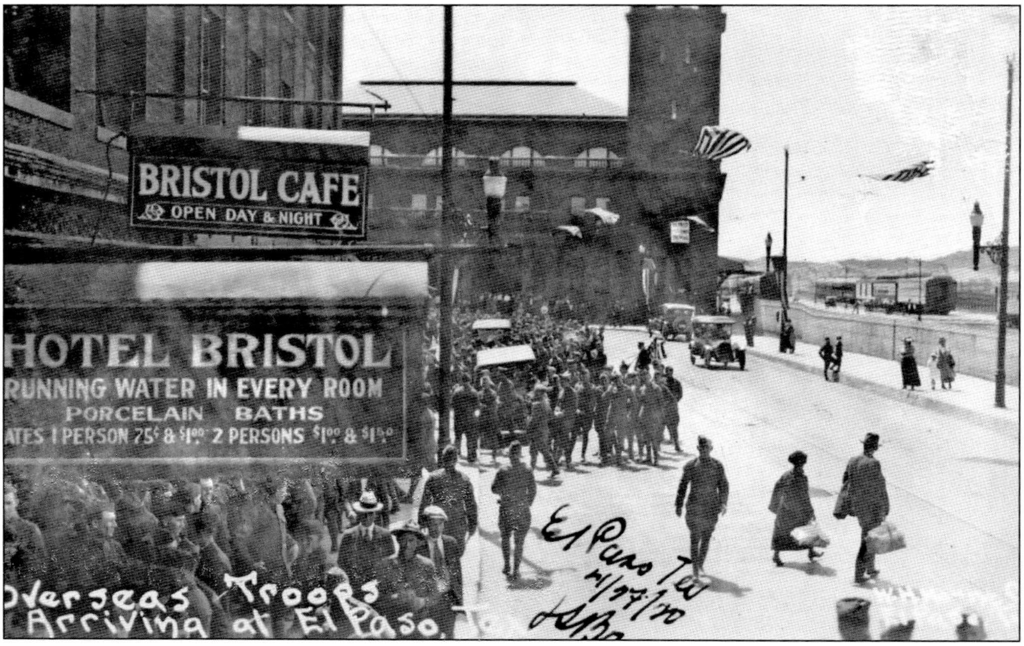


**Arriving Troops in the World War I Era.** In another W. H. Horne postcard view, the trolley line on San Francisco Street is visible as arriving troops wait for transportation on the street. The Bristol Hotel, known as one of the railroad hotels, provided respite for travelers for many years. Single-truck Birney streetcars on the Depot line often carried advertising reading "Take this car to hotels and Juarez."

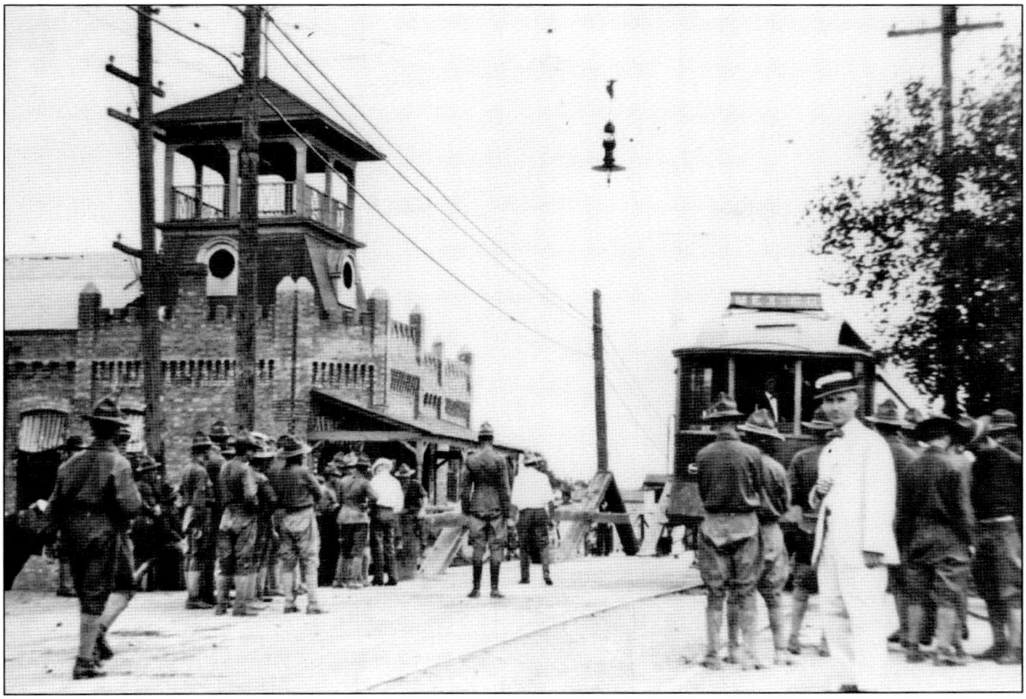

**Troops at the Bridge.** A major responsibility of troops in the Mexican Revolution era was to protect the international bridges. By appearance, this is the U.S. side of the Santa Fe Street Bridge. Reentering the United States is streetcar No. 81 or 83, the only two cars with railroad roofs. Not much weaponry is seen in this photograph.

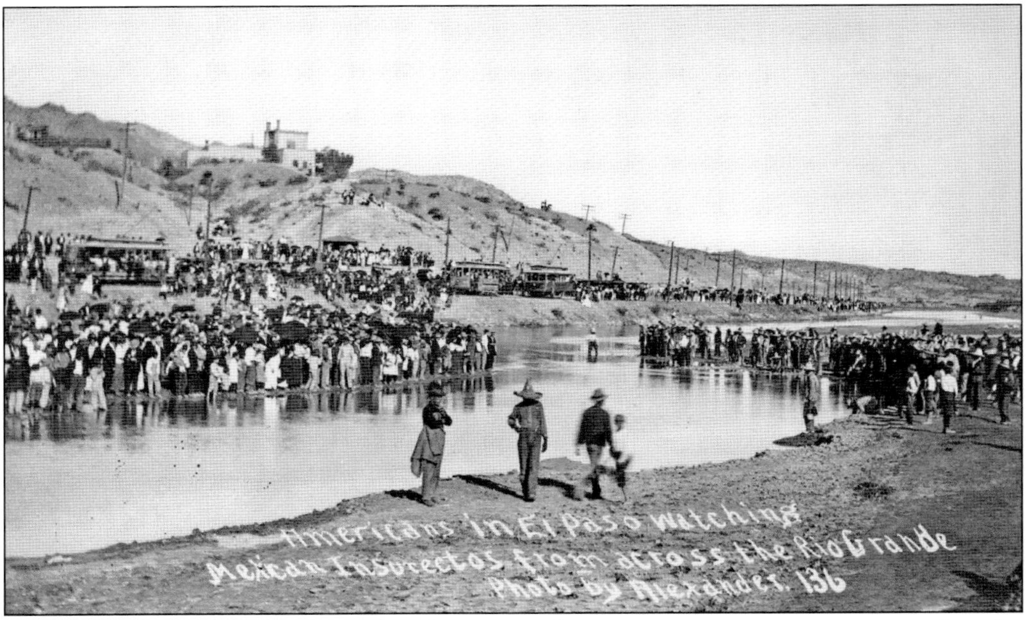


**Watching a Revolution.** Since the Mexican revolutionaries were at one time camped on the Mexican side of the Rio Grande a few miles upriver, it became a popular pastime for onlookers to travel by trolley out the Smelter line to watch the activities across the border. Here are both open and closed cars waiting for the hundreds of gawkers on both sides of the river.

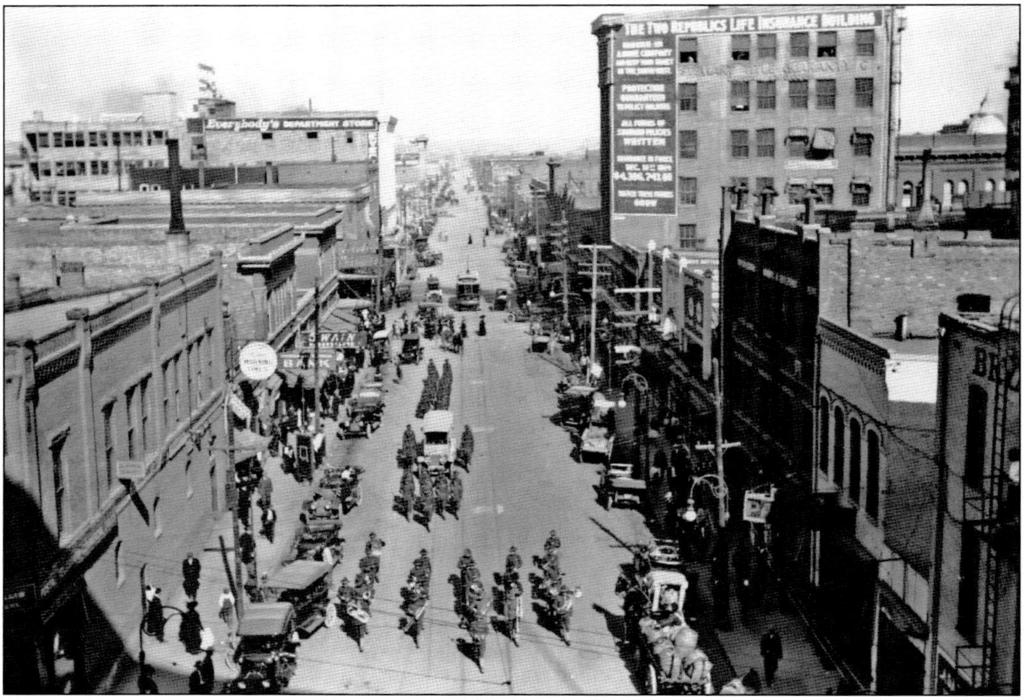


**A MILITARY PARADE.** What appears to be a military funeral procession makes its way down Texas Street with a streetcar following. Behind the band is a vintage ambulance with an honor guard, and there is even a riderless horse to complete the scene. The size of the cortege would indicate it was a high-ranking individual.

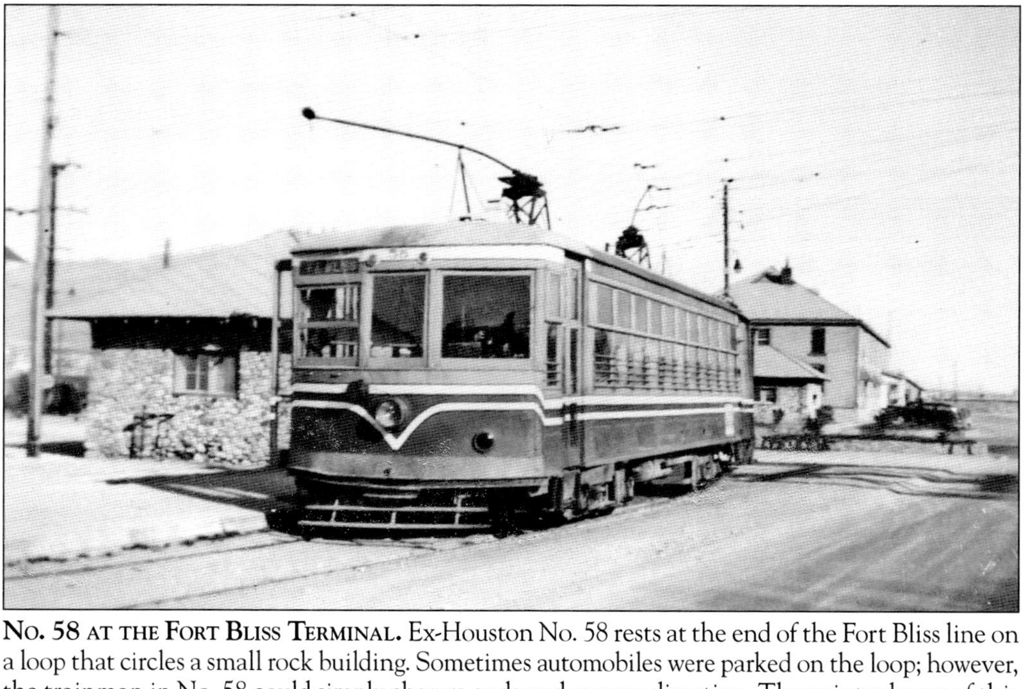

**NO. 58 AT THE FORT BLISS TERMINAL.** Ex-Houston No. 58 rests at the end of the Fort Bliss line on a loop that circles a small rock building. Sometimes automobiles were parked on the loop; however, the trainman in No. 58 could simply change ends and reverse direction. The paint scheme of this streetcar indicates the year is 1945 or 1946. The line was converted to buses in 1947.

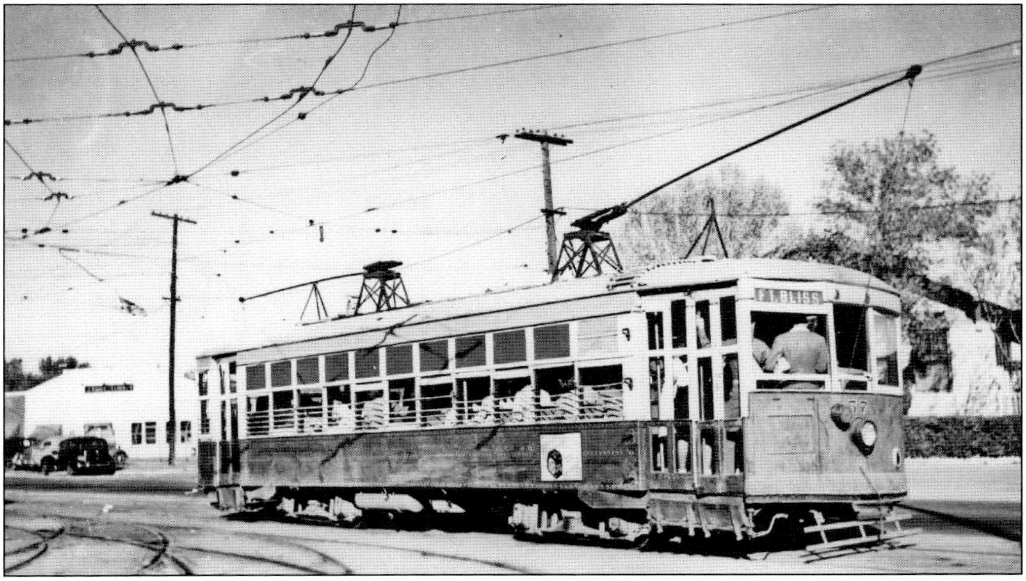

**No. 57 in Wartime.** Ex-Houston No. 57 is bound for Fort Bliss during World War II loaded with soldiers and with standing room only as it passes the carbarn on Cotton Street. Tracks entering the carbarn are on the left, and the bus barn is across the street. The building on the far right is the operator's lounge. No. 58 is still in El Paso Electric's red and white paint, prior to the City Lines takeover.

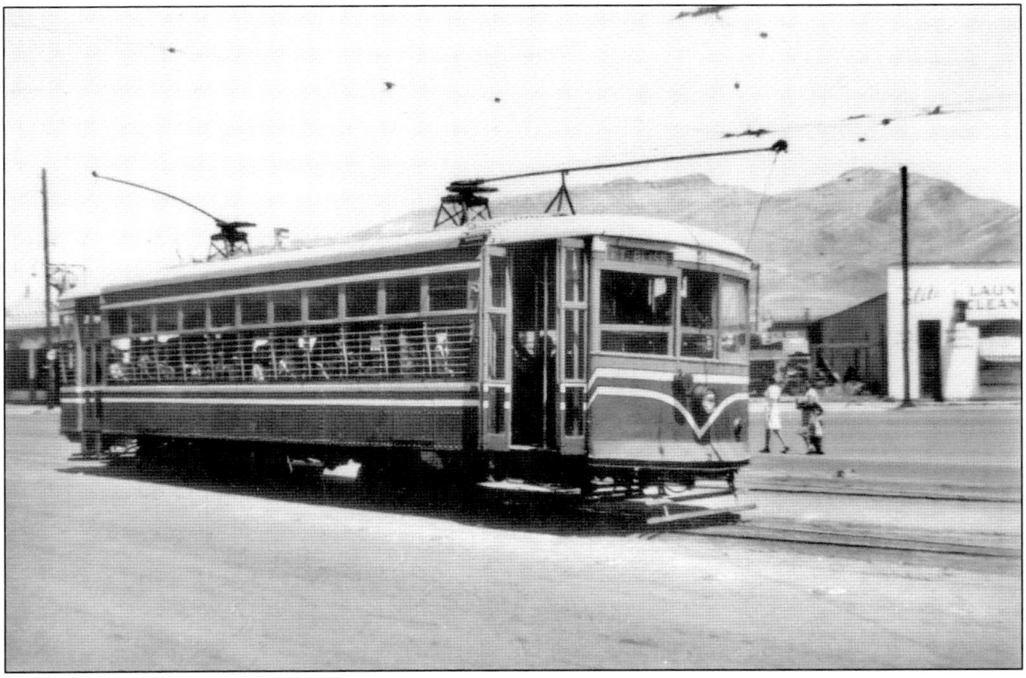

**Fort Bliss Car on Alameda Street.** Ex-Houston No. 51 has come off of Myrtle Avenue and will travel a short distance on Alameda Street before making a left turn on Piedras Street and crossing the Southern Pacific and Texas and Pacific Railroads at grade. It will climb Piedras up to the Five Points area, then go east on Tularosa Street. The Elite Cleaners is in the background.

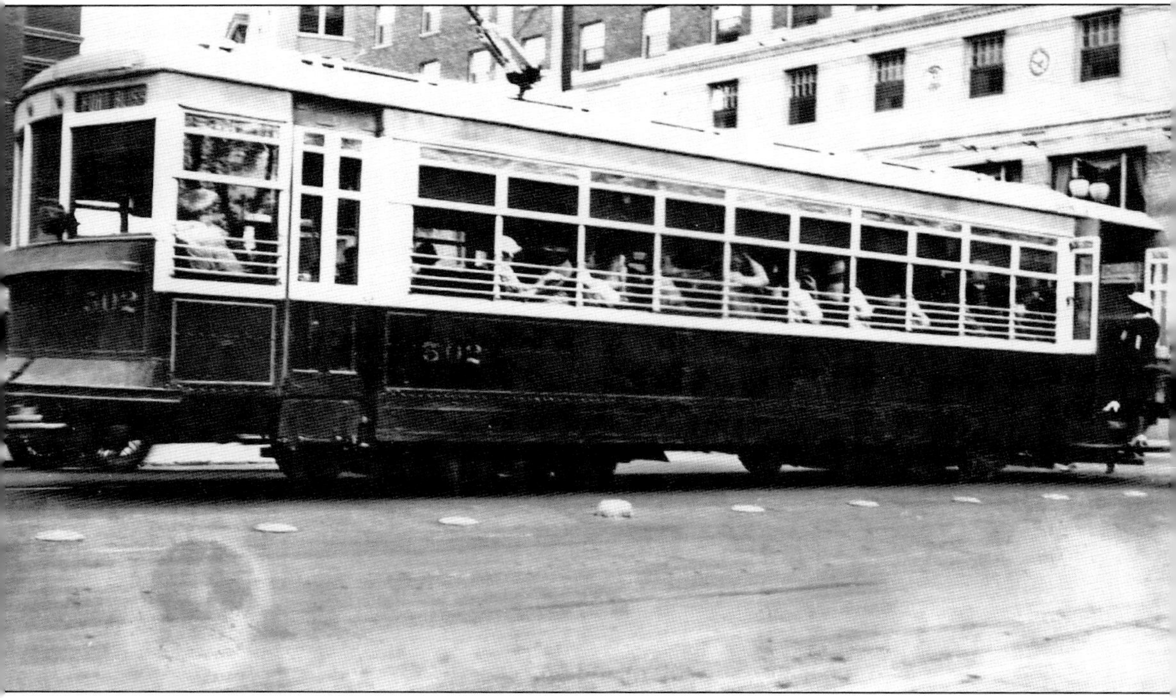

**No. 502 Downtown at Mills and Oregon Streets.** No. 502 was one of six single-end cars ordered for the Fort Bliss line in 1927, the last new car order placed by the El Paso Electric Company. These single-enders were fast, comfortable cars with deep leather seats. This scene is from around 1938 with Conrad Hilton's first high-rise hotel in the background. Boarding is a stylish matron in white hat, shoes, and gloves, hoping she will find a seat in the crowded car. After the Fort Bliss line was converted to buses in 1947, No. 502 was not scrapped, but in about 1950, it was sold to a farmer. (Courtesy of T. P. Taetsch Collection.)

# *Six*

# A Time of Transition 1930–1950

In the mid-1920s, the El Paso Electric Railway had reached its peak in electric rail service, with 63 miles of track, 17 routes, and more than 100 streetcars. About that time, the company became the El Paso Electric Company, with Power and Transportation Divisions. In 1929 and 1930, the first conversions to buses from streetcars occurred on the Smelter and Depot lines. The system remained stable until 1937, when the Highland Park, Manhattan Heights, Arizona Street, and the Government Hill lines were converted to buses. In 1938, the Mesa, High School, and Beaumont lines were converted; and in 1939 and 1940, the Sunset Heights and Second Ward lines were changed to bus service. By 1940, only the Fort Bliss, Park, and Juarez lines were left. There was a shuttle off of the Juarez line to the racetrack called the Hipodromo line, which lasted until 1945. After the Park and Fort Bliss lines went in 1947, all track was removed on Myrtle Avenue, leaving only San Antonio Street as the access to downtown from the carbarn on Cotton Street.

**Official Time-table El Paso Street Railway**

FRANKLIN PRINTING CO.

ALL CARS SCHEDULED FROM LITTLE PLAZA

| NAME | 1st Car | Schedule | Leaves Little Plaza | Last Car |
|---|---|---|---|---|
| Arizona | 5:48 a. m. | 12 min. | Even hour, 12, 24, 36, 48 min. after hour | 12:00 Midnight |
| Boulevard & Myrtle | 5:35 a. m. | 15 min. | To 7:50 p. m. 5, 20, 35, 50 min. after hour | |
| | | 20 min. | After 7:50 p. m. 10, 30, 50 min. after hour | 11:50 p. m. |
| Depot | 5:44 a. m. | 10 min. | 4, 14, 24, 34, 44, 54 min. after hour | 10:14 p. m. |
| Fort Bliss | 5:25 a. m. | 30 min. | 25, 55, min. after hour | 11:55 p. m. |
| Government Hill | 5:40 a. m. | 30 min. | To 8:10 p. m., 10, 40, min after hour | |
| | | 60 min. | After 8:10 p. m. 10 min after hour | 11:10 p. m. |
| Highland Park | 5:30 a. m. | 15 min. | To 7:00 p. m. even hr. 15, 30, 45 min. after hr. | |
| | | 20 min. | After 7:00 p. m. even hour, 20, 40 after hour | 12:00 Midnight |
| Manhattan Heights | 5:48 a. m. | 60 min. | 48 min. after hour | 11:48 p. m. |
| Mesa | 6:05 a. m. | 20 min. | 5, 20, 45 min. after hour | 11:45 p. m. |
| Mexico | 5:30 a. m. | 15 min. | To 7:00 p. m. even hour, 15, 30, 45 after hr. | |
| | | 12 min. | After 7:00 p.m. " 12, 24, 36, 48 min. after hr | 12:00 Midnight |
| Washington Park | 5:30 a. m. | 15 min. | To 2:00 p. m. 15, 30, 45 min. after hour | |
| | | 9 min. | After 2:00 p. m. to 7:00 p. m. 9, 18, 27 etc. | |
| | | 15 min. | After 7:00 p. m. 15, 30, 45 min. after hour | 12:00 Midnight |
| Smelter | 5:20 a. m. | 20 min. | 20, 40 min. after hour | 12:00 Midnight |
| Sunset | 5:50 a. m. | 20 min. | 10,30,50 min. after hour | 11:50 p. m. |
| Second Ward | 5:16 a. m. | 12 min. | 4, 16, 28, 40, 52 min. after hour | 12:00 Midnight |
| Race Track | 3 cars daily | 6:15 a. m. | 11:15 a. m. 5:45 p. m. | |
| Interurban | Leaves both terminals every hour from 6:00 a. m. to 11:00 p. m. | | | |

RETURNING TO LITTLE PLAZA CARS LEAVE AS FOLLOWS

| | |
|---|---|
| Arizona | Returns every 12 min. from 6:00 a. m. |
| Boulevard & Myrtle | Returns every 15 min. from 6:05 a. m. |
| Depot | Returns every 10 min. from 5:50 a. m. |
| Fort Bliss | Returns every 30 min. from 5:43 a. m. |
| Government Hill | Returns every 30 min. from 6:08 a. m. to 6:38 p. m. then 60 min. to 12:08 a. m. |
| Highland Park | Returns every 15 min. from 5:53 a. m. to 6:50 p. m. then 20 min. to 12:08 a. m. |
| Manhattan Heights | Returns every 60 min. from 6:25 a. m. |
| Mesa | Returns every 20 min. from 6:15 a. m. |
| Mexico | Returns every 15 min. from 5:45 a. m. |
| Washington Park | Returns every 15 min. from 5:52 a. m. to 2:00 p. m. then 9 min. to 7:00 p. m. |
| Smelter | Returns every 20 min. from 5:40 a. m. |
| Sunset | Returns every 20 min. from 6:00 a. m. |
| Second Ward | Returns every 12 min. from 5:28 a. m. |
| Race Track | Returns 6:45 a. m., 11:45 a. m., 6:15 p. m. |

**EL PASO STREET RAILWAY TIMETABLE.** An interesting and rare piece of ephemera, this timetable, sponsored by the Popular Dry Goods Store, a downtown icon, shows the routes and times of operation in the mid-1920s. Most lines had service until midnight. A few of the heavier patronized lines, such as Fort Bliss, were known to have "owl" cars, with hourly service from midnight to 5:00 a.m. Notice that cars are scheduled to leave from Little Plaza, on Mills Street between Oregon and El Paso Streets, also known as Pioneer Plaza. Most car lines started the day leaving from Little Plaza around 5:30 a.m. That would obligate the trainmen to show up at the carbarn by 4:30 a.m. to get their assignment, do their paperwork, and check out their assigned car before departing.

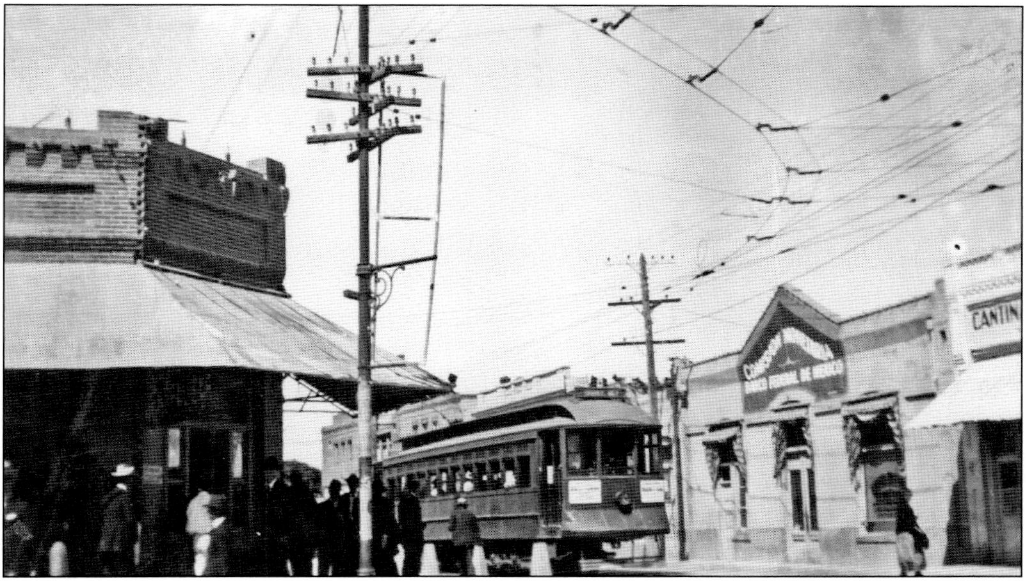

**A Railroad Roof-Heavy Car in Mexico.** No. 81 or 83, carrying a heavy load of riders, rounds the corner of Lerdo Street and Avenida 16 de Septiembre in Ciudad Juarez. These cars, built by the Laconia Car Company, were originally open cars, rebuilt later to closed cars and renumbered upward. The concrete pylons near the front entrance of the streetcar are meant to provide a safe loading space in the street.

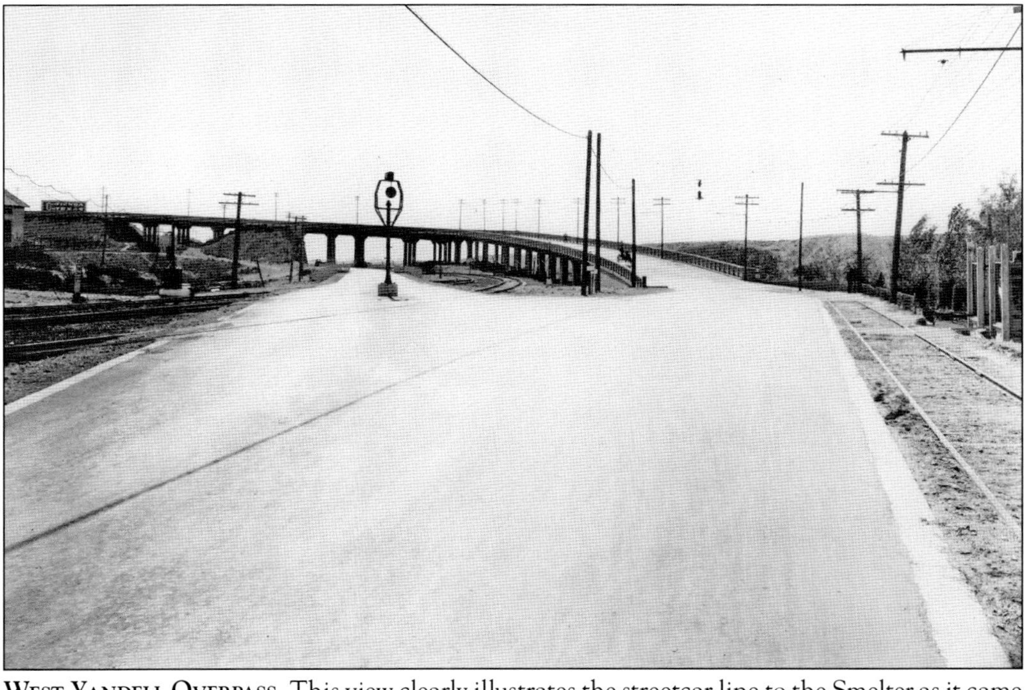

**West Yandell Overpass.** This view clearly illustrates the streetcar line to the Smelter as it came off the concrete overpass on West Yandell Street down to the side of Paisano Street, then known as Upper Valley Road. The railroad (left) is the Santa Fe line to Las Cruces, New Mexico. The wig-wag crossing signal was typical in those days. The original Hart's Mill would be to the right of the photograph.

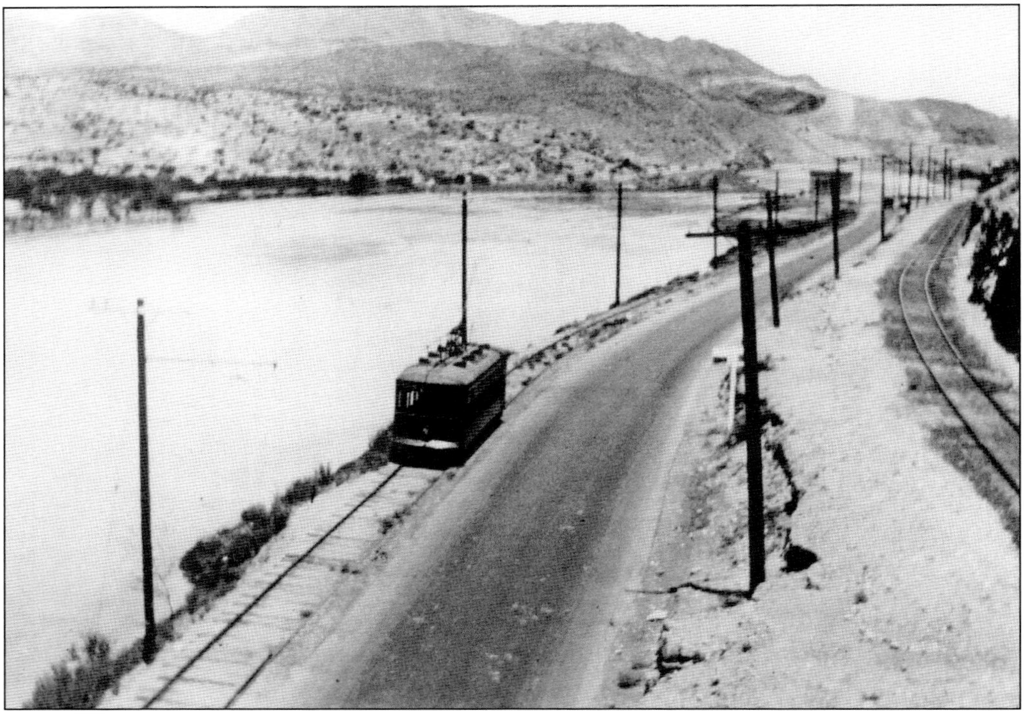

**Smelter Streetcar.** The American Smelting and Refining facility on Paisano Street was the destination of many riders on the Smelter streetcar line. At the end of the line, there were other industries, including the Southwestern Portland Cement and El Paso Brick Companies. From left to right are the Rio Grande River, a single-truck Birney on the Smelter line, the highway to Las Cruces, and the Santa Fe Railway.

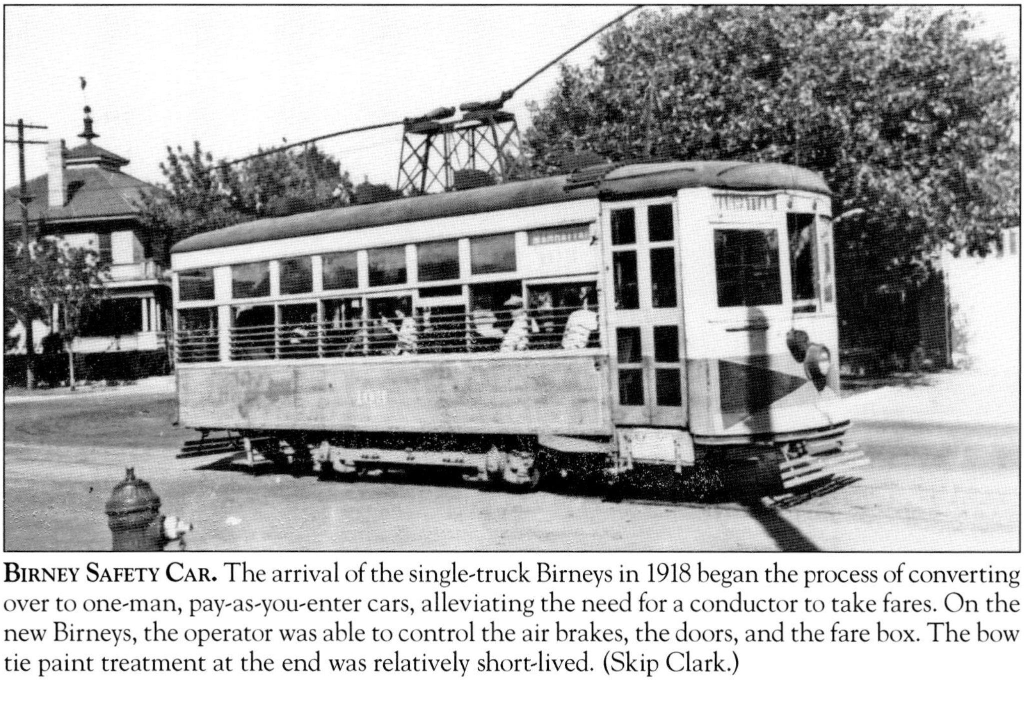

**Birney Safety Car.** The arrival of the single-truck Birneys in 1918 began the process of converting over to one-man, pay-as-you-enter cars, alleviating the need for a conductor to take fares. On the new Birneys, the operator was able to control the air brakes, the doors, and the fare box. The bow tie paint treatment at the end was relatively short-lived. (Skip Clark.)

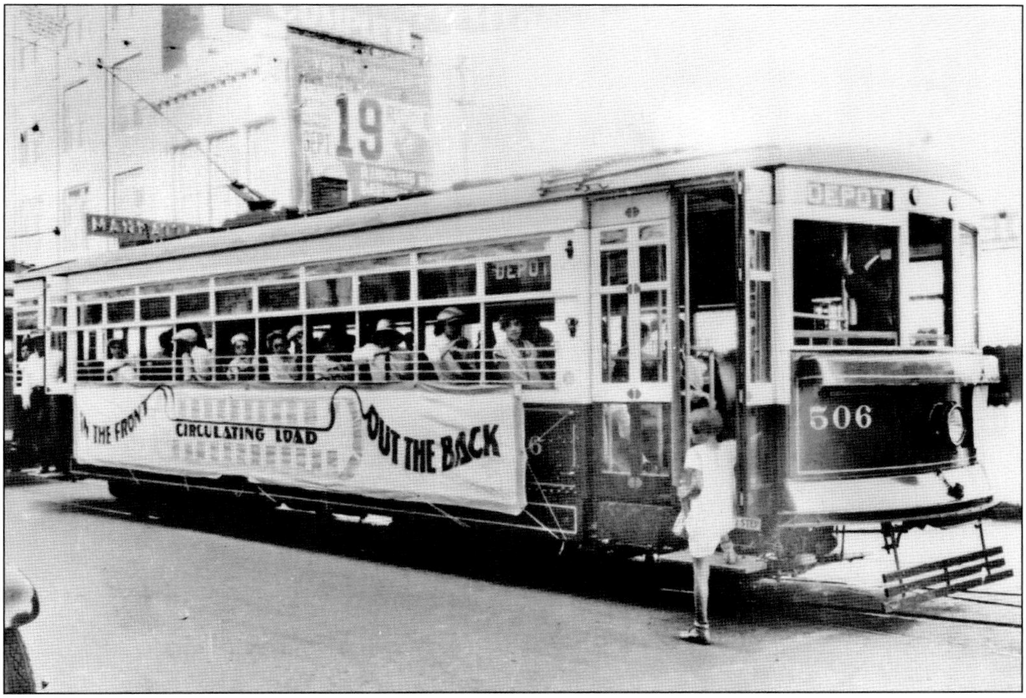


**The Company Promotes Ridership.** The El Paso Electric Company was cognizant of the need for advertising its services. That included some advertising banners on the cars, especially when the new Fort Bliss cars came in 1927. This one on No. 506 touted a circulating load. No. 506 would later be destroyed in a collision with a Texas and Pacific (T&P) passenger train at the Piedras Street crossing in 1941. (Courtesy of Skip Clark.)

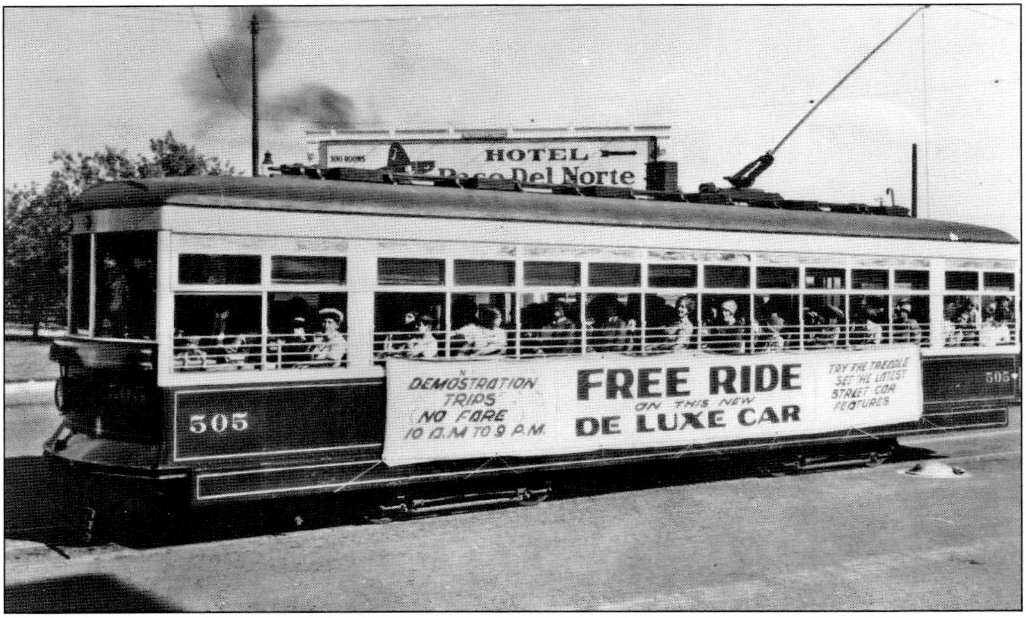


**A Free Ride.** With the arrival of the new 500-series Fort Bliss cars, free rides were given to the public from downtown to the depot, a short ride but one that would give the public a taste of riding in the new cars. No. 505 has a skirt attached to the car body. (Courtesy of Skip Clark.)

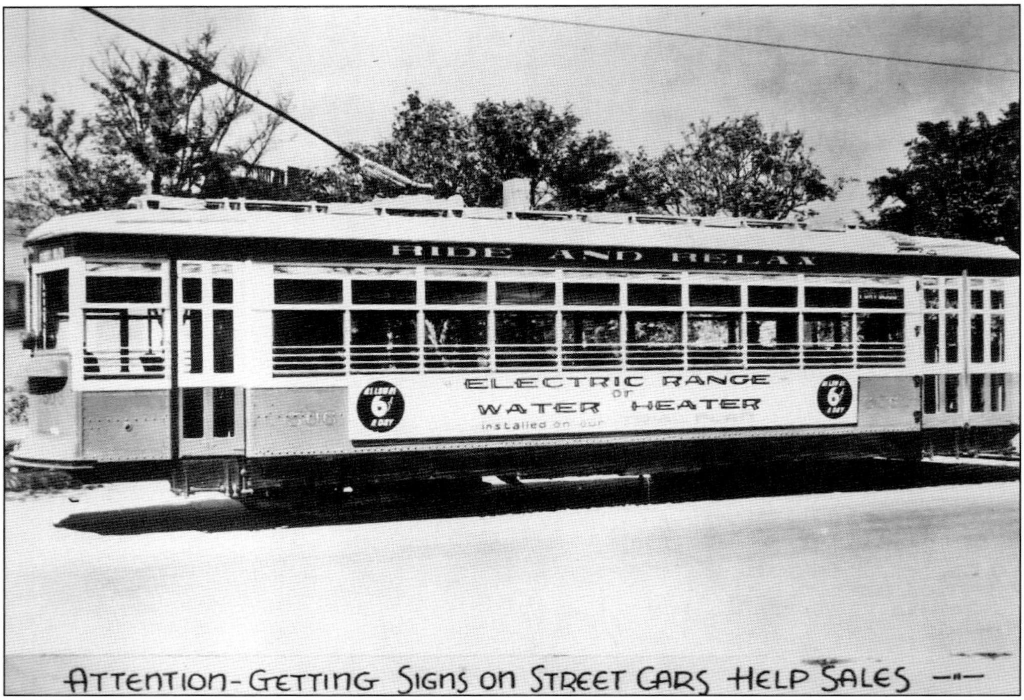


**ADVERTISING ELECTRICITY USES.** The El Paso Electric Company did from time to time use its cars to advertise the services of the Power Division. Here this 500-series Fort Bliss car carries a banner advertising electric appliances. The color scheme of this car was red and white with a blue band at the top.

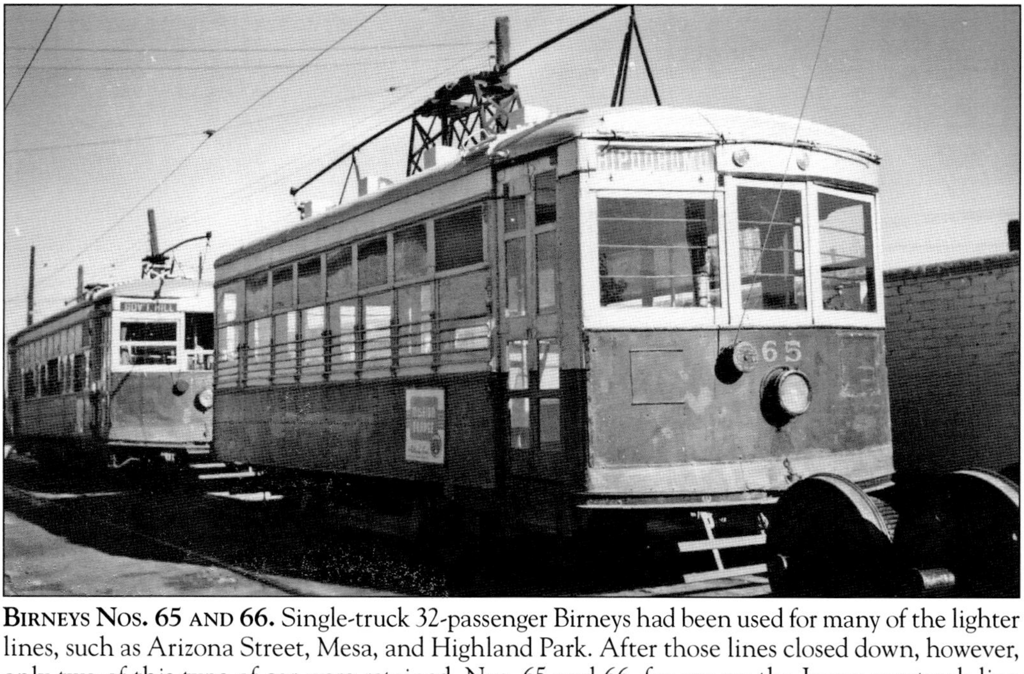


**BIRNEYS NOS. 65 AND 66.** Single-truck 32-passenger Birneys had been used for many of the lighter lines, such as Arizona Street, Mesa, and Highland Park. After those lines closed down, however, only two of this type of car were retained, Nos. 65 and 66, for use on the Juarez racetrack line known as Hipodromo.

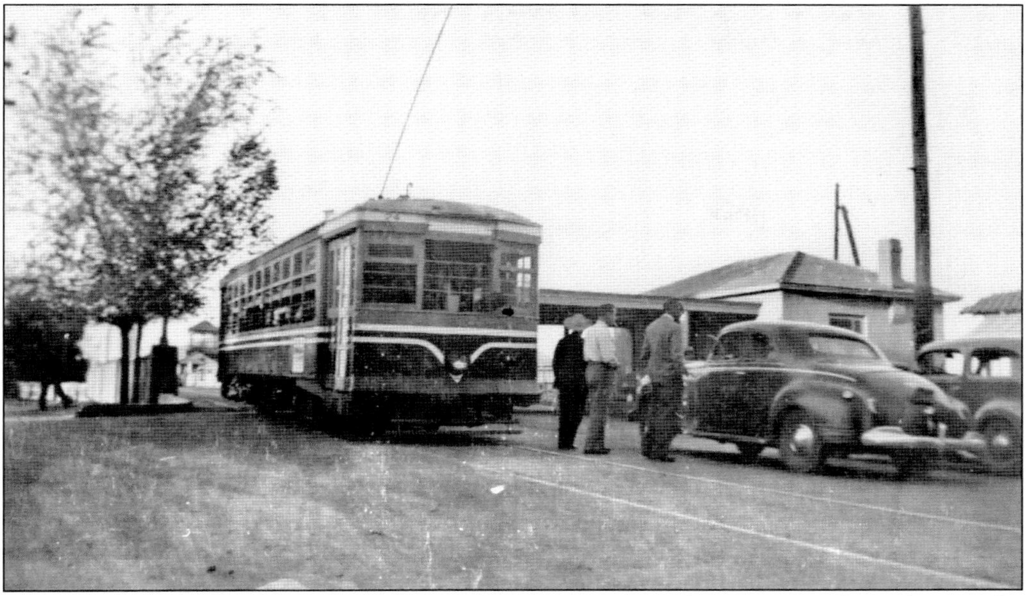

**The Stanton Street Bridge.** No. 74, one of the cars that was often rebuilt, is shown here in the mid-1940s ready to cross into Mexico from Stanton Street to Lerdo Street. The streetcar is in the left lane as the driver of the Dodge business coupe is being queried by the customs official.

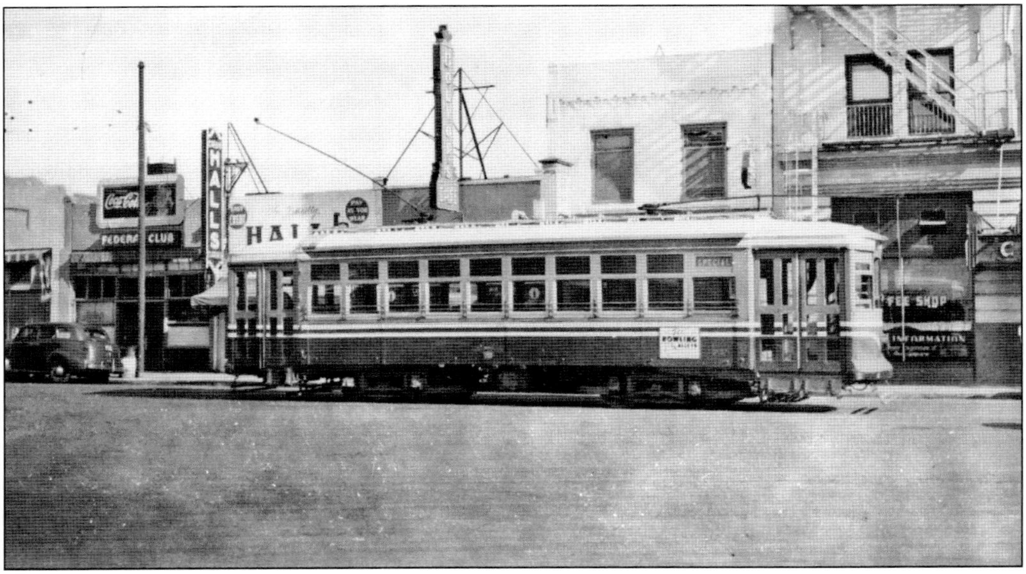


**No. 73 on San Antonio Street.** In this 1944 photograph, No. 73 is on San Antonio Street in downtown. No. 73 at this block would indicate it is traversing the Juarez loop. A few years later, No. 73 would go south to Torreon, Mexico.

# MODERNIZED STREET CARS

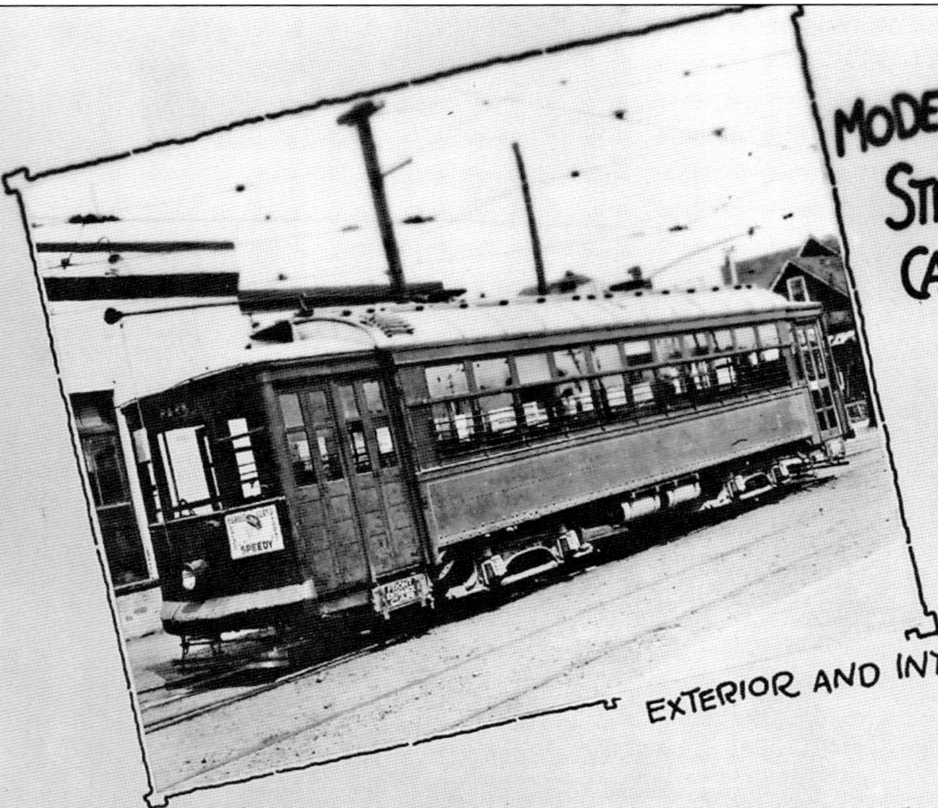


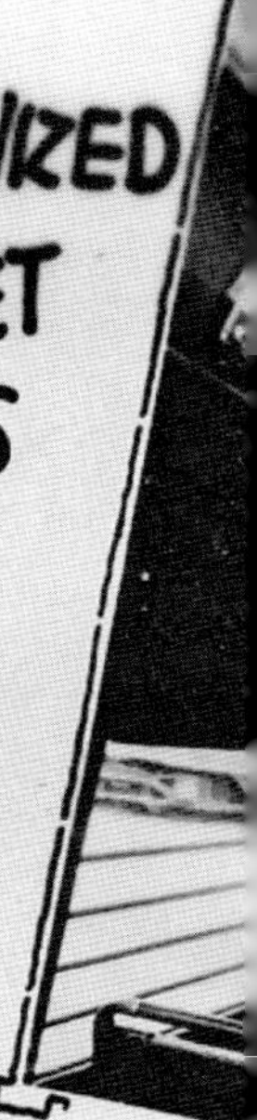

EXTERIOR AND INTERIOR OF C

PLATE No. 9

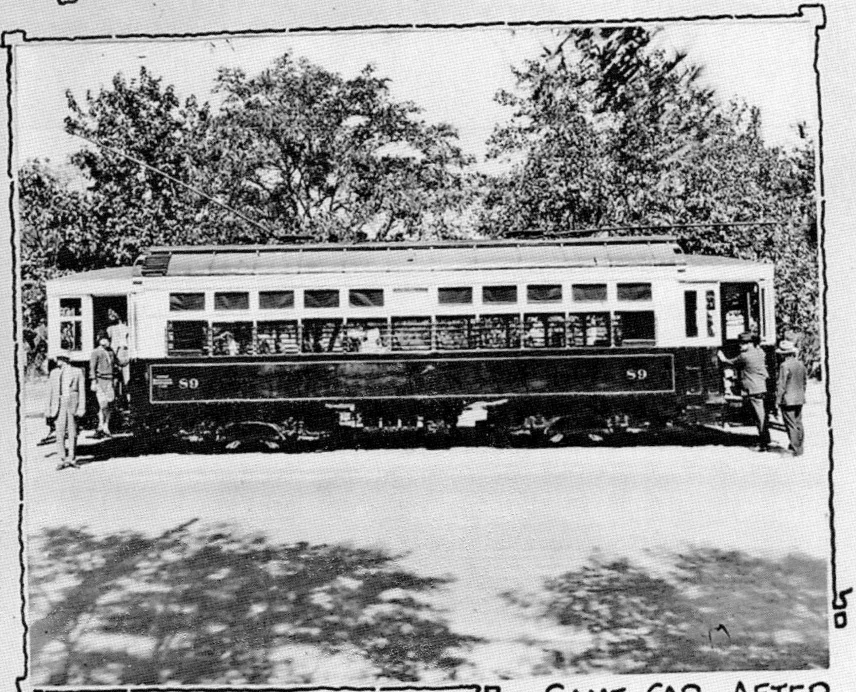

SAME CAR AFTER MODERNIZ

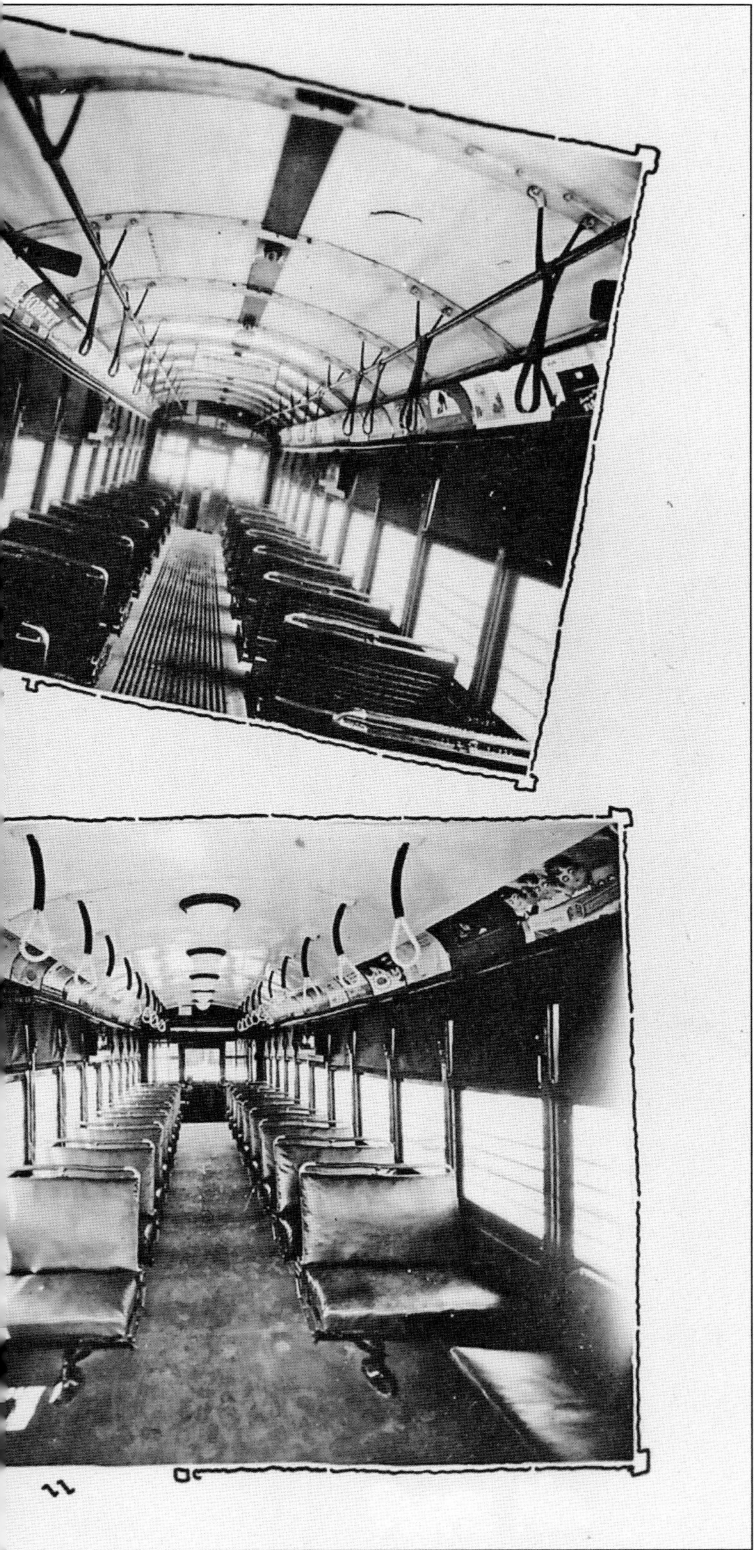

**MODERNIZED STREETCARS.** The 12 Stone and Webster, or "turtle roof," cars, Nos. 85 to 96, which came in 1912 and 1914, were given a remodeling or modernization in 1930 and 1931 as evidenced by this Electric Company advertisement. Not only did they get a new red-and-white paint scheme to replace the old Pullman green, the interiors were redone with new ceilings, new lighting fixtures, and new seating. This was done in the company shops at a much lower cost than purchasing new cars. At the same time, these cars had their running gear overhauled and renewed, including brakes, traction motors, truck assemblies, and wheels.

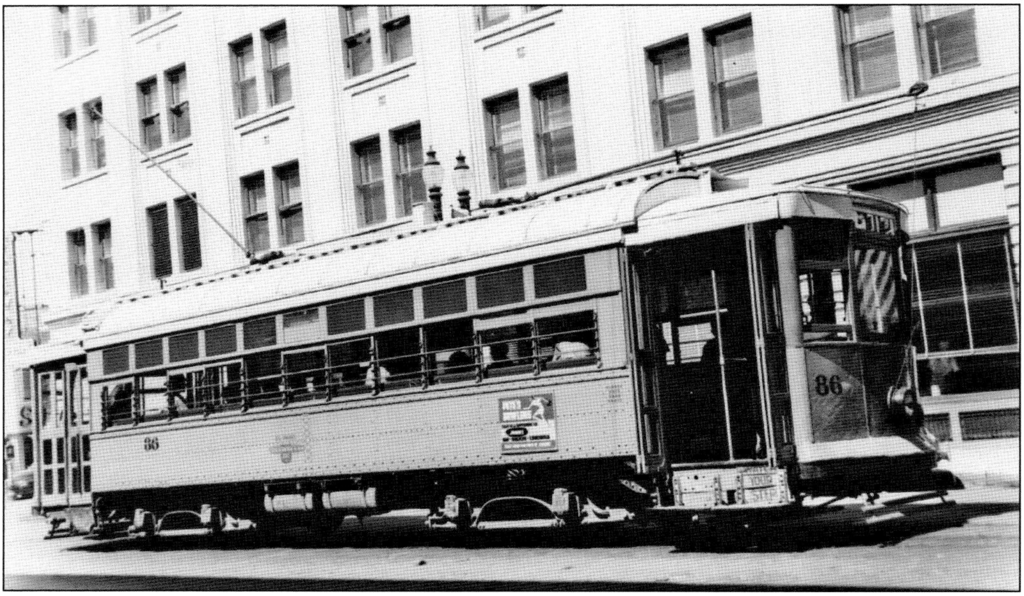


**No. 86 at the Gateway Hotel.** The "turtle-top," or Stone and Webster–style, roof is clearly seen here in this view of No. 86 in front of the Gateway Hotel on Stanton Street, loading for the Juarez line. There is an air scoop at each end, which assists ventilation. These were four-motor cars with St. Louis 47B trucks.

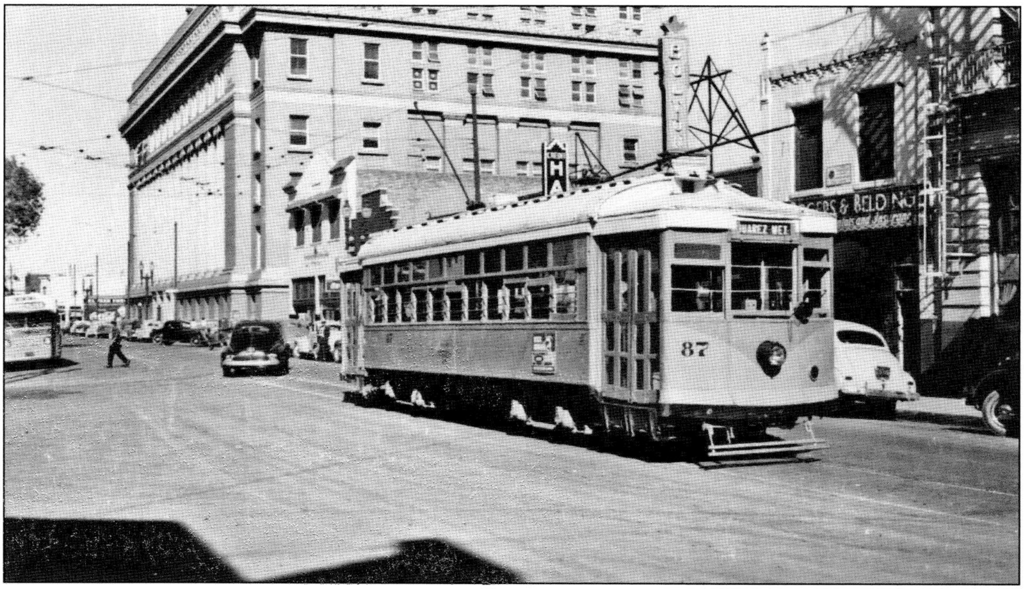


**No. 87 Passing the County Courthouse.** No. 87 is westbound on San Antonio Street from the carbarn to join the Juarez loop. Just above the GM "Curbliner" bus, notice the overhead catenary curve. This turn back from Myrtle to San Antonio Streets was added in 1943.

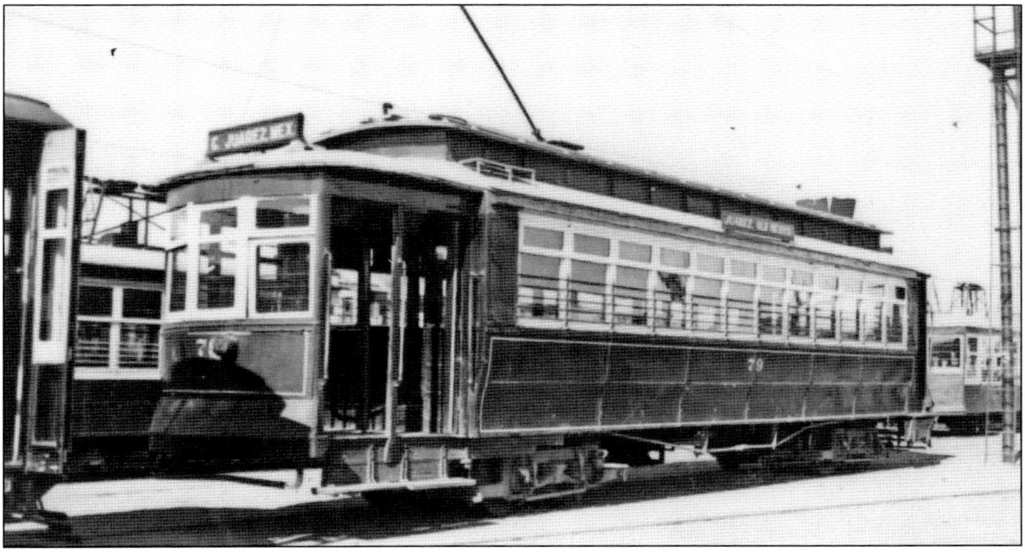


**Survival of a Monitor-Roof Car.** No. 79 was unique in that it was the only car with a monitor roof that did not get rebuilt to an arch roof. No. 79 dates back to 1907, having been delivered as an open car. It was rebuilt to a closed car about 1912 and ran for more than 30 years.

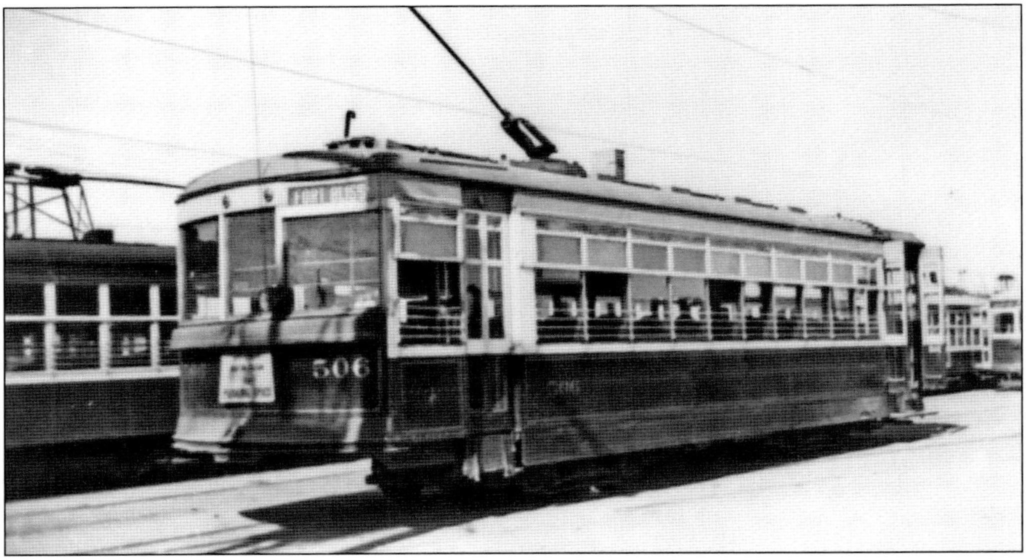


**No. 504 with Skirts.** No. 504 carries only one trolley pole since it was built as a single-ender, with motorman controls only at one end. This car was built for the Fort Bliss line and needed a loop at each end of the line. No. 504 shows fenders installed on the sides in this photograph. The idea was to reduce noise and to be more aesthetically appealing. (Courtesy of Skip Clark.)

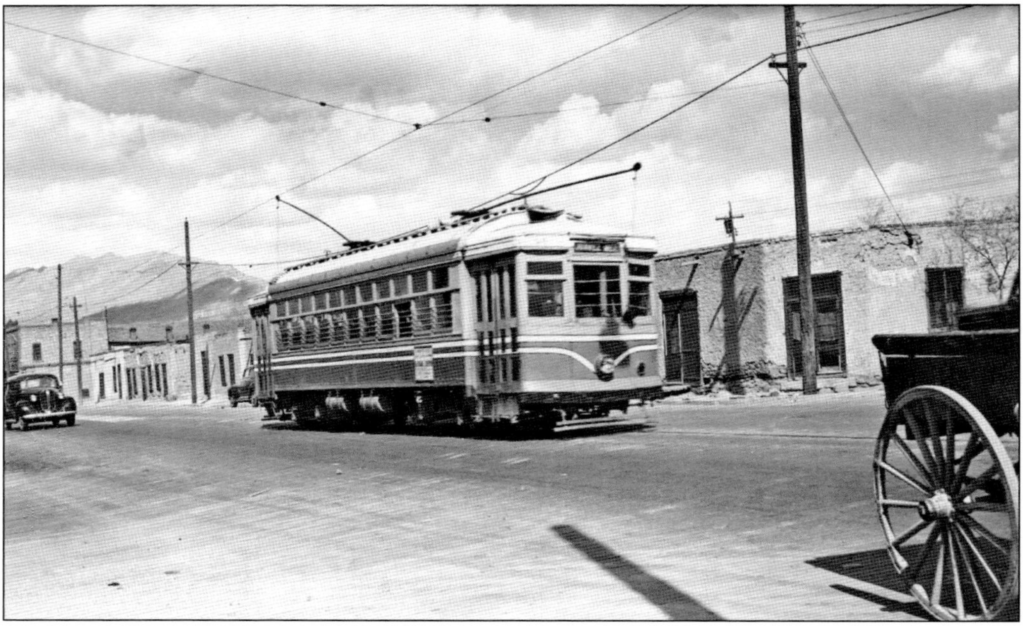

**Cars, Wagons, and Streetcars.** Adobe tenements still lined this portion of Stanton Street when this image was taken in 1945. No. 96 is the last of the second series of Stone and Webster roof cars. The second series, delivered in 1914, had two motors and maximum traction trucks.

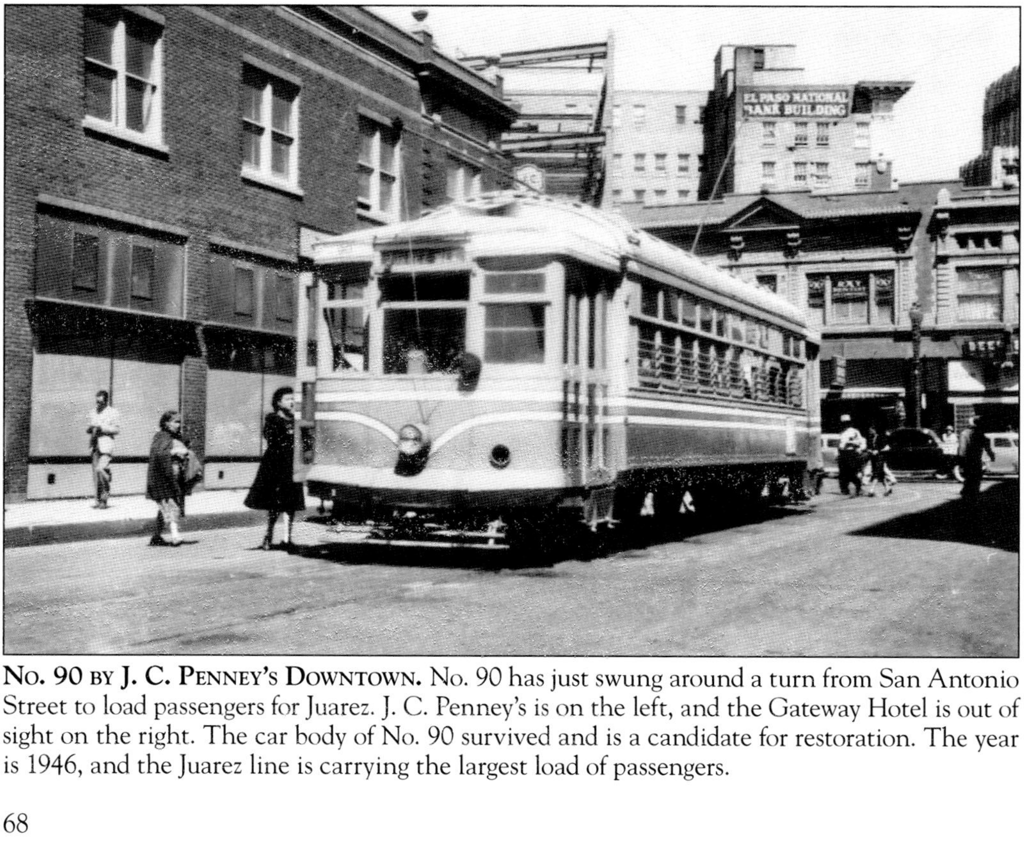


**No. 90 by J. C. Penney's Downtown.** No. 90 has just swung around a turn from San Antonio Street to load passengers for Juarez. J. C. Penney's is on the left, and the Gateway Hotel is out of sight on the right. The car body of No. 90 survived and is a candidate for restoration. The year is 1946, and the Juarez line is carrying the largest load of passengers.

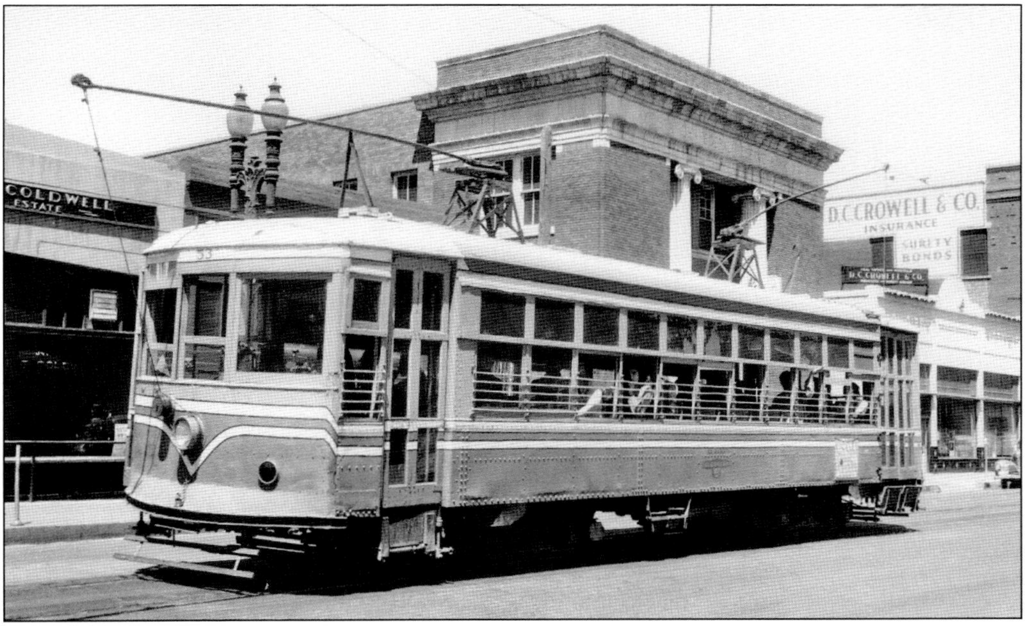


**SEPTEMBER 16, 1946.** It is a hot day in postwar El Paso as No. 53 comes in from either the Park or Fort Bliss lines. The only relief is the ability to open the window. The tall building behind the trolley is the Federal Reserve. No. 53 will unload and load at this point on Myrtle Avenue before swinging left onto San Antonio Street and going back out. (Courtesy of John Bromley Collection.)

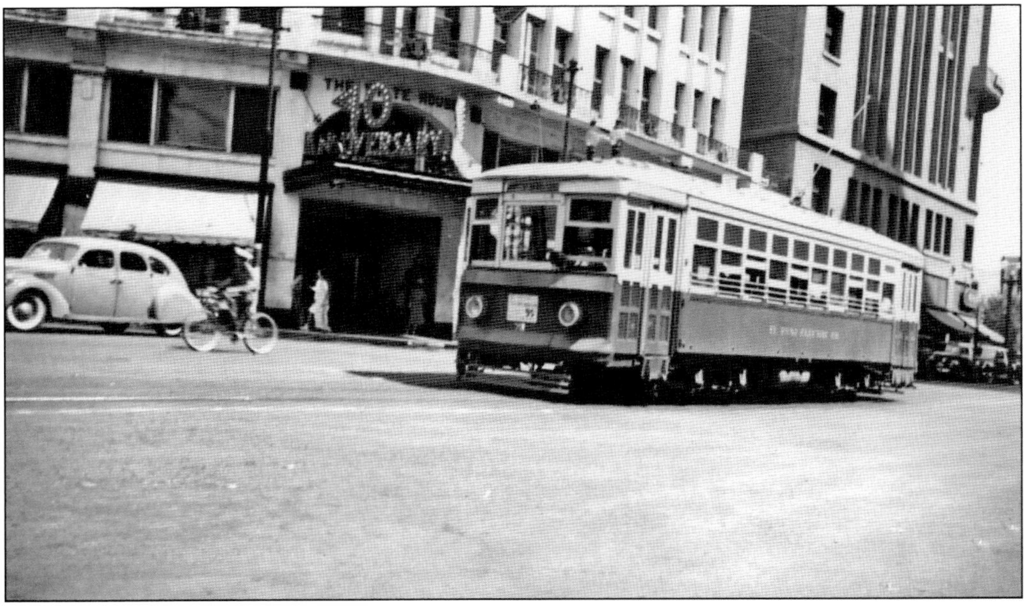

**CAR NO. 73.** No. 73 by this time (June 22, 1940) had been rebuilt to have twin headlights. This was an experiment that did not work, and the cars that had been so modified were returned to single center headlights. A Western Union telegraph messenger boy passes by the White House Department Store and a parked snazzy-looking car, possibly a Lincoln Zephyr. (Bob Crockett photograph, courtesy of Cliff Scholes.)

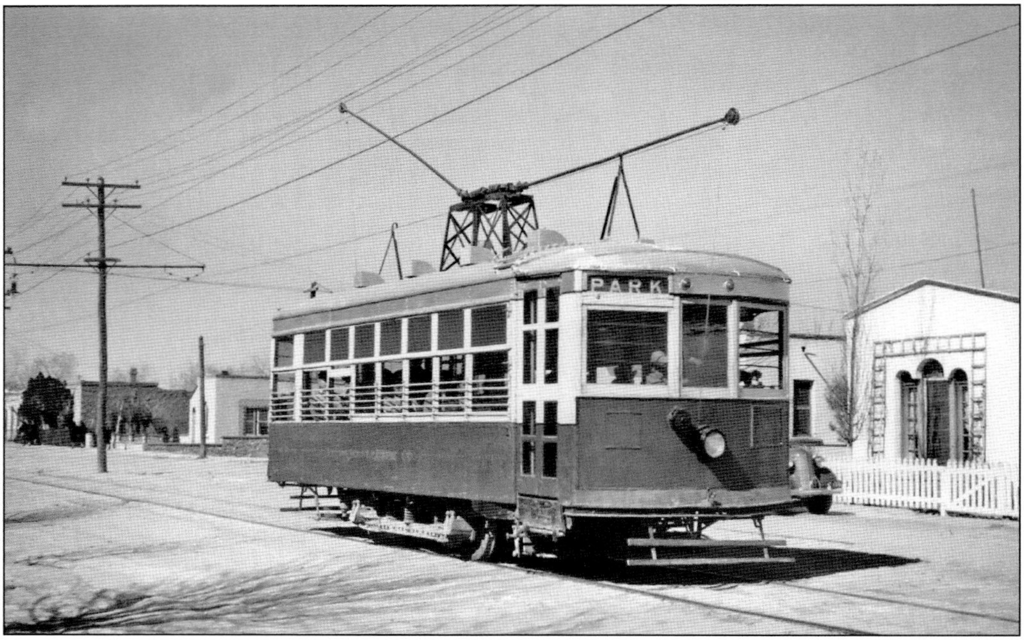


**No. 65 in 1943.** Birney No. 65 is carrying a Park destination sign, but it is believed that the car is actually on the Hipodromo line in Ciudad Juarez according to the surroundings. No. 65 routinely served the racetrack line. The paint scheme on this car at this time was white over red with a top silver band and roof. (Courtesy of John Bromley.)

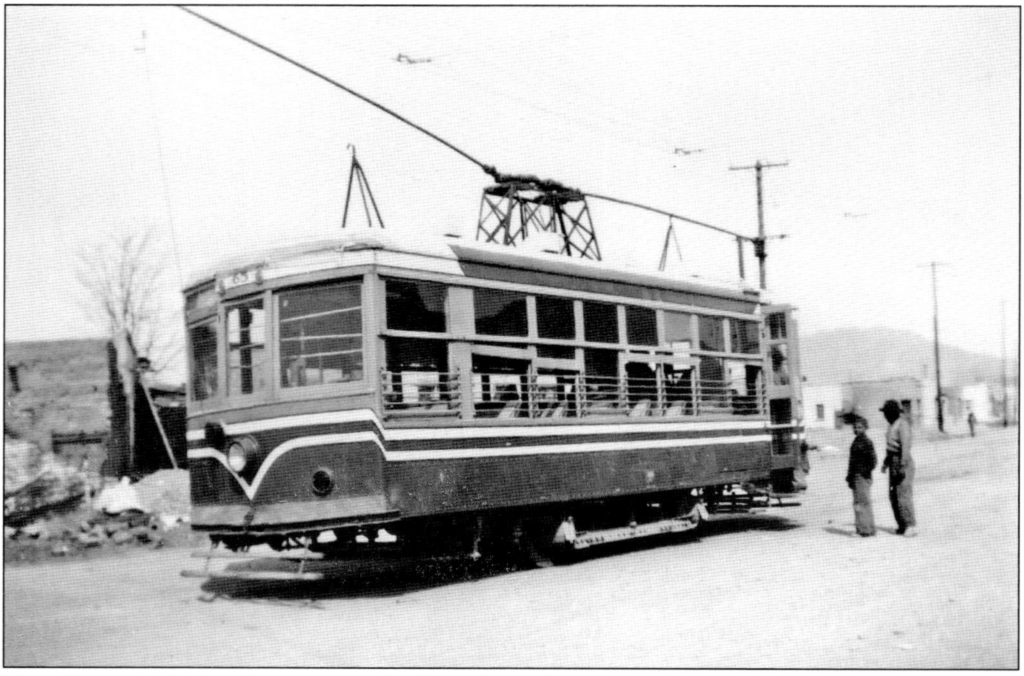

**No. 65 in 1945.** No. 65 is seen on the Hipodromo line in 1945, the last year of its operation. By this time, No. 65 was owned by El Paso City Lines, who bought the Transportation Division of the electric company at the end of 1943. The color scheme in this photograph is lime green over orange with white stripes. The two boys are waiting expectantly.

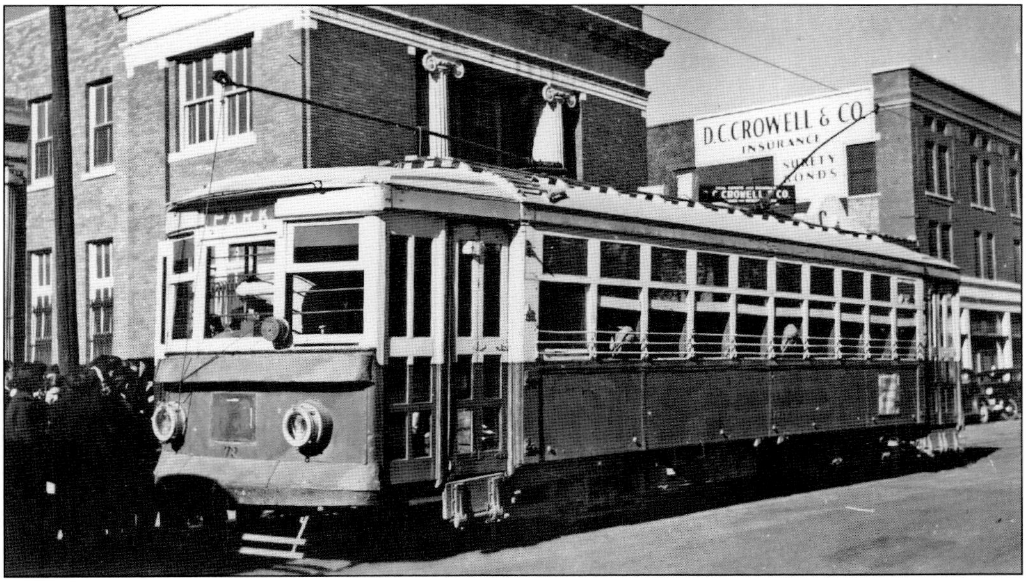


**No. 73 on the Park Line.** No. 73 was said to have been rebuilt so many times, it hardly resembled the original. In its original state, it had a monitor roof, later rebuilt to an arch roof. Here it is stopped on Myrtle Avenue. No. 73 would be sold to Torreon, Mexico, in the late 1940s and would run there until 1952. (Barney Neuberger photograph, courtesy of PDNSPS.)

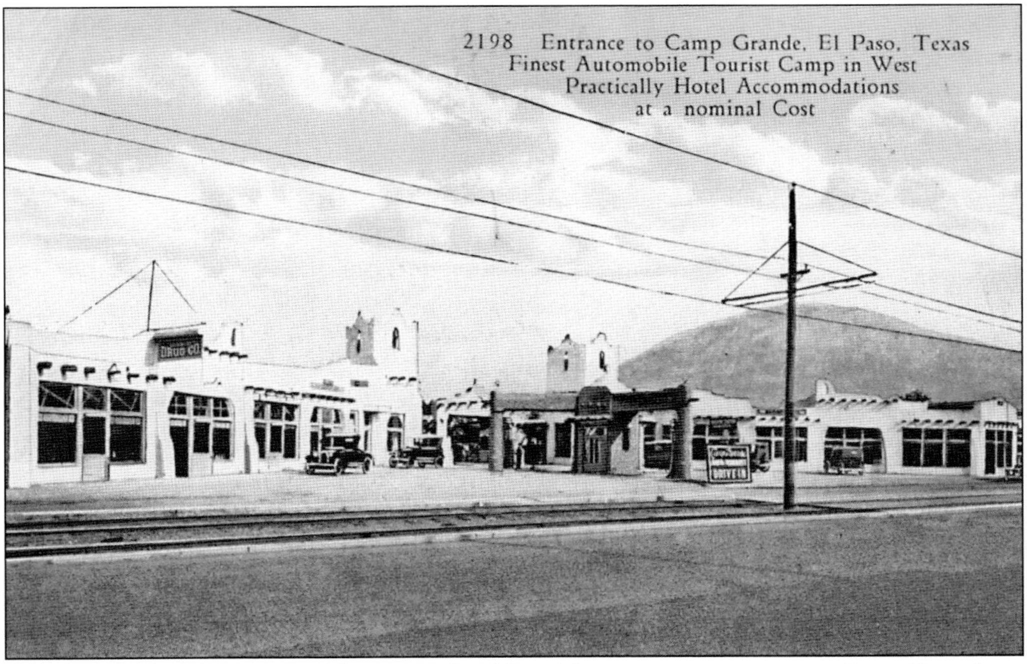


**Camp Grande on Alameda.** Claiming to be El Paso's largest auto tourist camp, Camp Grande on Alameda Street, on the edge of the city, provided accommodations for the traveling motorist. It also was a pickup spot for auto tours to Juarez and other sights in the area. The camp was served by the Park line streetcars, whose double tracks can be seen in the median in this postcard view.

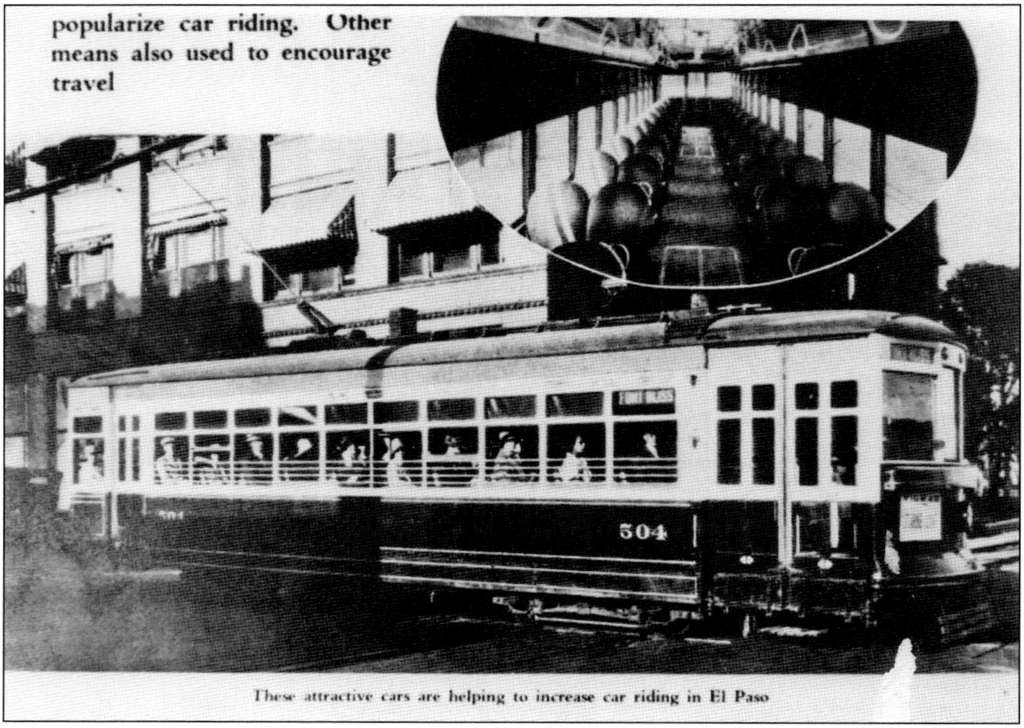


**CAR NO. 504 ON STANTON STREET.** In this photograph from the *Electric Railway Journal* of 1927, a view of the interior of the car is shown. No. 504 is southbound on Stanton Street, approaching downtown, inbound from Fort Bliss. The building in the background is the Southern Pacific office building, originally that of the El Paso and Southwestern Railroad, which was absorbed by the Southern Pacific in 1924.

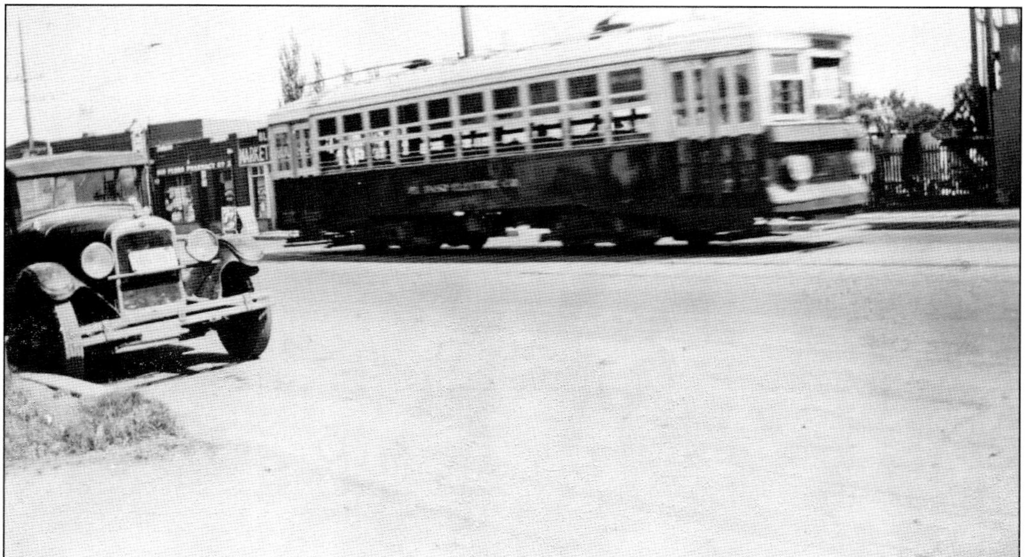


**NO. 73 ON THE JUAREZ LINE.** This 1938 view shows No. 73 passing a Model A on the Juarez line in June 1938. This streetcar still sports the twin headlight modification and is in the El Paso Electric Company's white-over-red paint scheme. (T. P. Taetsch photograph, courtesy of PDNSPS.)

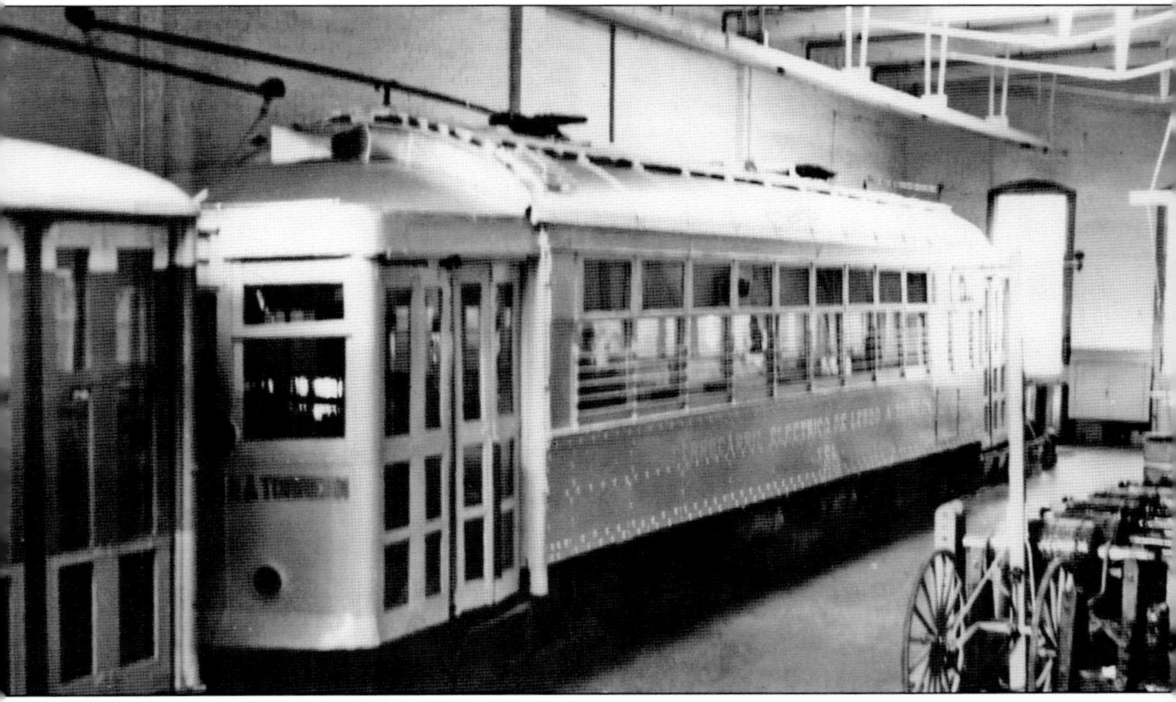

**HEADED FOR MEXICO.** After the closure of the Park and Fort Bliss lines in 1947, Nos. 73 and 74, as well as some of the 85–96 series Stone and Webster roof cars, were sold to the Torreon, Mexico, transit line, Ferrocariles Electricos de Lerdo a Torreon. This Cotton Street carbarn photograph shows a Stone and Webster car after being painted and lettered for the sale to Mexico. It was renumbered 21 and in Mexico ran in Torreon, Gomez Palacios, and Lerdo from 1948 to 1952 or 1953. In El Paso, they had been remodeled in 1931 to longitudinal seating to accommodate border inspection but were returned to transverse seating for the sale to Mexico. An old-timer who worked for El Paso City Lines relates a story that the representative for the Mexican transit company arrived in El Paso with a satchel full of cash to pay for the cars. They made the trip to Mexico loaded on flatcars.

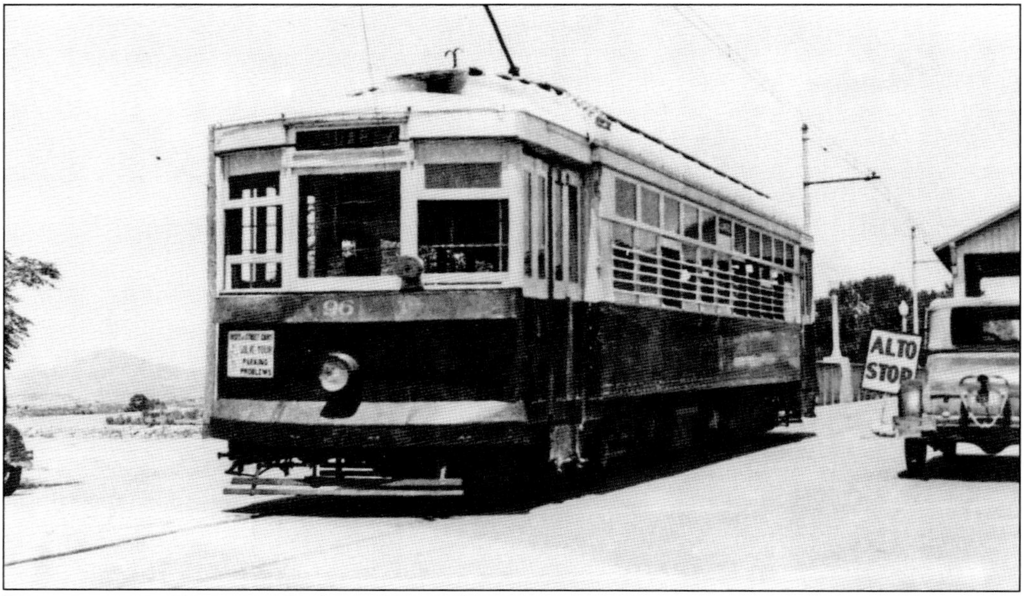


**NO. 96 ON THE BRIDGE.** The last of the order of Stone and Webster cars, No. 96, moves forward on the Santa Fe Street Bridge toward U.S. Customs. On the concrete bridges built in the 1920s, streetcars occupied the left lane. There was a pedestrian walkway on the side protected from traffic by a waist-high divider.

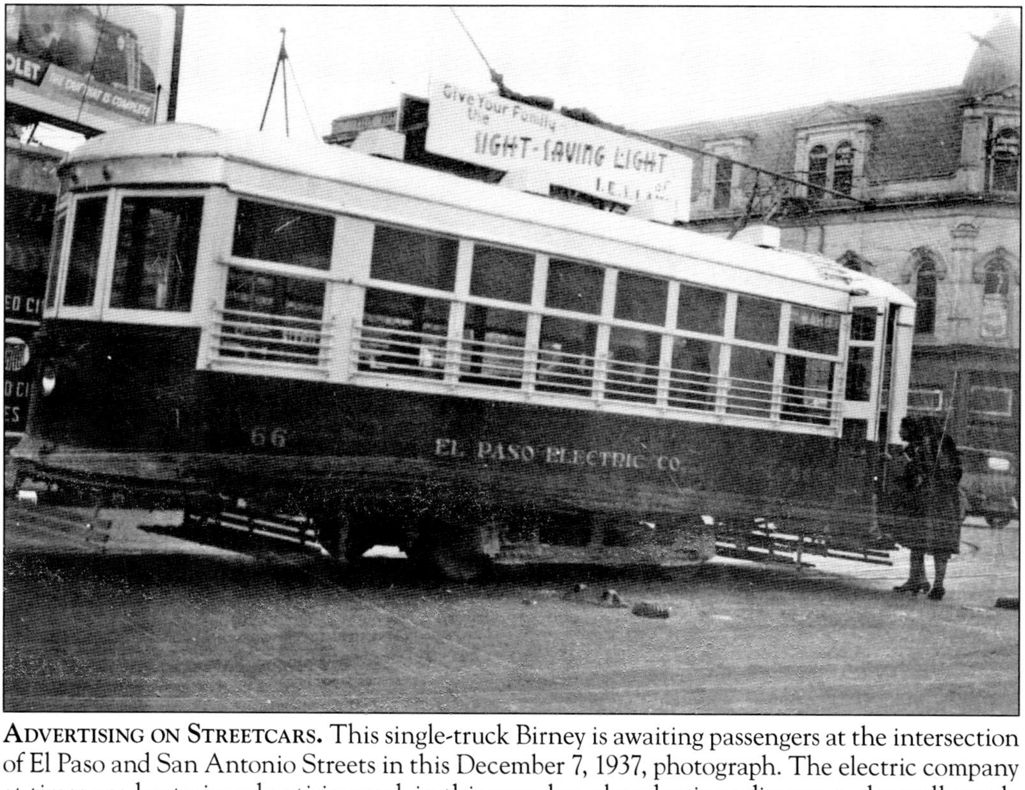


**ADVERTISING ON STREETCARS.** This single-truck Birney is awaiting passengers at the intersection of El Paso and San Antonio Streets in this December 7, 1937, photograph. The electric company at times used exterior advertising and, in this case, has placed a sign adjacent to the trolley pole tower extolling the benefits of certain types of electric lighting.

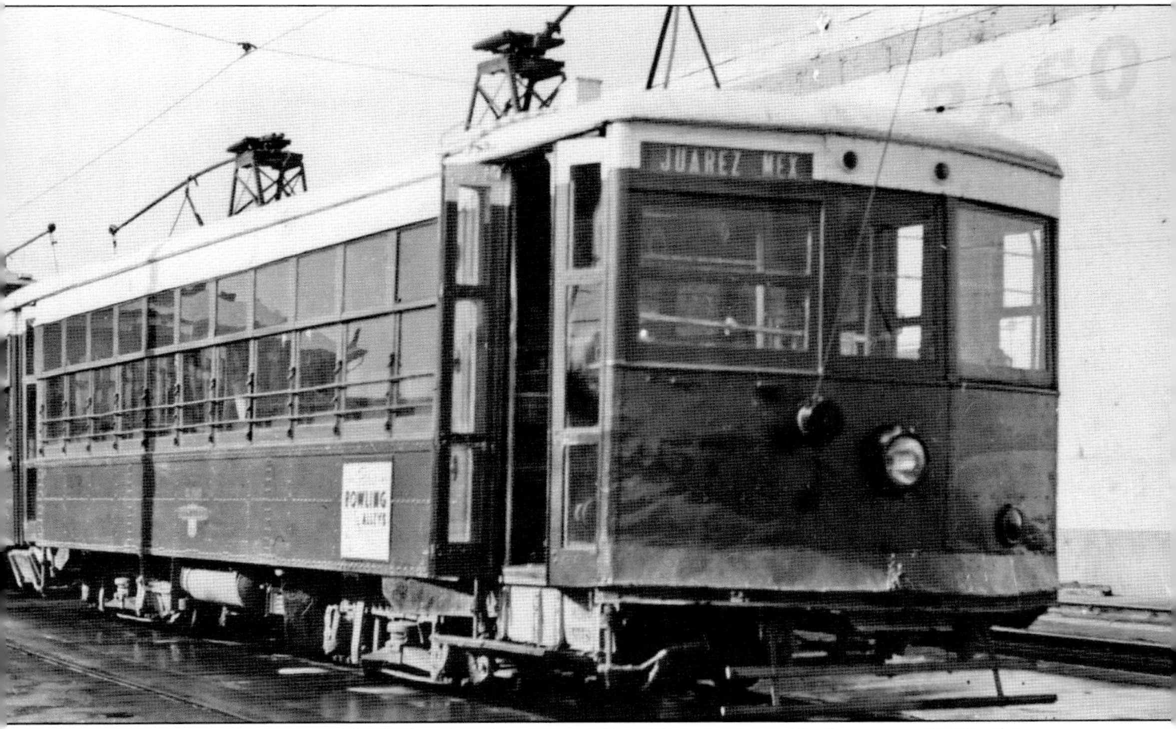


**No. 57 at the Carbarn.** Built by the American Car Company in St. Louis in 1922, this car worked on the Houston system before coming to El Paso in 1940. El Paso Electric paid $7,000 each for the 10 cars of a type known as double-truck Birney Safety cars. Numbered from 50 to 59, these cars had a lower roof line than did the Stone and Webster roof cars. Therefore, like the single-truck Birneys, they needed towers to mount the trolley poles to reach the overhead wire. No. 57 is on an outside track at the barn, already painted in El Paso City Lines' fruit salad paint scheme. This image was taken on December 17, 1947, four months after the closure of the Park and Fort Bliss lines, freeing No. 57 to work on the Juarez line. (Richard J. Anderson photograph, courtesy of PDNSPS.)

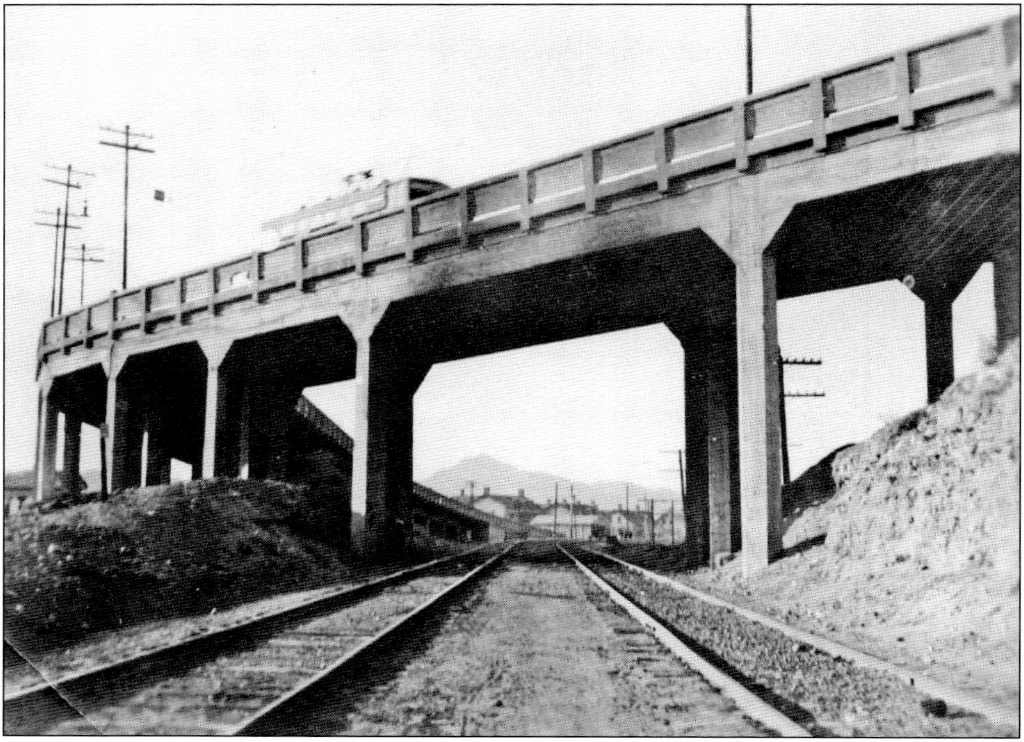

**ON THE YANDELL OVERPASS.** This Birney car is inbound from the Smelter line on the West Yandell Street overpass. Steam engines have left smoke smudges on the bridge as the view is down the route of the Santa Fe Railway, known as the Panhandle and Santa Fe for the segment from El Paso to the New Mexico border. In the distance (center) are the buildings of old Fort Bliss.

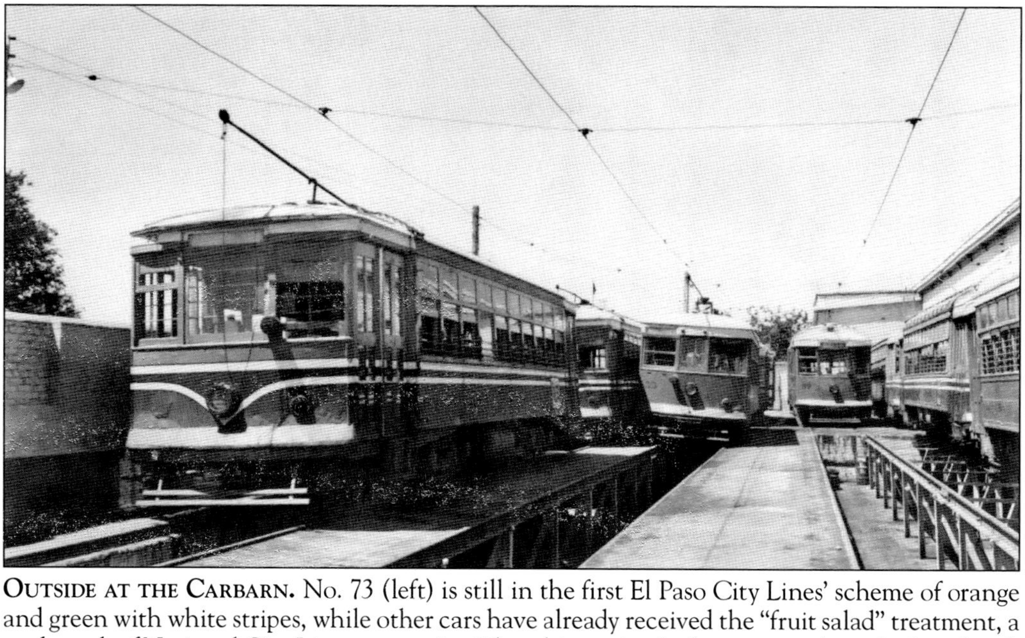

**OUTSIDE AT THE CARBARN.** No. 73 (left) is still in the first El Paso City Lines' scheme of orange and green with white stripes, while other cars have already received the "fruit salad" treatment, a trademark of National City Lines properties. The white-striped scheme was relatively short-lived, lasting only from 1944 to 1946. The fruit salad scheme would last through the 1950s.

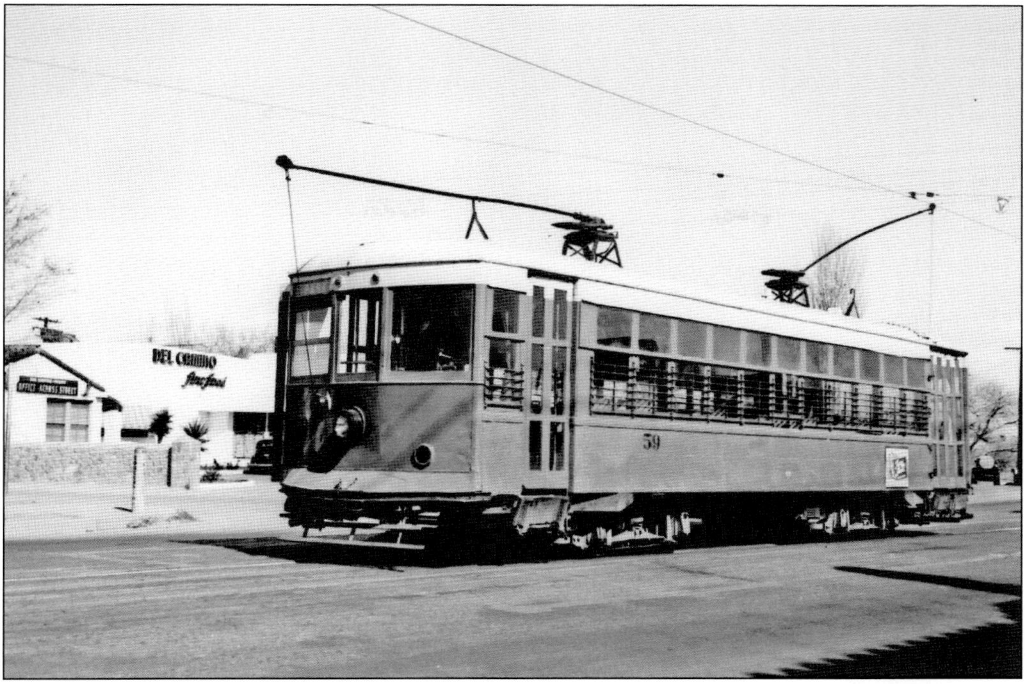


**At the End of the Park Line.** Ex-Houston car No. 59 pauses at the end of the Park line on Alameda Street, near Concepcion Street, with the Del Camino Courts in the background. On the way back to town, this car will pass Washington Park and the Evergreen Cemetery. The paint scheme and the Park line date this image as late 1946 or early 1947.

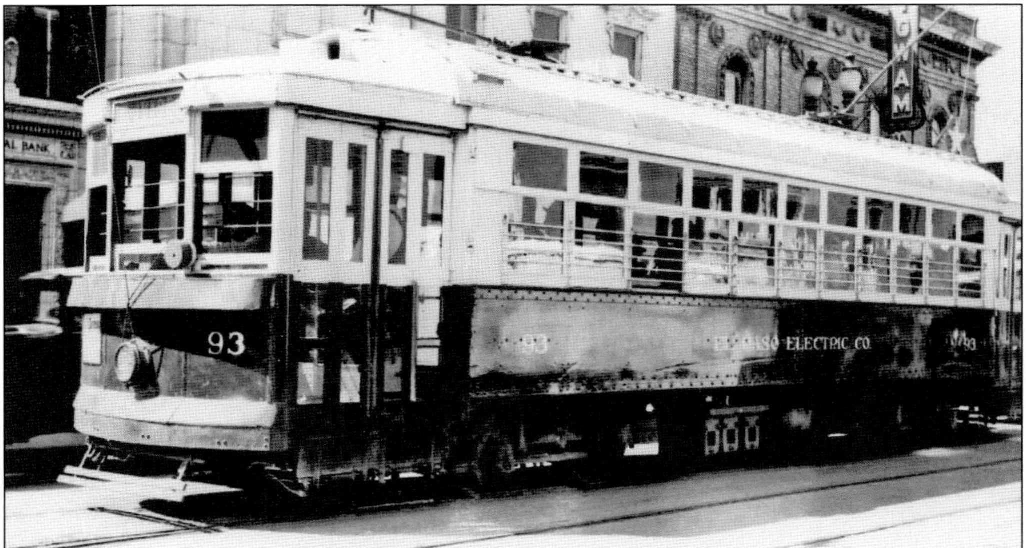


**No. 93 Passing the Wigwam Theater.** The time period is the early to mid-1930s as No. 93, delivered in 1914, is sporting a brand-new paint job and interior remodeling. No. 93 is on San Antonio Street and is approaching the intersection with Oregon Street where the Second Ward line crosses San Antonio. The hood over the headlight is to reduce glare in the motorman's eyes.

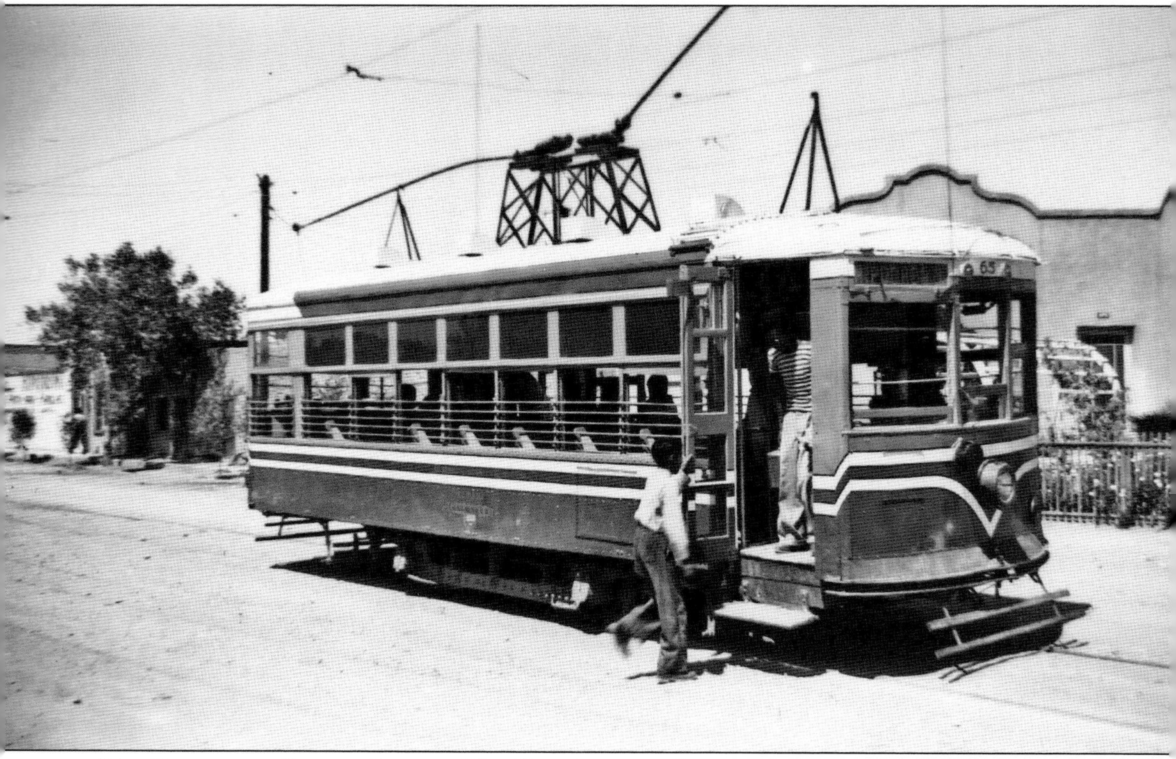

**THE RACETRACK LINE IN JUAREZ.** The Hipodromo, or Racetrack, line in Ciudad Juarez was built about 1912 to serve the horse racetrack in Juarez. It was a popular distraction for El Pasoans because wagering was illegal in the state of Texas at the time. In earlier days, there was through service from downtown El Paso. In later days, service was handled by a single-truck Birney as a shuttle connecting with Juarez cars at Avenida 16 de Septiembre. The original line made a loop near the racetrack on the property of the local light and power company. The line followed a number of streets getting out to the racetrack and was double tracked down Hipodromo Avenue, later Insurgentes Avenue. Most of these streets were unpaved at the time. In 1935, the line was cut back to the brewery. Patronage dwindled with loss of the racetrack, which was destroyed by fire, even though there was some attempt to interest patrons in the Brewery Park destination. El Paso City Lines, which had taken over the streetcars in 1944, abandoned the Hipodromo line in 1945.

*Seven*

# The Carbarn and Work Cars

The carbarn on Cotton Street dates back to 1910 in its present form. There were four bays inside with maintenance pits and four tracks outside, some with work pits. Fire was a concern with early streetcar companies since there was always woodwork, painting, and upholstery work going on with paints, varnishes, and other flammable materials stored. The Cotton Street barn is believed to be the first commercial building in El Paso to have been fitted with a sprinkler system. Nevertheless, there were fires, and one destroyed the south portion of the barn, which was then left uncovered from that period forward. With the maintenance facilities existing in the carbarn, workers were able to remodel and rebuild whenever necessary. It was reported in a transit journal that the El Paso Electric Railway could completely rebuild a Birney car from the ground up in eight days.

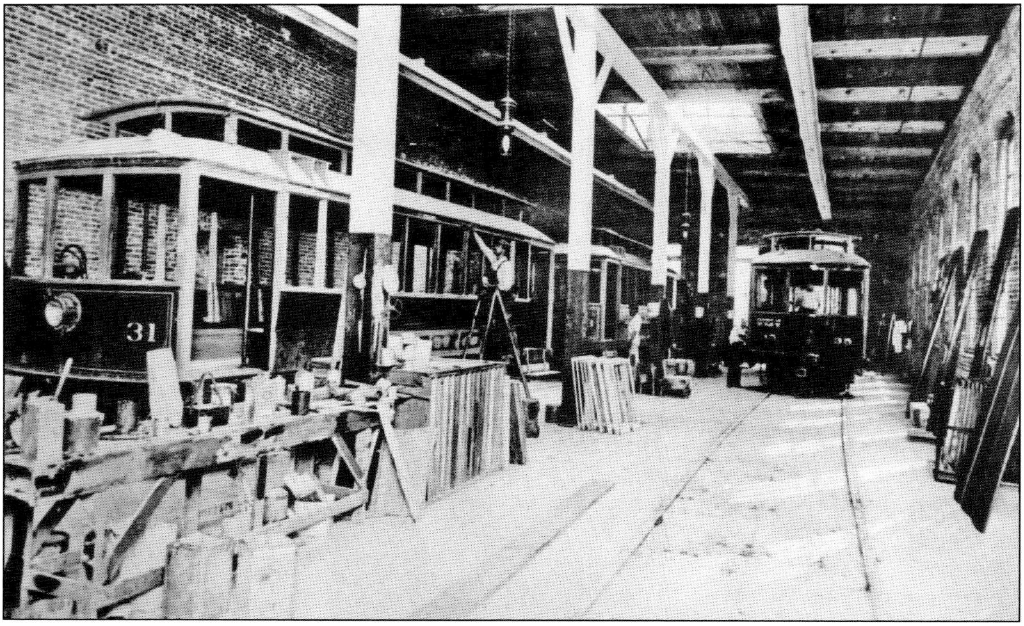

**REBUILDING AND REMODELING.** In this interior carbarn photograph, several 30-series cars are getting rebuilt. Unlike motor vehicles, streetcars can run indefinitely with the proper maintenance, so it was not unusual for a car to be rebuilt several times in its lifetime. In this instance, these cars are being remodeled from semi-convertible cars to full closed cars. (W. L. Bess photograph, courtesy of Henry Leinbach Jr. Collection.)

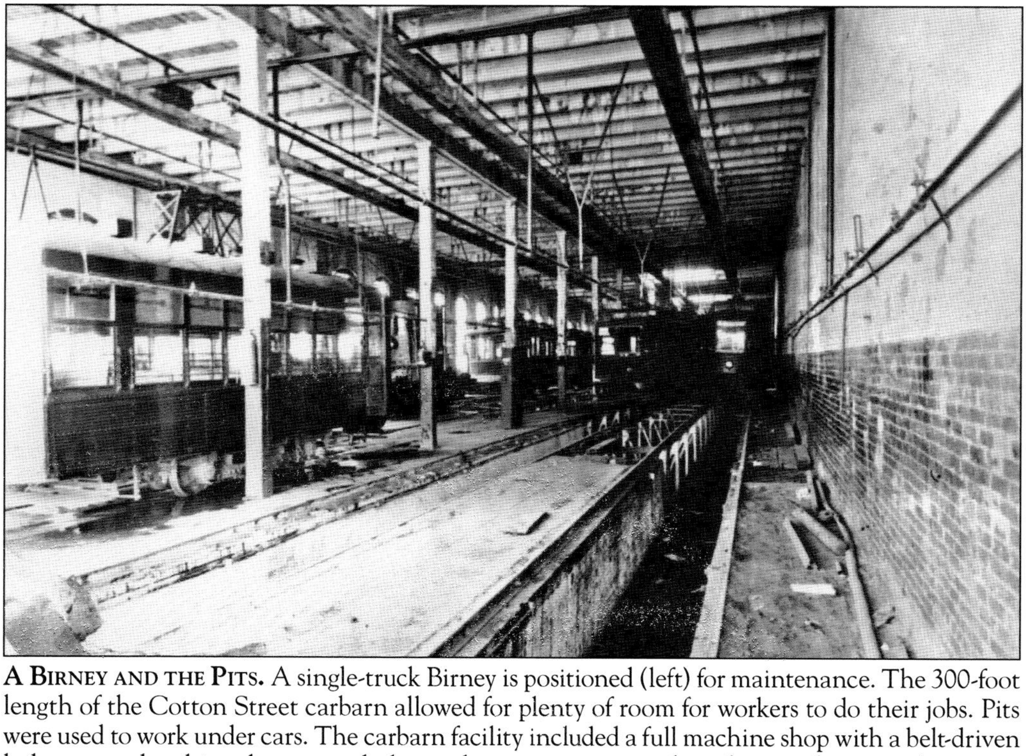

**A BIRNEY AND THE PITS.** A single-truck Birney is positioned (left) for maintenance. The 300-foot length of the Cotton Street carbarn allowed for plenty of room for workers to do their jobs. Pits were used to work under cars. The carbarn facility included a full machine shop with a belt-driven lathe, a woodworking shop, an upholstery shop, a motor rewinding shop, and a paint shop.

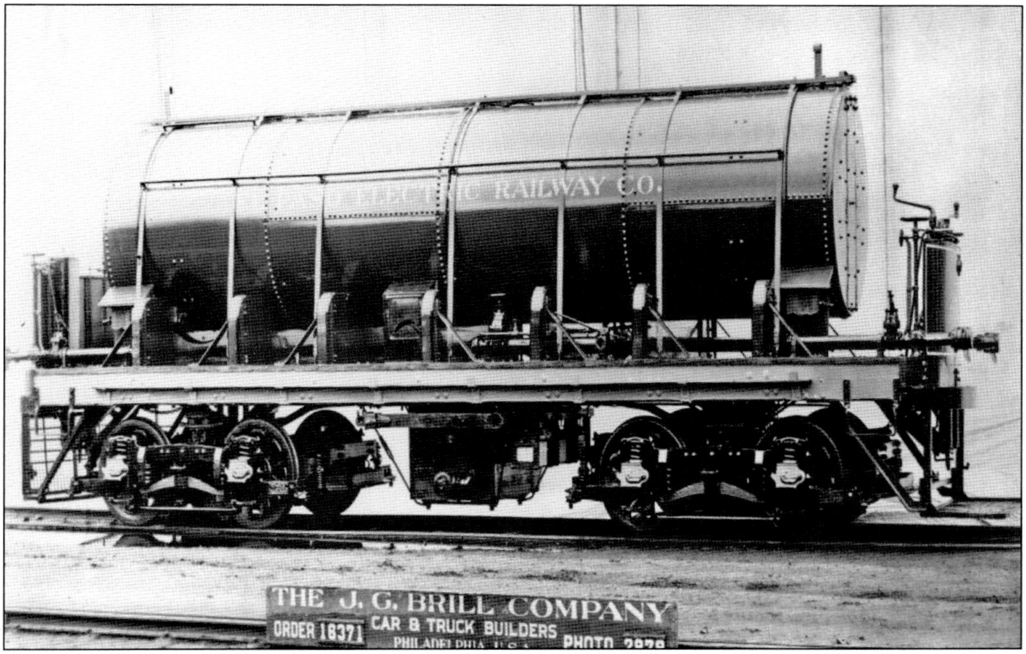


**A Sprinkler Work Car.** This is a builder's photograph of a sprinkler car lettered for the El Paso Electric Railway Company. It is a self-propelled car with controls at the front. Trolley poles have not yet been installed. In the early days, most car-line streets were not paved, and by city ordnance, the street railway company was encumbered to sprinkle streets periodically to keep the dust down.

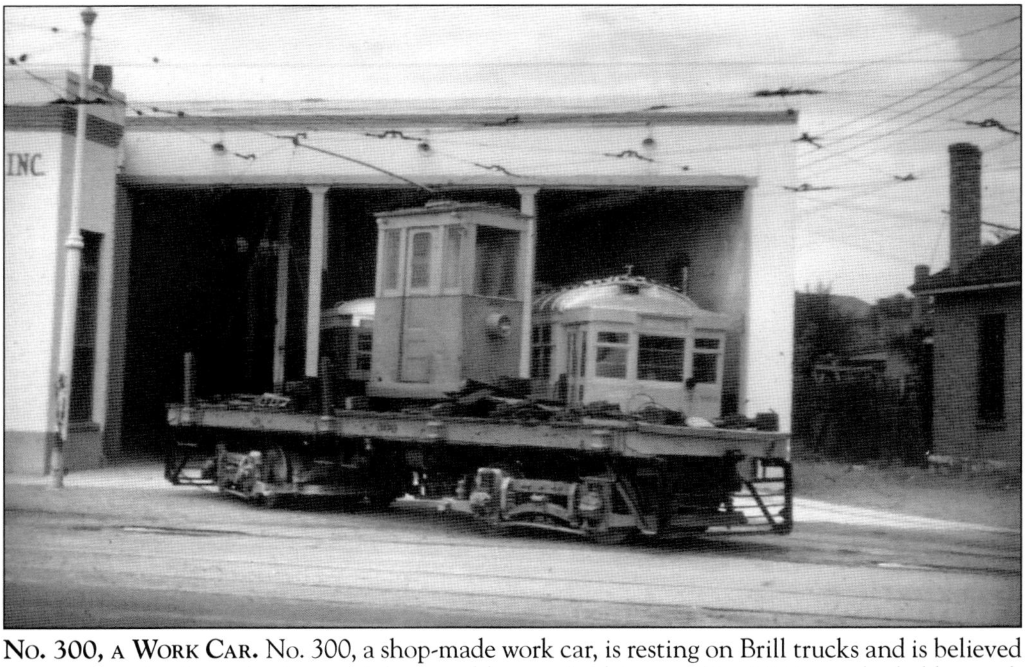


**No. 300, a Work Car.** No. 300, a shop-made work car, is resting on Brill trucks and is believed to have been built on the frame of the sprinkler car. In this view, No. 300 is on the ladder track in front of the carbarn, and the reader gets a peek at one of the Stone and Webster cars in new paint prior to delivery to Torreon, Mexico.

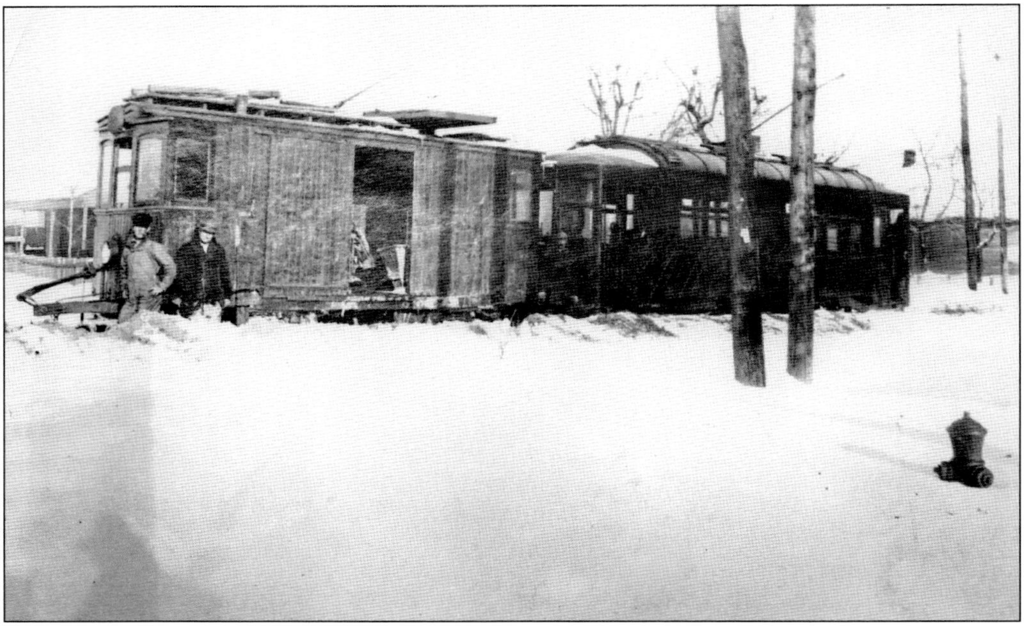

**An Unusual Winter for El Paso.** The streetcar company rarely needed a snowplow, but it did keep one in reserve. It is seen here on San Antonio Street trying the clear the track after a winter storm. There were few occasions when the weather would shut down a line, but this may have been one of them.

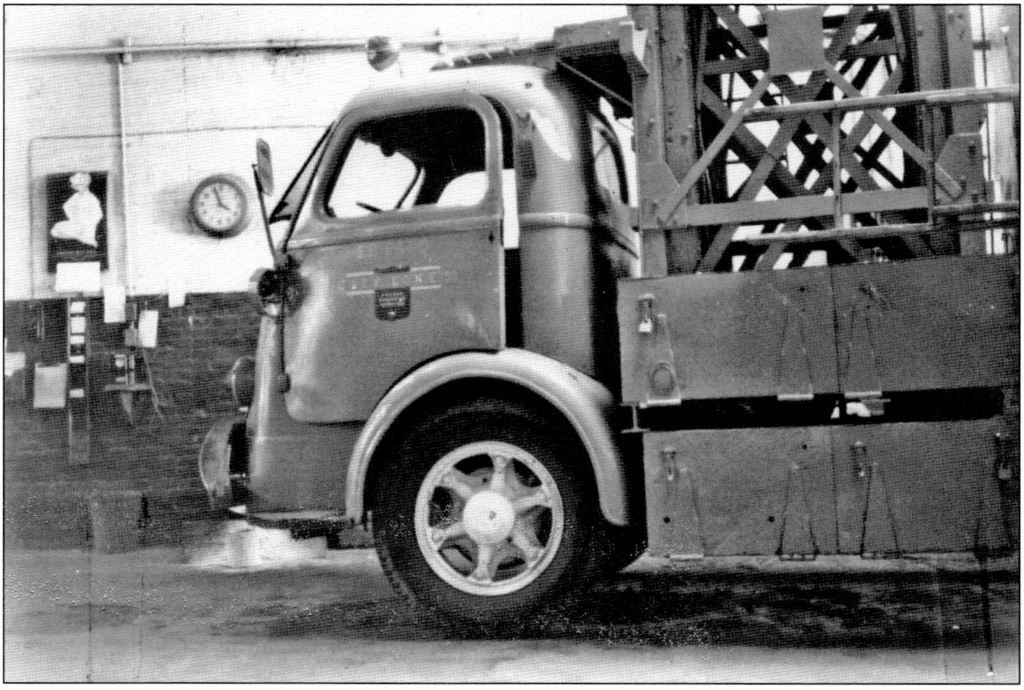

**Overhead Line Truck.** Here is a peek at the 1938 International line truck resting in the carbarn in 1971 near the end of the operations by El Paso City Lines. On the wall is a pinup and time clocks for maintenance personnel. Three entities used this truck: the El Paso Electric Company, El Paso City Lines, and Sun City Area Transit (SCAT).

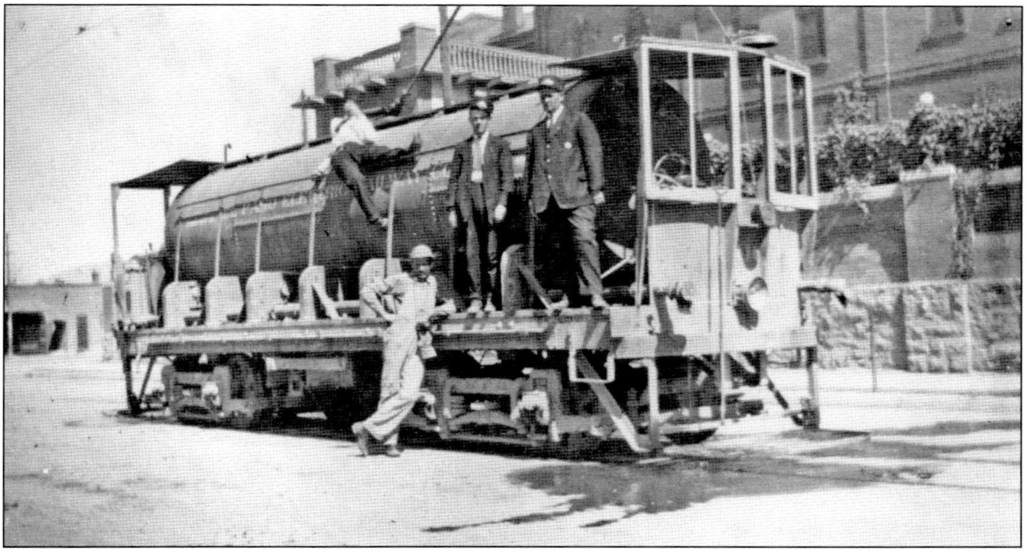

**Sprinkler at Work.** This Brill sprinkler car is seen at work in a photograph from the Dennis Lane Collection. The crew of four poses informally. Two are operators, and two are maintenance people. After reaching El Paso, the company added a front windshield and shade for the motorman's comfort. It appears to be a double ender, capable of moving in both directions.

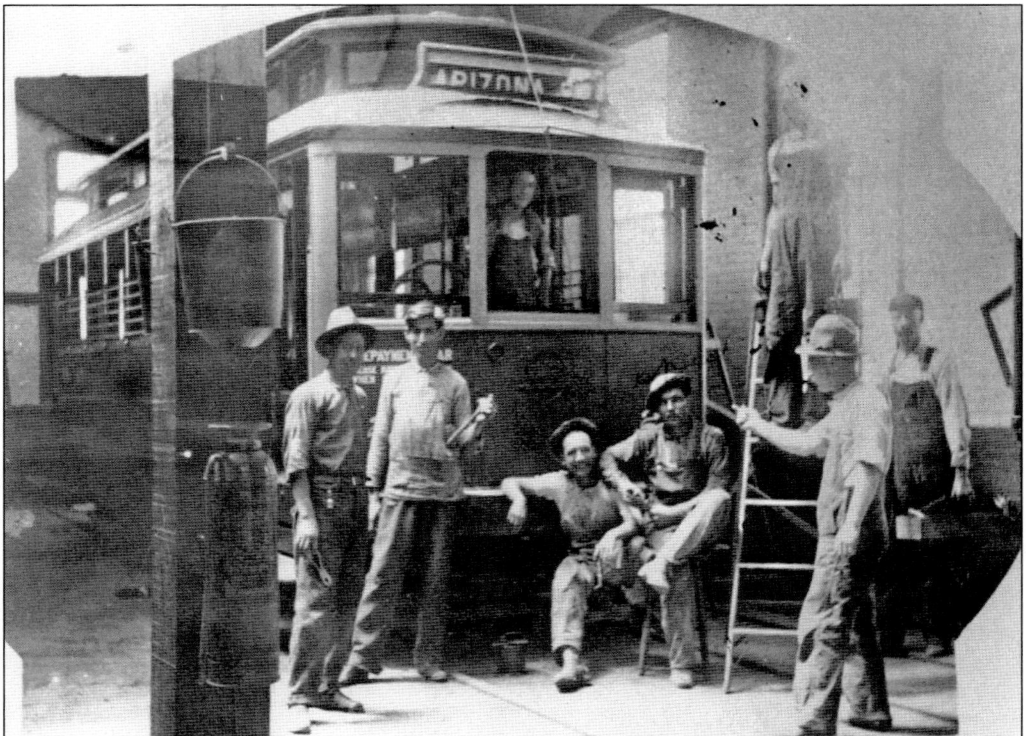

**Carbarn Work Crew.** Seven unidentified carbarn workers are seen in this view. The car is off the Arizona Street line and is a prepayment car, which indicates that it has been converted to a one-man operation. The motorman or trainman would operate the car, open and close the doors, and take fares. The fire extinguisher and water bucket are visible on the pole (left).

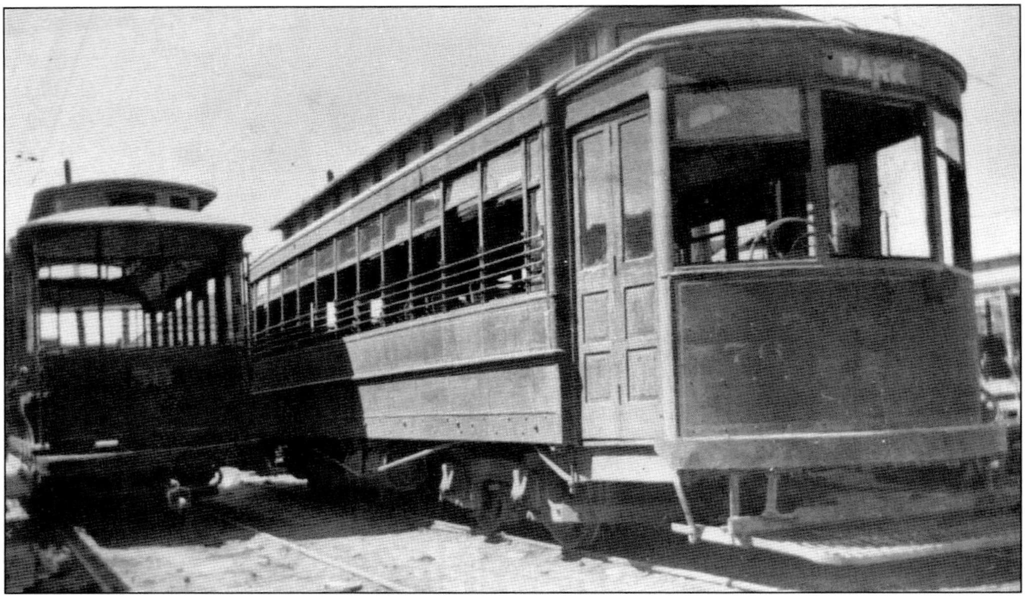


**In the Storage Yard.** In this photograph from the Dennis Lane Collection and taken before 1910, No. 76 is in the storage yard on the east side of Cotton Street, across from the carbarn. There were nine storage tracks on the east side of the street, which was later to become a bus barn. Next to No. 78 is an open trailer, No. 56, which was scrapped by 1912.

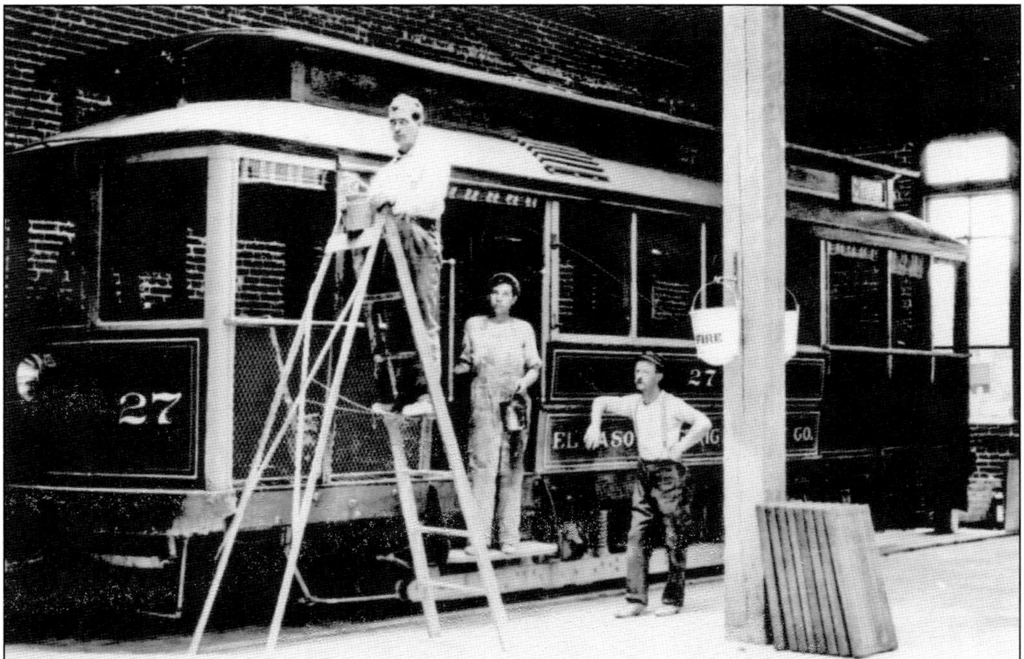


**Painting and Varnishing.** These unidentified maintenance workers are refinishing No. 27. The carbarn crew included painters, woodworkers, machinists, welders, electricians, and upholsterers. No. 27 is being remodeled to a full closed car without the semi-convertible feature. In later years, the paint shop was isolated near the back of the carbarn.

**Lifting a Heavy Load.** The overhead block-and-tackle rig in the carbarn could be used to lift heavy loads off the pit track when necessary. This traction motor and truck assembly is being worked on in the motor rewinding section of the shop. The street railway company advertised to the public that proper maintenance procedures were a high priority.

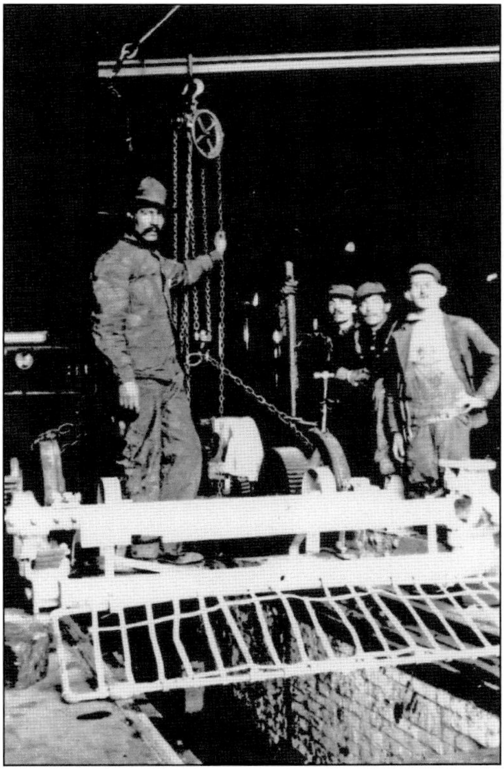

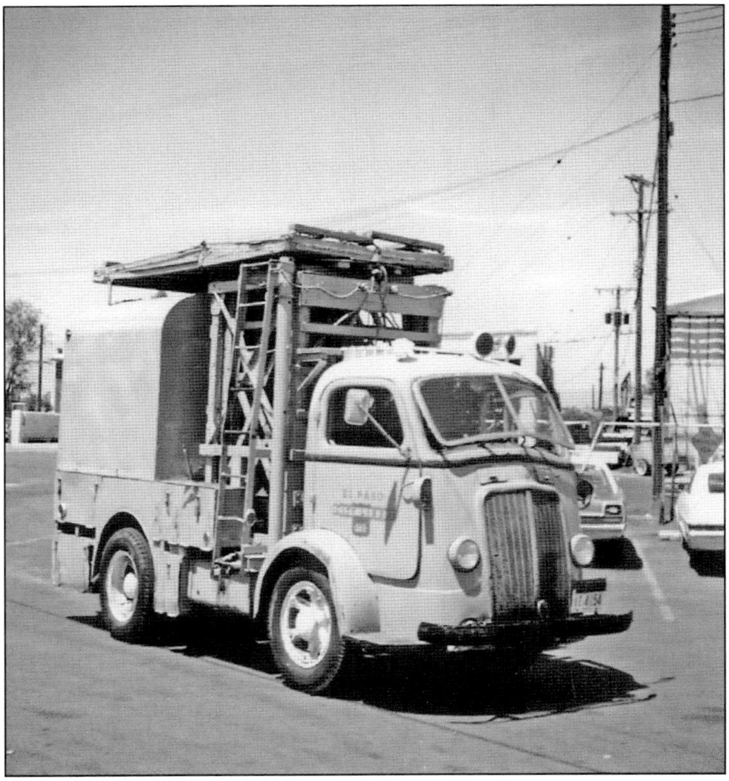

**A 1938 International Line Truck.** For many years, El Paso City Lines, and later the City of El Paso, used this 1938 International platform tower truck for overhead wire maintenance. The truck had a wooden platform that could be raised hydraulically. There had been a trolley work car before 1945 used on the lines, but apparently management felt the truck would be more flexible in getting to the problem areas.

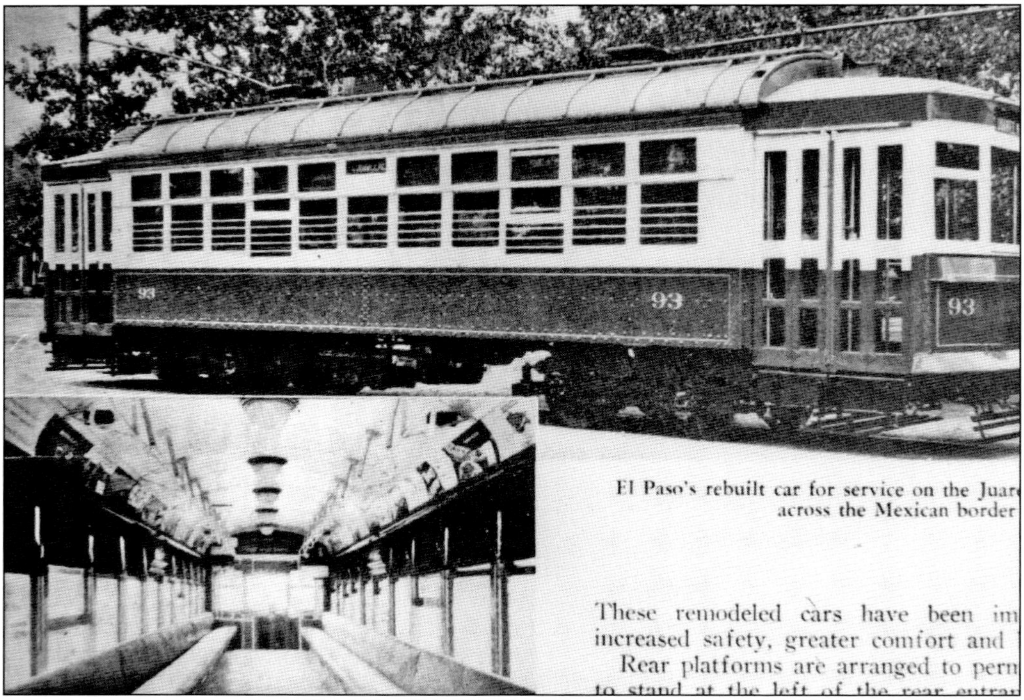


**No. 93 after Remodeling.** The 1930 and 1931 remodeling of the 1912 and 1914 Stone and Webster roof cars saved the local streetcar company a considerable amount of money and avoided the need for purchasing new cars in the depths of the Great Depression. No. 93 was consigned to the Juarez line and, therefore, received the longitudinal seating, as seen in the photograph from the *Electric Railway Journal.*

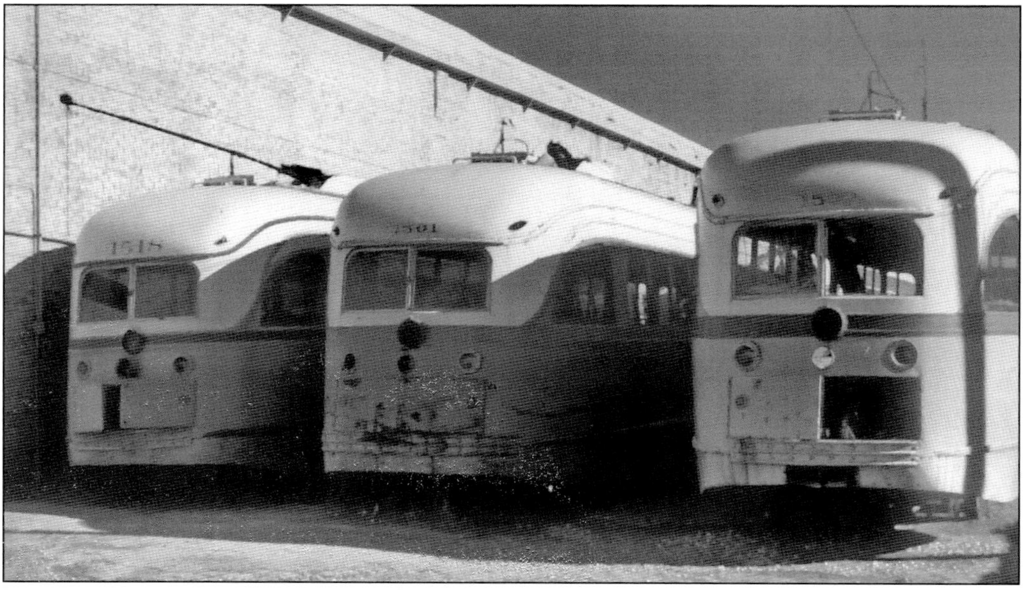


**Maintenance in the PCC Era.** These three PCC streetcars—from left to right, Nos. 1518, 1501, and 1507—have been relegated to the back of the outside storage tracks and have been cannibalized for parts. No. 1501 did not receive the 1960s or the 1970s paint schemes, indicating it has been out of service for some time. All three were soon to be scrapped.

# *Eight*

# Accidents and Derelicts

El Paso streetcar historians have managed to track down some of the cars disposed of in the 1947–1949 period and after the PCCs arrived from San Diego in 1950. Many of the car bodies were not scrapped but rather were lifted off their trucks and motors, and were sold to whoever wanted them. Some ended up as diners, some as apartments, some as chicken coops, and some even as bracero housing on a farm. Four of the Fort Bliss 500-series cars were found on a farm in Columbus, New Mexico, being used as cotton trailers.

Accidents plagued most streetcar companies, and the El Paso Electric Railway was no exception. Due to the number of lawsuits from people jumping on and off open cars, the state legislature outlawed open cars in 1912, forcing companies to remodel open cars to closed or semi-convertible styles.

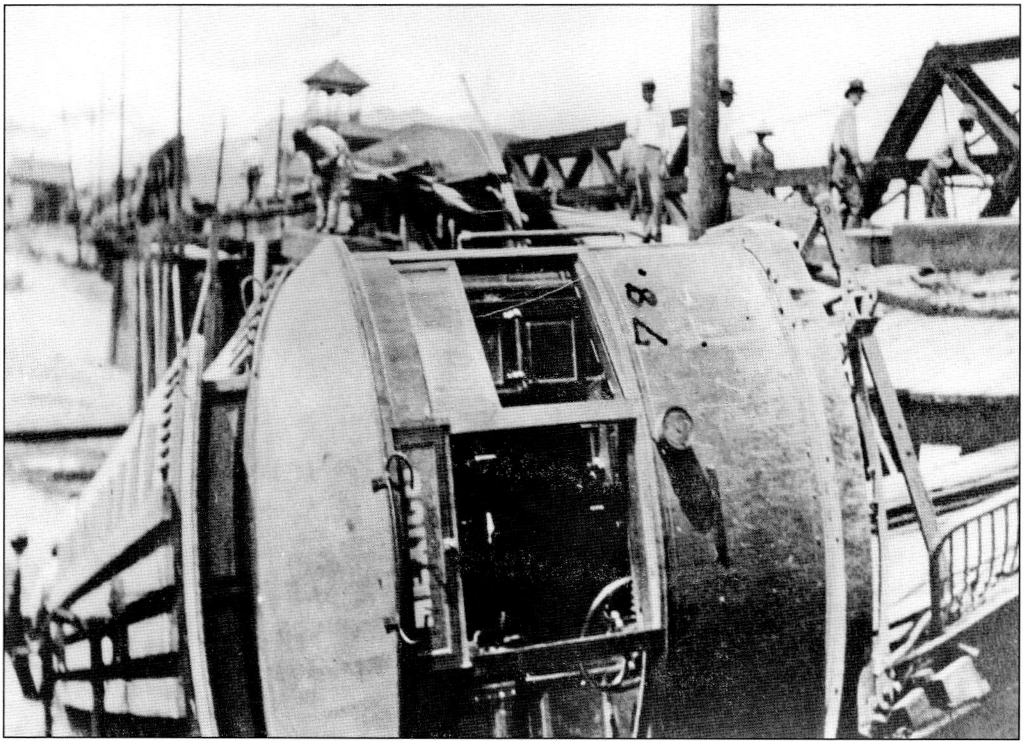


**BRIDGE COLLAPSES UNDER STREETCAR.** Both the original Stanton Street Bridge and the Santa Fe Street Bridge were built in the late 1800s to carry lightweight early trolleys, buggies, and horses. With the advent of streetcar technology, the cars became bigger and heavier. The above photograph is a close-up frontal view of No. 78 after falling through the Santa Fe Street Bridge. This incident occurred about 1915. The photograph below was taken from the dry riverbed, showing a number of spectators observing the proceedings. At this point, the heavy crane needed has not yet been brought to the site. The bridge was rebuilt and reinforced, but a concrete bridge would not come until the 1920s. (Both, courtesy of EPPL.)

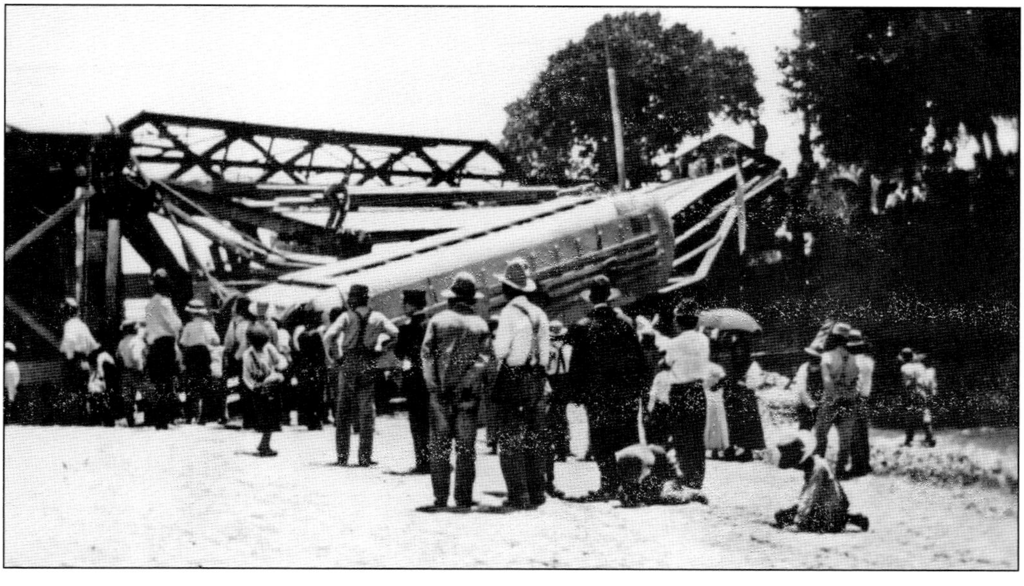

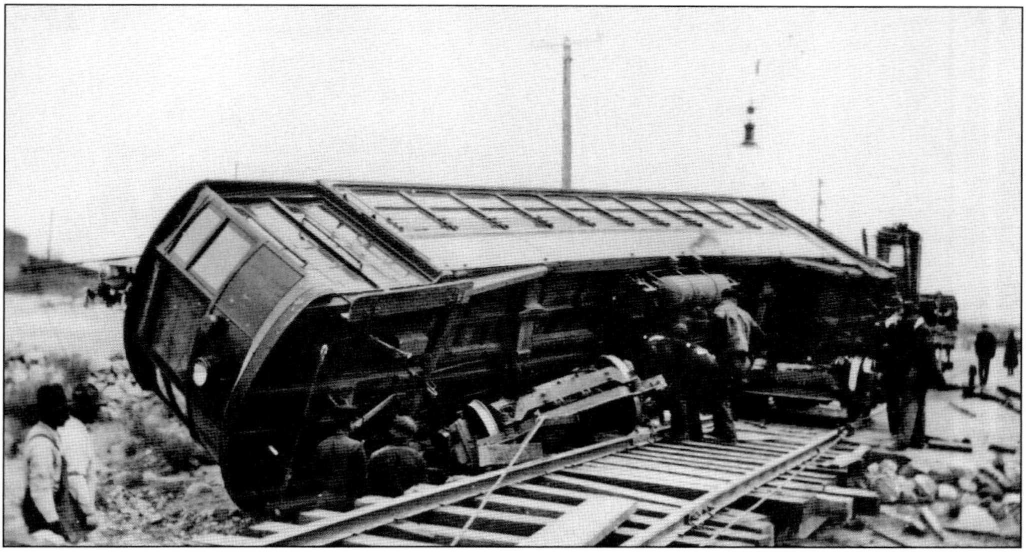

**Accident on the Fort Bliss Line.** Built in 1906, the Fort Bliss line passed through some open countryside before neighborhoods grew up around the line. Alta Vista, Altura Park, and Grandview were a few of the neighborhoods on the Fort Bliss line. In the 1909 pre–World War I photograph above, this 70-series car has left the tracks. Crews are working to secure the trucks before attempting to right the car. In the photograph below, this unidentified matron can barely conceal her annoyance at the delay. The El Paso Electric Railway did have a work car for just such an occurrence.

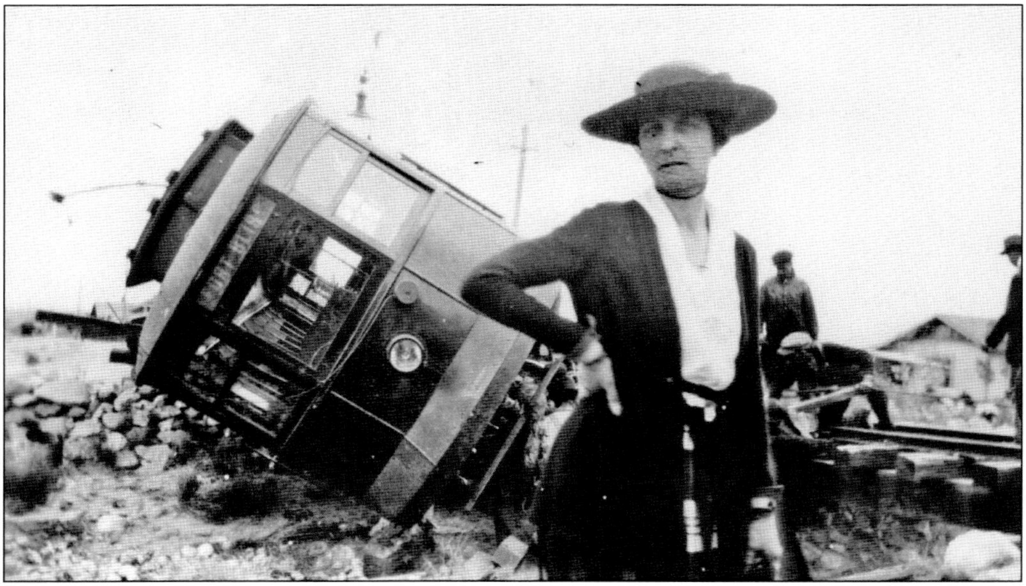

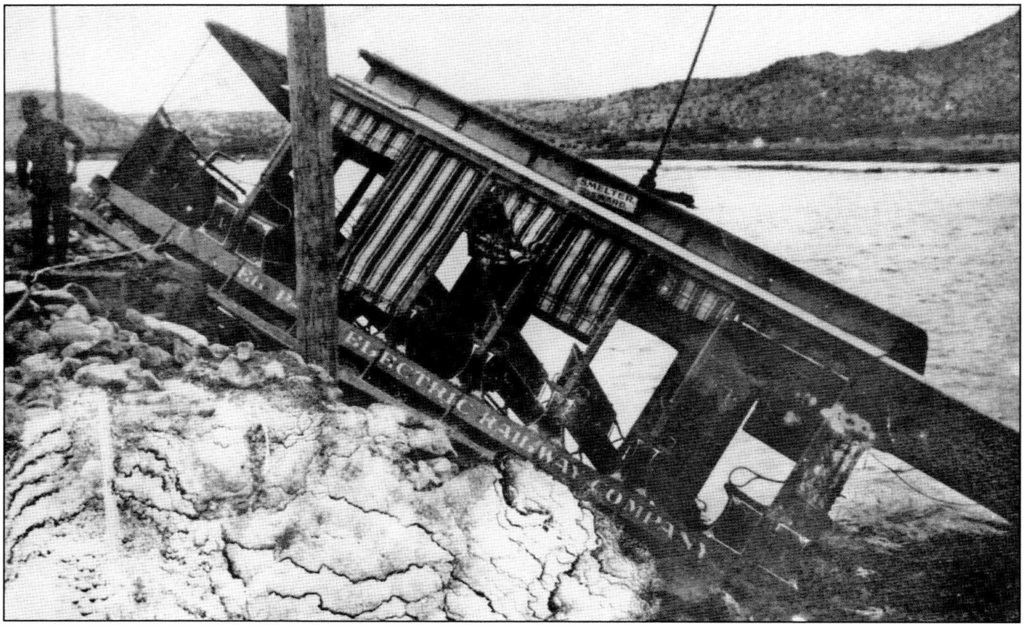


**In the Rio Grande.** This open car, built in 1902, has jumped the track on the Smelter line and has ended up in the Rio Grande. Likely the cause was high water erosion and flooding on the river. The Smelter line often carried workers to the ASARCO copper smelter. The frequent flooding caused the Smelter line to be converted to buses by 1930. (Courtesy of EPPL.)

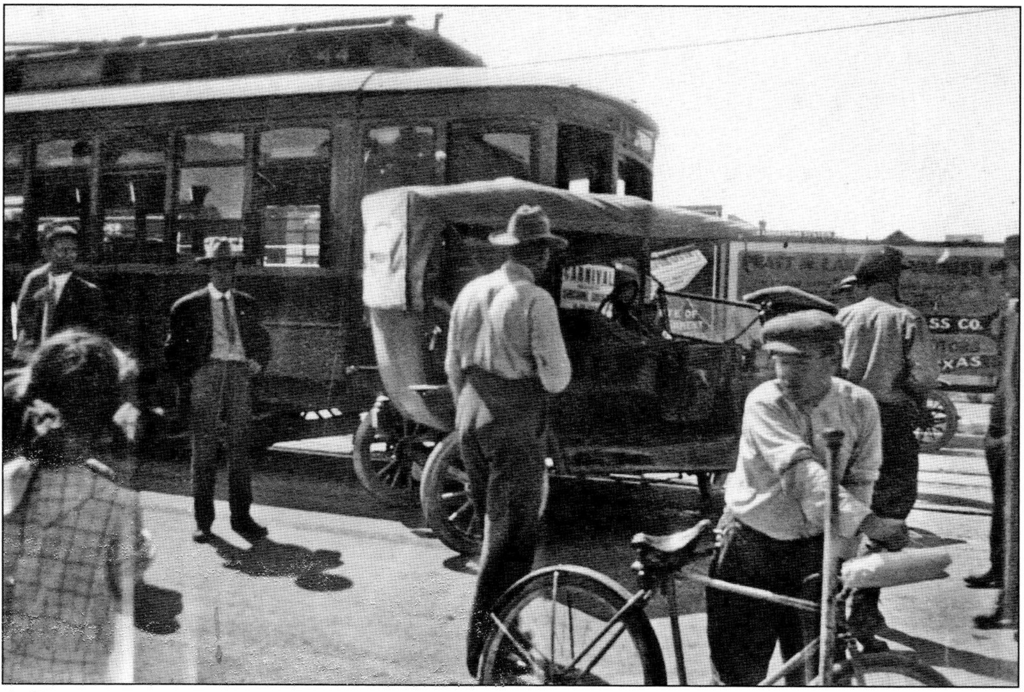


**A Streetcar and a Model T on Yandell Street.** This accident, involving a 40-series streetcar on the Highland Park line, occurred on Boulevard Avenue, later Yandell Street. The Model T auto was no match for the much heavier streetcar. The streetcar company regularly trained trainmen to try to avoid accidents.

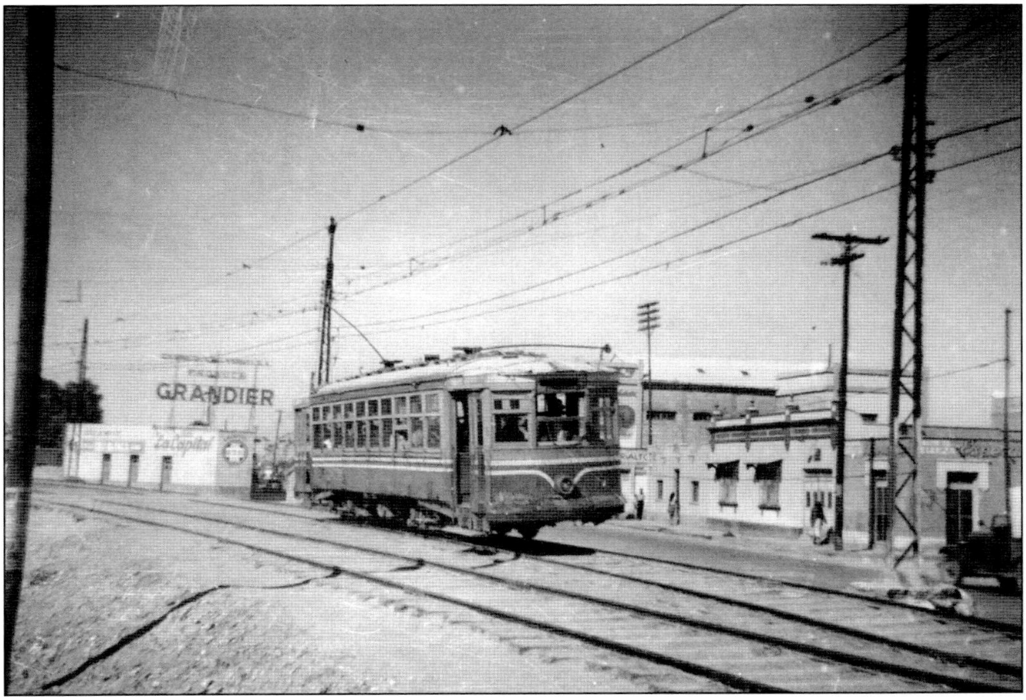


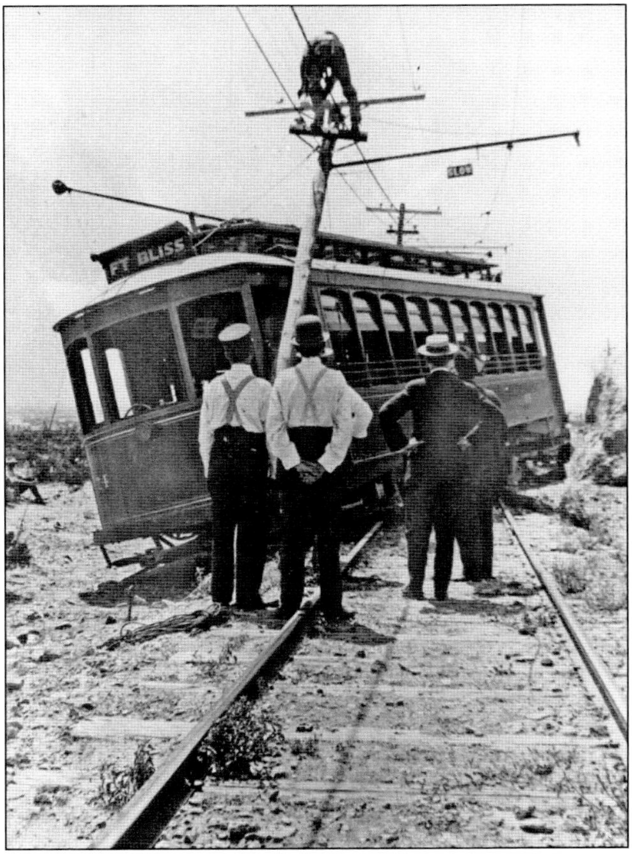


**No. 74 in 1910 and in 1952 in Mexico.** No. 74, still in El Paso City Lines colors, was one of the cars sold to the Torreon-to-Lerdo electric railway in Mexico about 1948 after the closure of the Fort Bliss and Park lines in 1947. Above, No. 74 is on a double-track right-of-way between Torreon, Gomez Palacios, and Lerdo. That line lasted until the end of 1952. In the second image (at right), the same No. 74 is seen in about 1910 in a derailing on the fort Bliss line. A lineman is on the pole as crewmen watch. The sign on the overhead says "slow." No. 74 was later rebuilt to an arched roof and was one of the longest lasting cars in the inventory.

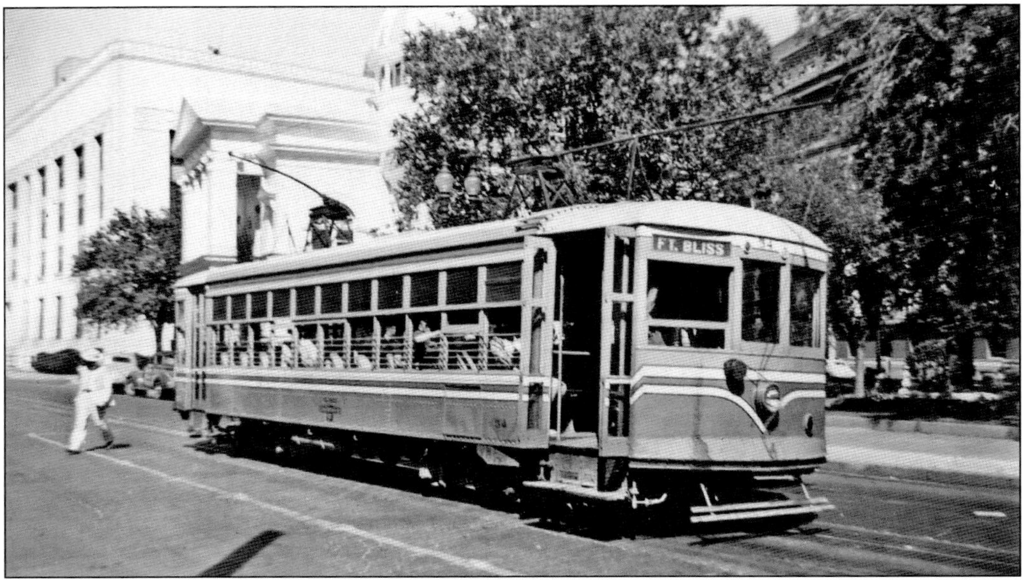


**No. 54 Decaying in the Desert.** Ex-Houston car No. 54 (above) is shown inbound on the Fort Bliss line. The loading area was adjacent to the city hall, the county courthouse, and the Federal Building. After loading, No. 54 will make a wide swing to the left and head back east on San Antonio Street. During World War II, these cars carried heavy loads as gasoline and rubber were rationed. Many years later, the body of No. 54 (below) is seen resting in the desert near Chaparral, New Mexico, slowly succumbing to the elements. The individual who bought the car body from City Lines placed it here as a quail hunting lodge, an activity that was curtailed by the gentleman's age and the growth of ranches in the areas.

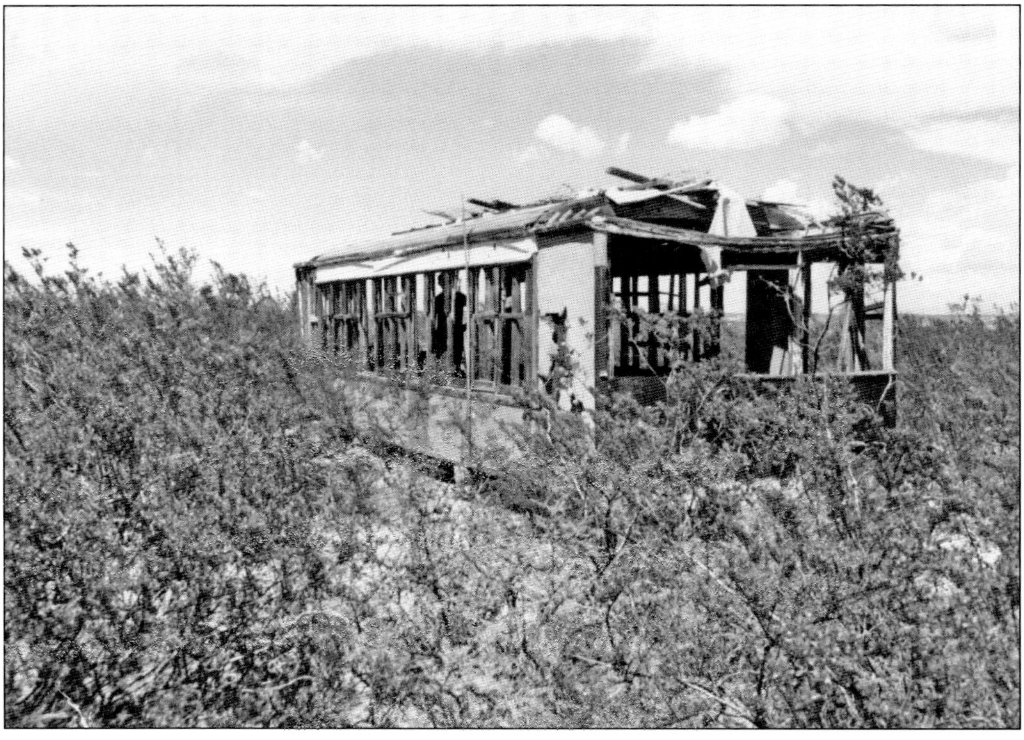

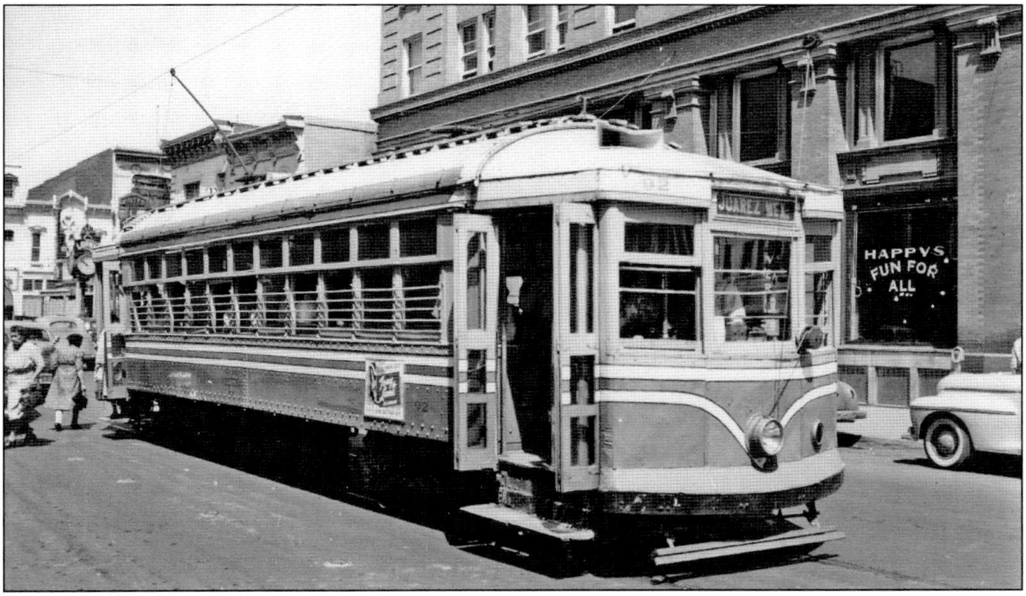


**No 92 and Taqueria 62, One and the Same.** No. 92, the car that later became a taco diner in Juarez, is seen in this image (above) in the first block after turning east from El Paso Street. The date is May 24, 1946, and one of the ladies who have exited the rear door of the car is crossing the street behind the streetcar, an unsafe habit. A somewhat ignoble end to the career of this Stone and Webster–type car, it ended up in Ciudad Juarez as a diner, Taqueria 62. It is actually No. 92, from the second group of similar cars arriving in 1914. The number was confirmed on-site by the author; however, the car has since been scrapped.

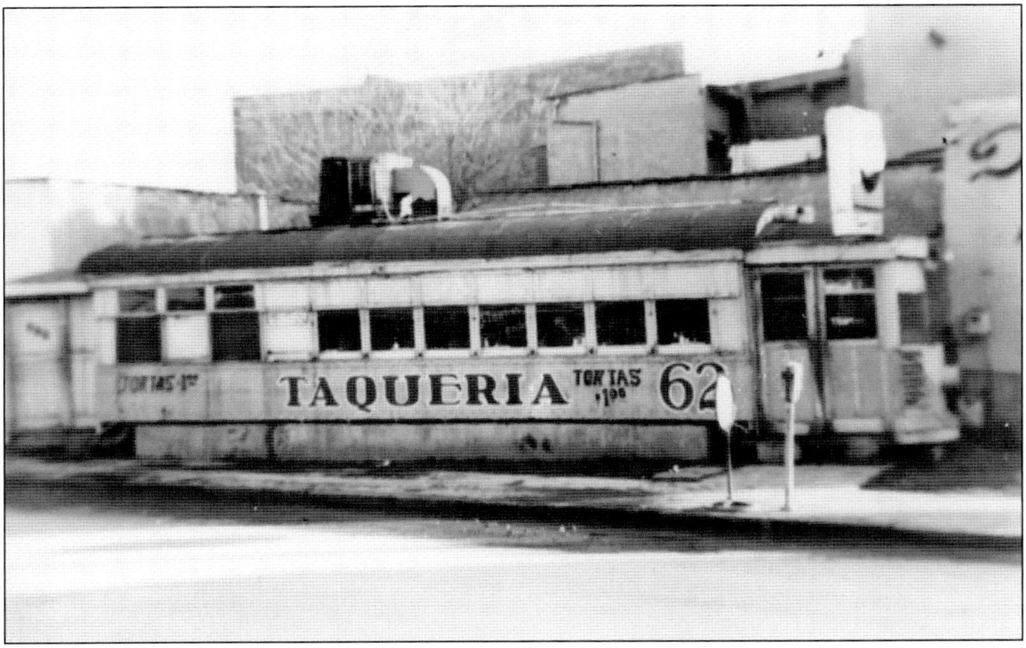

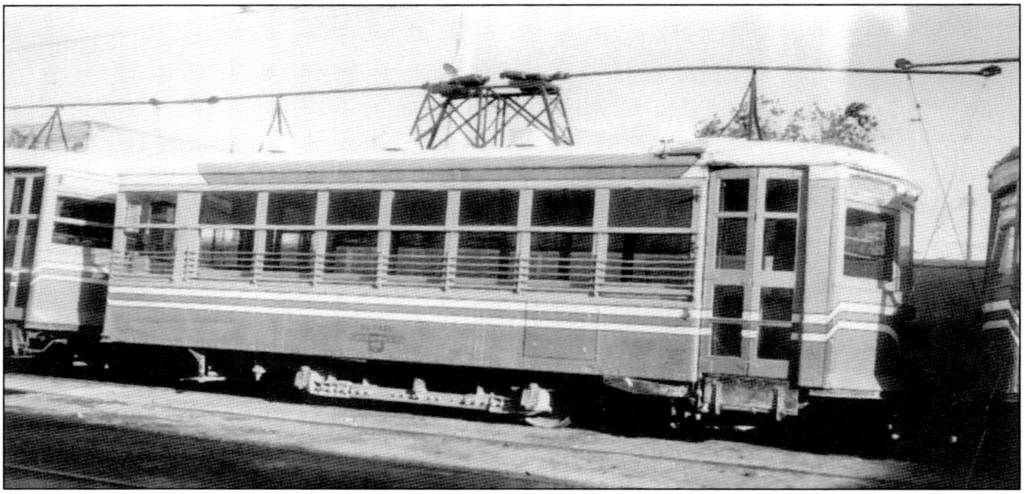

**Birney No. 66.** One of two Birneys lasting into the 1940s, No. 66 (above) is on the far track on the outside lot of the carbarn about 1945. The fence behind the cars was once a wall before a fire destroyed the roof and walls of the addition. The roof was never rebuilt, and the four outside tracks were primarily used for storage. No. 66 (below) also served for many years as a diner near the Phelps Dodge Refinery on North Loop Road. This was one of the two Birneys retained until 1945. After its use as a café, it sat abandoned on North Loop Road for several years before being hauled away as junk. (Above, courtesy of Barney Neuberger; below, courtesy of O. A. Goessl.)

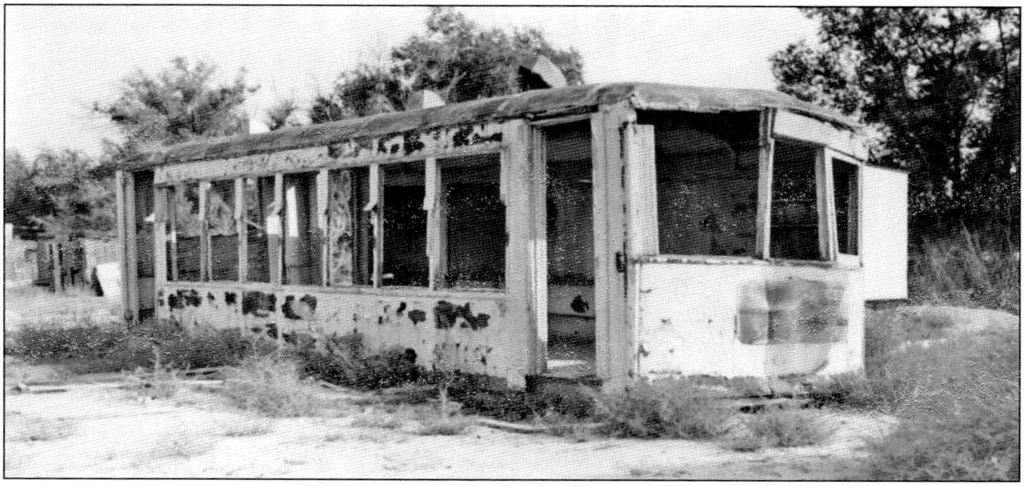

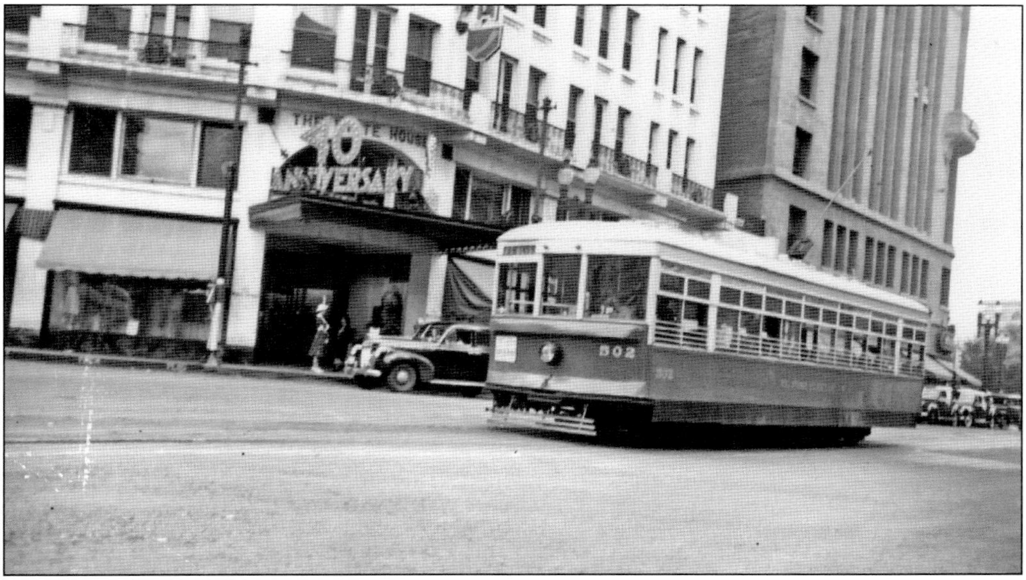


**No. 502 in 1940 and in 2000.** In competition with Popular Dry Goods was the White House, a well-known and luxurious department store that opened at this location in 1912. Fort Bliss car No. 502 (above) passes by the front of the White House, advertising its 40th anniversary on June 22, 1940. The White House at one time had the longest escalator in the country. In the second image (below), No. 502 is shown on a farm in southern New Mexico being used as a cotton trailer. About 1950, it was bought by a farmer and used for bracero housing. Later the ends and tops were cut off, wheels were added underneath, and it became a cotton trailer. (Above, Bob Crockett photograph, courtesy of Cliff Scholes.)

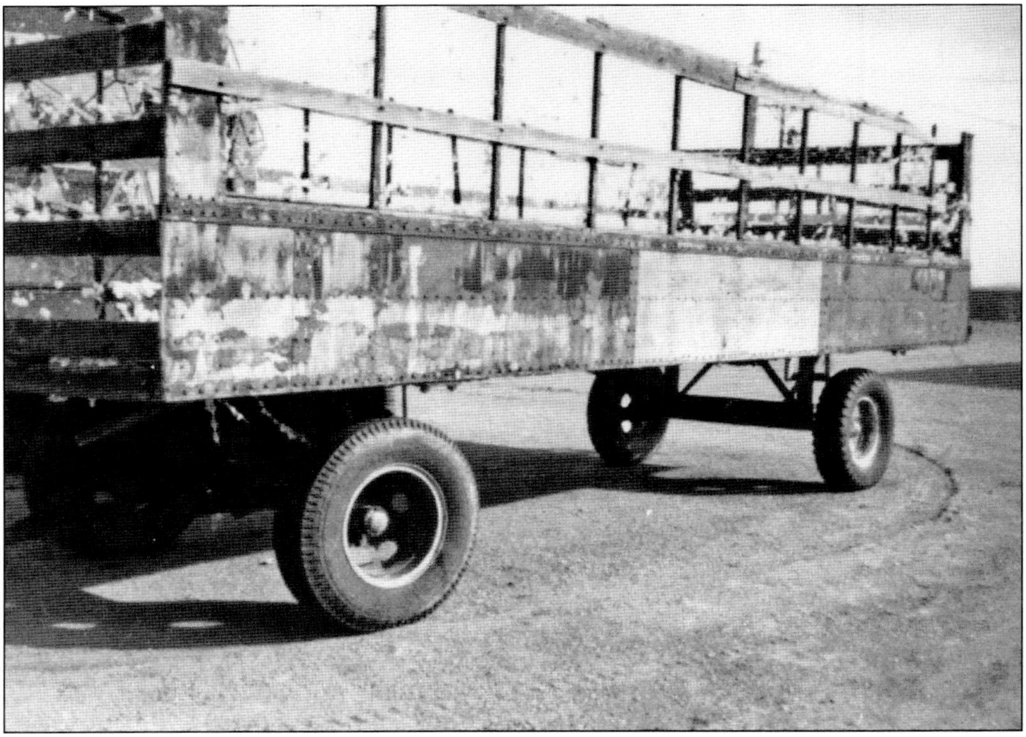

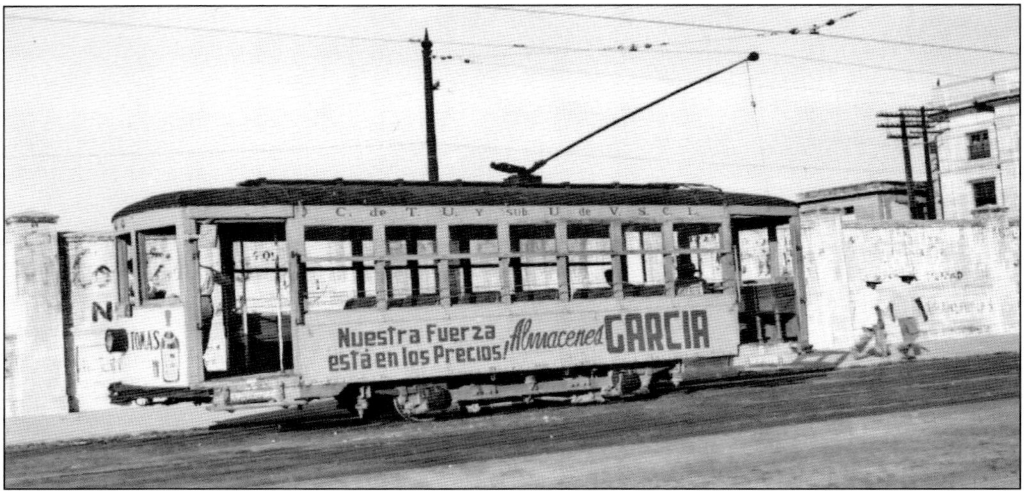


**In Veracruz, Mexico.** This ex–El Paso single-truck Birney streetcar was one of the 100 series sold to Mexico after 1937. Here it is running in Veracruz on Mexico's gulf coast, complete with advertising. It has been modified with extra doors. Built in 1921, it ran in Veracruz until the early 1980s.

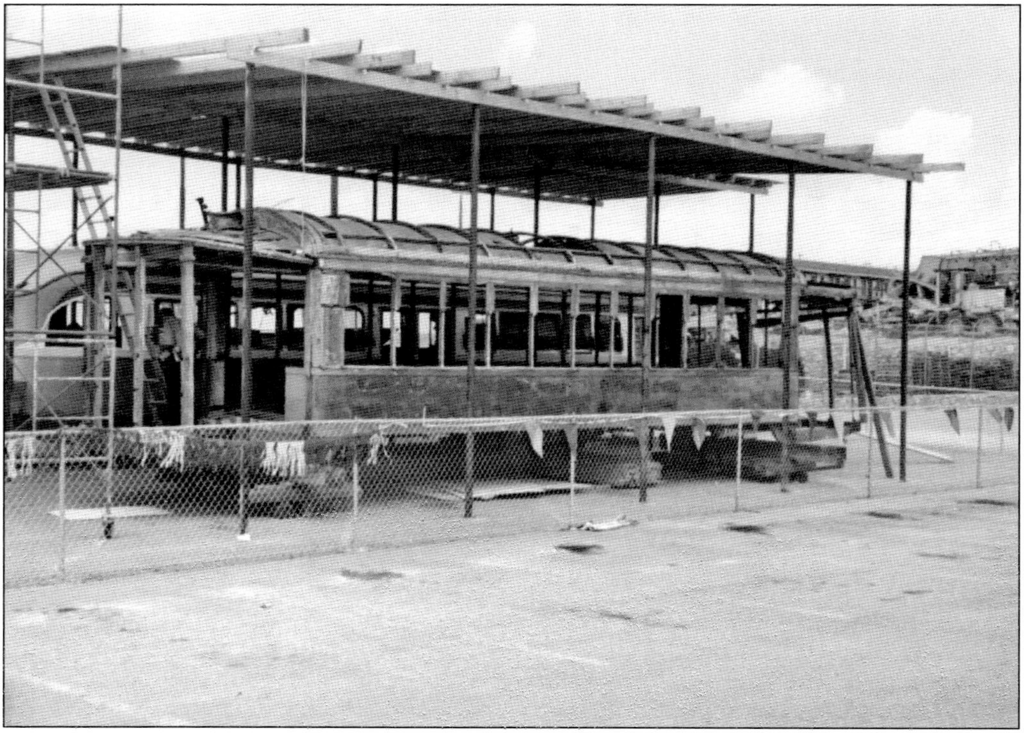

**Car No. 90.** Stone and Webster–type car No. 90 is shown here in recent years starting a restoration process at the El Paso Job Corps Center. Apparently the El Paso Electric Company and later El Paso City Lines did not strip paint when changing paint schemes, as workers found all the old layers of paint in the removal process.

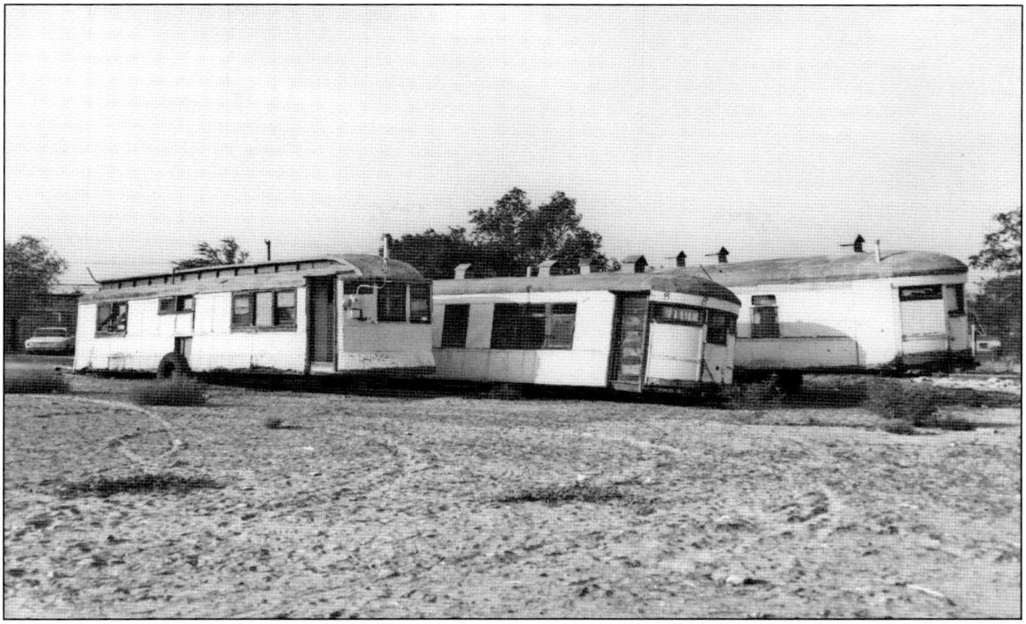

**Recycling Streetcars.** In the early days, it was more profitable for the street railway company to sell their discarded car bodies than it was to scrap them. In the foreground is railroad-roofed No. 81 and two of the original El Paso–to–Ysleta interurban cars after having been used as apartments on a lot on Alameda Street in the 1960s. (Courtesy of H. J. Leinbach Jr. Collection.)

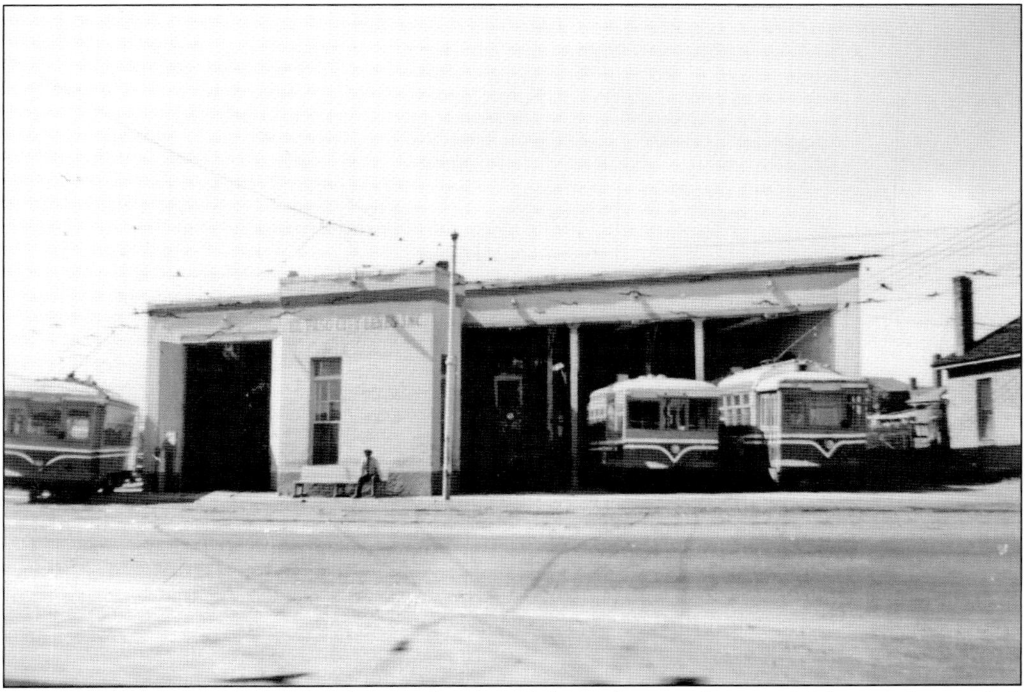

**Carbarn in 1945.** This is a wide outside view of the carbarn in late 1945. The war has ended, and the streetcar fleet is aging. A single-truck Birney (left) is waiting on the ready track as a motorman sits on the outdoor bench awaiting his next assignment. Some of these cars have been in service since 1912 and will be replaced by PCCs by 1950.

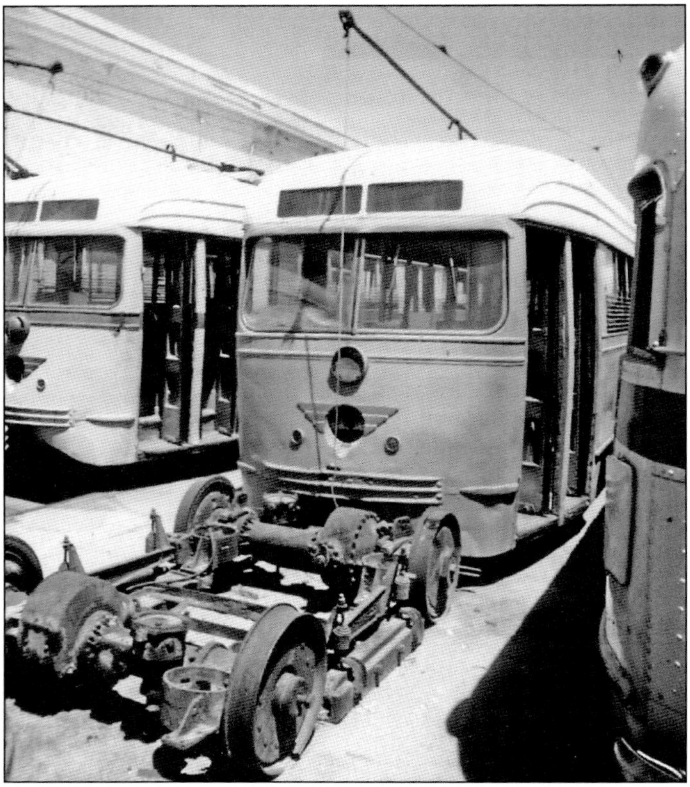

**Cannibalizing PCCs at the Barn.** This exterior carbarn view shows two streetcars out of service and being cannibalized for parts. The traction truck in front of the car in the foreground is a Clark B-2 truck, used on the early versions of PCC streetcar built by the St. Louis Car Company.

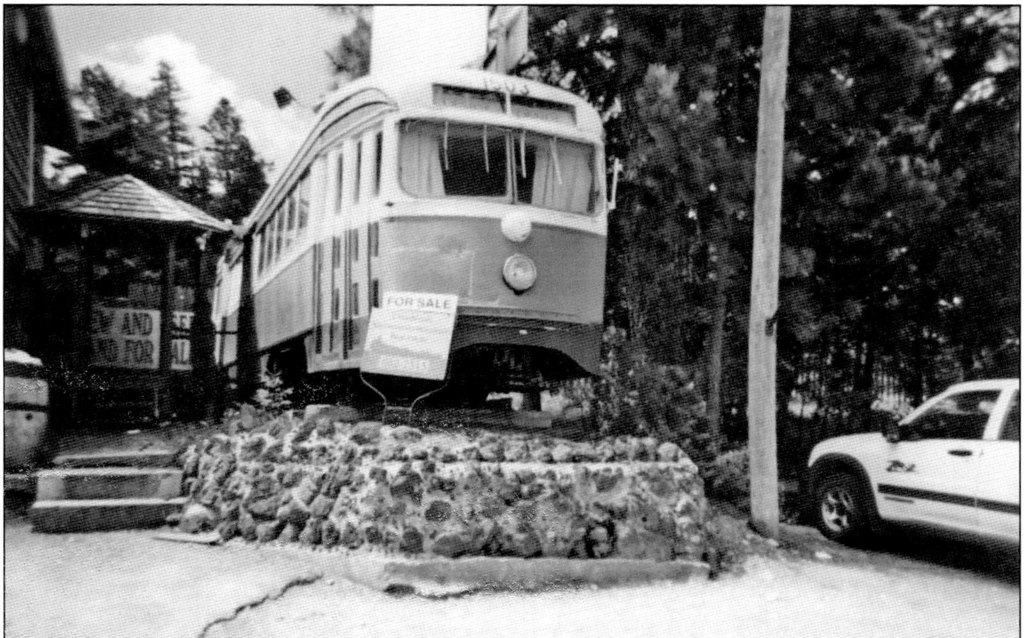


**PCC Streetcar No. 1503.** This ex–El Paso PCC streetcar, No. 1503, is shown in Cloudcroft, New Mexico, serving as a real estate office. Several cars were sold to individuals in 1986. No. 1503 was No. 503 in its time in San Diego. It has since found a home at the Baltimore Trolley Museum.

## *Nine*

# The International Bridges

After the organization of a mule-powered streetcar line in 1882, a bridge was built at the foot of Stanton Street over to Lerdo Street in Ciudad Juarez. Prior to this time, crossing the border involved a makeshift ferry. The 1882 bridge was a wooden structure easily strong enough to support the mule car line and horses and wagons. There was a flood, however, about two years later, and the whole structure had to be rebuilt in 1884. At that time, the Santa Fe Street bridge had not yet been built, so the mule cars both entered and left Mexico via the Stanton Street Bridge. By 1888, there was congestion, with cars often delayed at the bridge switch waiting for a car to pass in the opposite direction.

By that time, Zach White and his Santa Fe Street Railway were lobbying for permission to build a new international bridge at the foot of Santa Fe Street. Permission was obtained, and the new bridge was opened for pedestrian traffic on June 1, 1889, and opened to streetcars about two weeks later. After the consolidation of the mule car companies by Anson Mills in the following two years, a loop on the Juarez line was in place; thereafter cars entered Juarez on the Stanton bridge and returned to the United States side via the Santa Fe Street Bridge. This arrangement continued throughout the lifespan of the streetcar line, even after the construction of the new concrete bridges, Stanton in 1924–1925 and Santa Fe Street four years later.

The tolled bridges were owned by the El Paso Electric Company and later the El Paso City Lines. This situation would ultimately lead to the demise of the streetcar line. Traffic was heavy on the line, and streetcars tried to maintain a 10-minute headway. In 1939, for example, the company carried more than nine million passengers, most of them on the Juarez line.

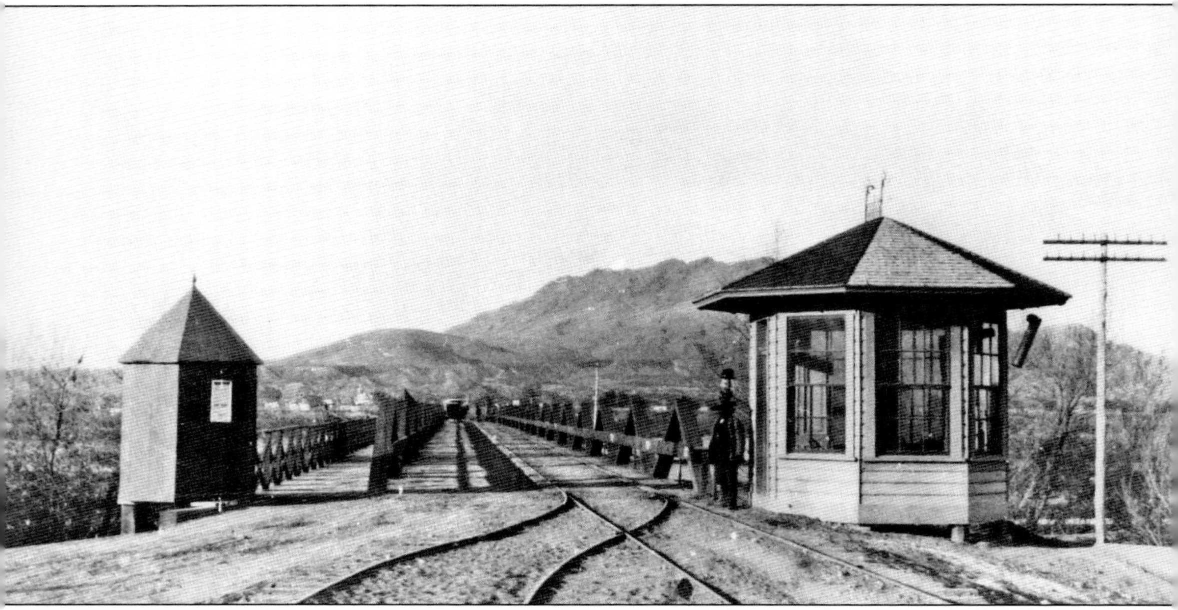

**Mule Car Days.** This is an early view of the Stanton Street Bridge in the mule car days. The view is from the Mexican side looking toward El Paso. Nothing is paved, but the transit company has provided a separate walkway for pedestrians. The electric pole (right) indicates electricity was available, but the new electric cars have not yet been introduced at the time of this photograph. The rail switch dates from the time that the Stanton Street bridge was the only international bridge for the mule cars prior to the construction of the Santa Fe bridge. In those days, one car might have to wait for the other to clear before proceeding. The El Paso and Juarez Traction Company owned this bridge and later the Santa Fe Street Bridge. Both were always tolled. (Courtesy of EPPL.)

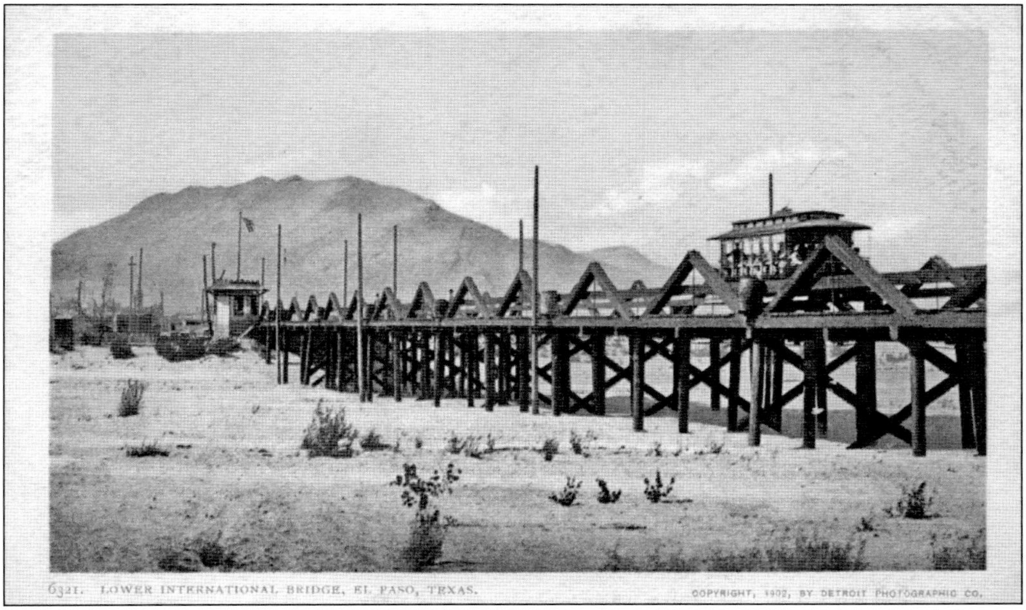


**EARLY OPEN CAR ON THE BRIDGE.** A single-truck open car of the type that inaugurated electric car service in 1902 hurries across the international bridge in this postcard view. At this time, the nine-bench cars were sufficient to carry the passenger loads, but that changed quickly, and by the end of 1902, the El Paso Electric Railway was ordering more new cars to handle the cross-border traffic.

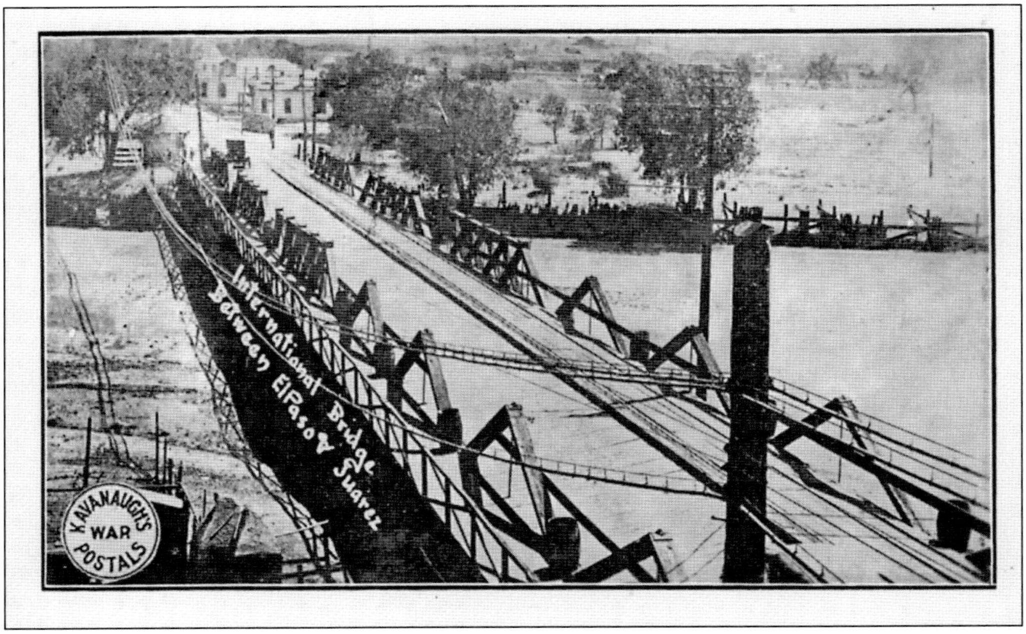


**INTERNATIONAL BRIDGE DURING WORLD WAR I.** In a postcard view taken in the World War I era, a buggy crosses into Mexico over what appears to be the Santa Fe Street Bridge. In this view, steel pylons are visible along the river's edge to prevent erosion from periodic flooding.

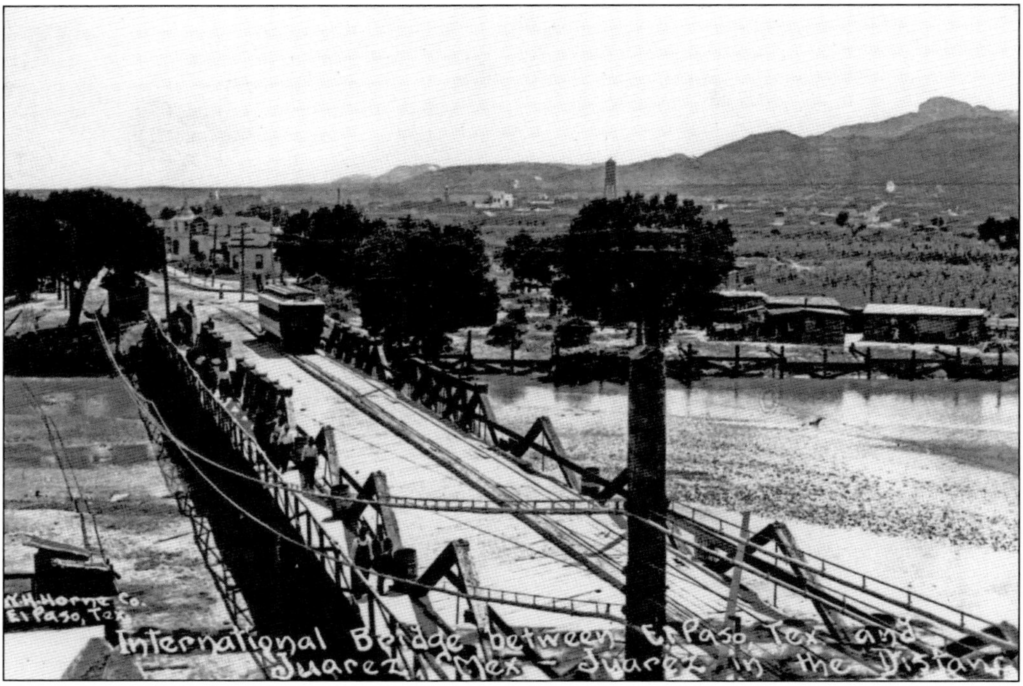


**Closed Car.** In a later view by W. H. Horne, a double-truck closed car leaves Mexico on the same bridge. By this time, some houses have sprung up on the Mexican side, and it appears more commerce is taking place. The newer and heavier cars would soon prove too heavy for the early bridges.

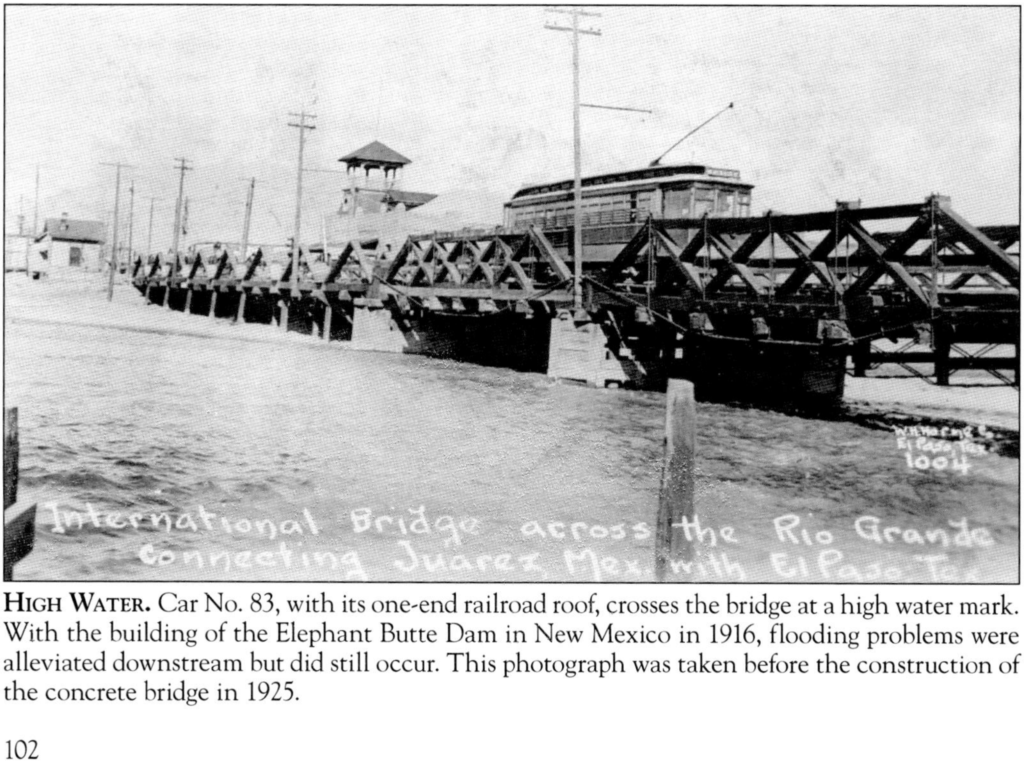


**High Water.** Car No. 83, with its one-end railroad roof, crosses the bridge at a high water mark. With the building of the Elephant Butte Dam in New Mexico in 1916, flooding problems were alleviated downstream but did still occur. This photograph was taken before the construction of the concrete bridge in 1925.

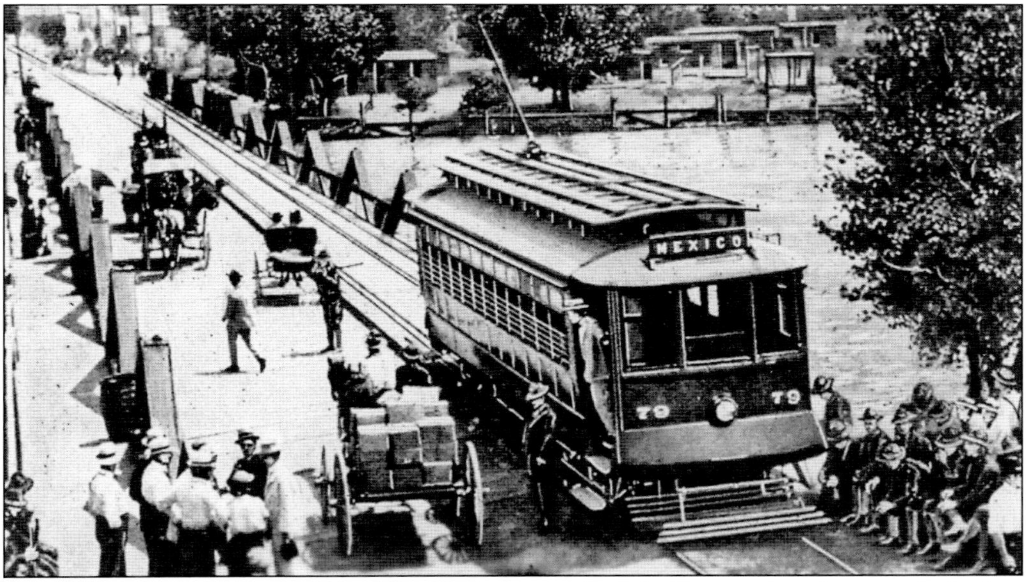


**REVOLUTIONARY TIMES ON THE BRIDGE.** With the number of soldiers and civilians on the bridge, it appears to be a scene from Mexican Revolution times. No. 79 was rebuilt from a four-motor double-ended open car to a four-motor single-end closed car. This was one of the heaviest cars in the system. No automobiles are yet on the scene.

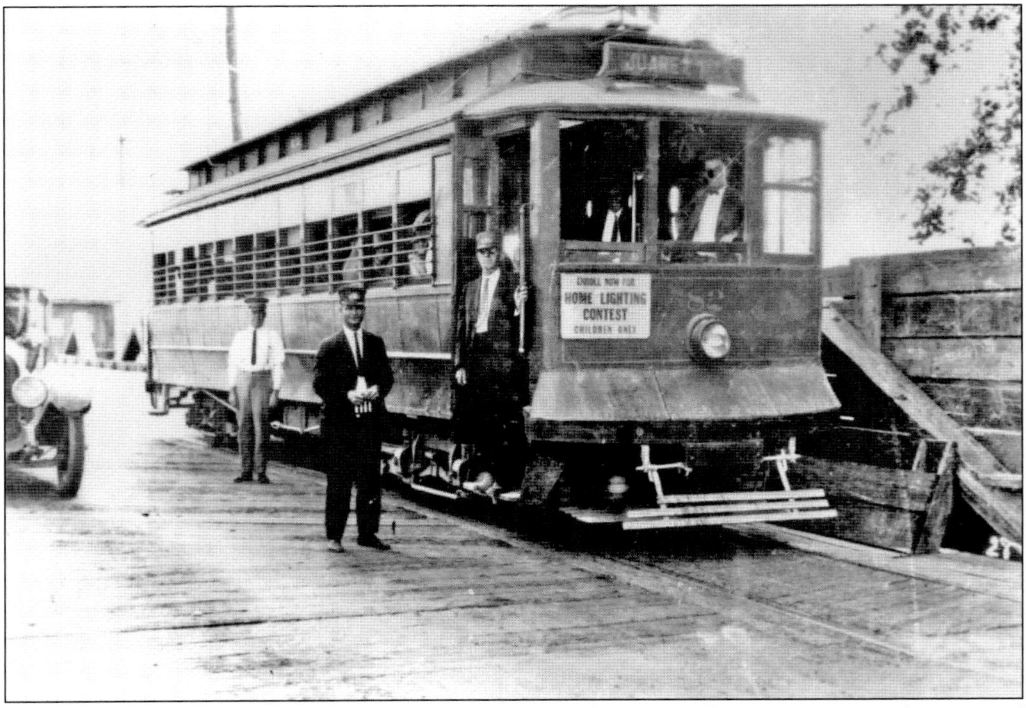


**NO. 82 AND A LIGHTING CONTEST.** Car No. 82, rebuilt from an earlier open car, stands on one of the early wooden international bridges in this photograph from the Dennis Lane Collection. No. 82 is sporting a sign announcing a home lighting contest with the admonition "children only." Leaves on the tree and shirtsleeves seem to indicate it is not a Christmas lighting contest.

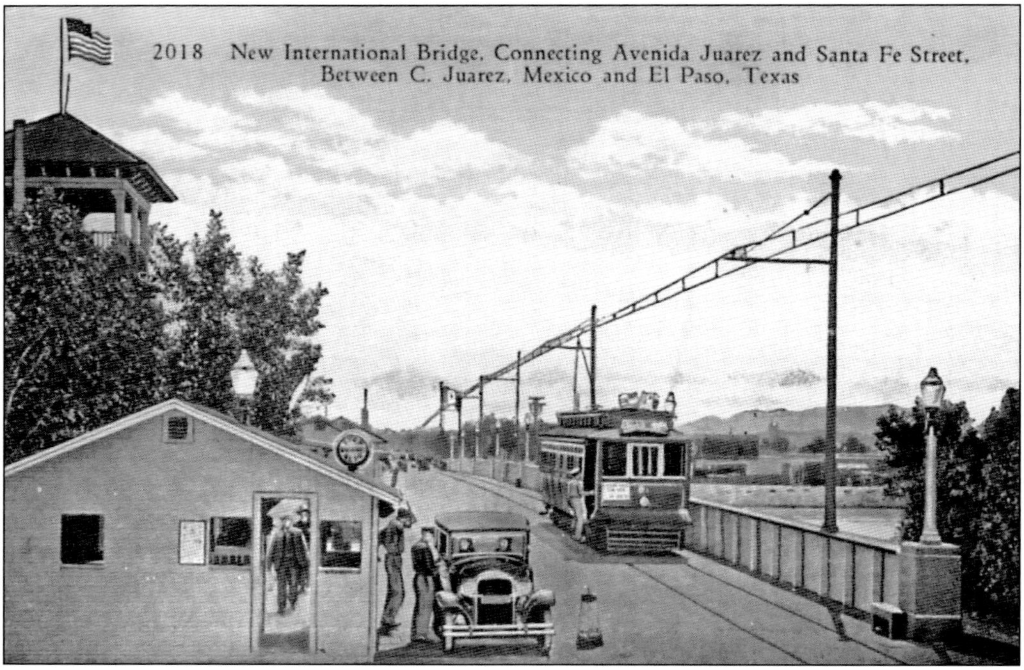


**A New Concrete Bridge.** About 1925, new concrete bridges replaced the old wooden structures at the foot of Stanton and Santa Fe Streets. Larger customs facilities were also installed. The Santa Fe Street Bridge, in this postcard view, connected with Avenida Juarez on the Mexican side. It was northbound for auto and streetcar traffic.

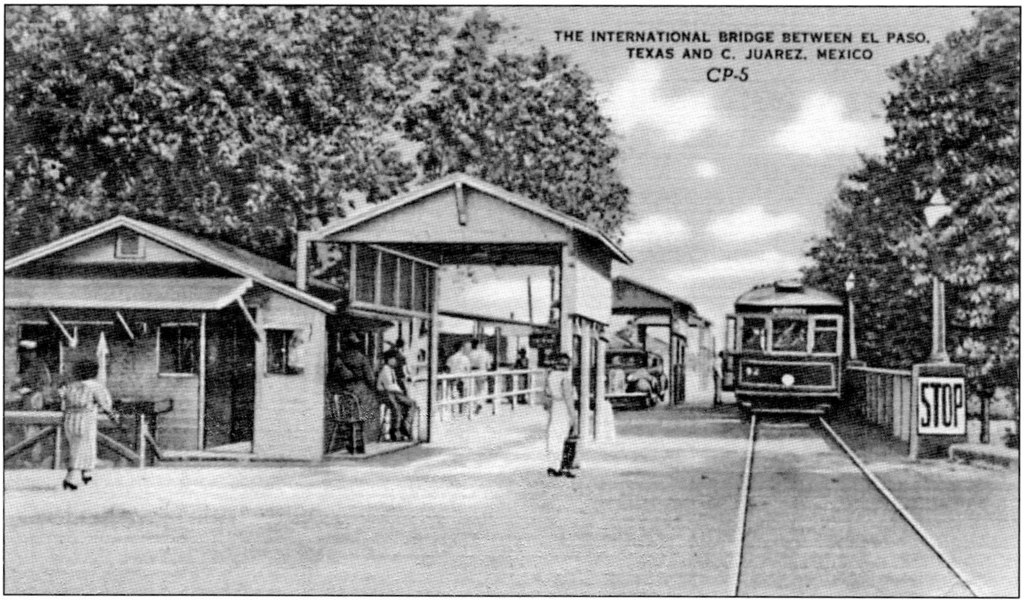


**Shading the Collectors.** By the 1940s, two sheds have been added to protect the customs officials and passengers from the sun and heat. No. 92 is from the second order of Stone and Webster roof cars from the St. Louis Car Company in 1914. These two motor cars had maximum traction trucks and were used until the PCCs came in 1950.

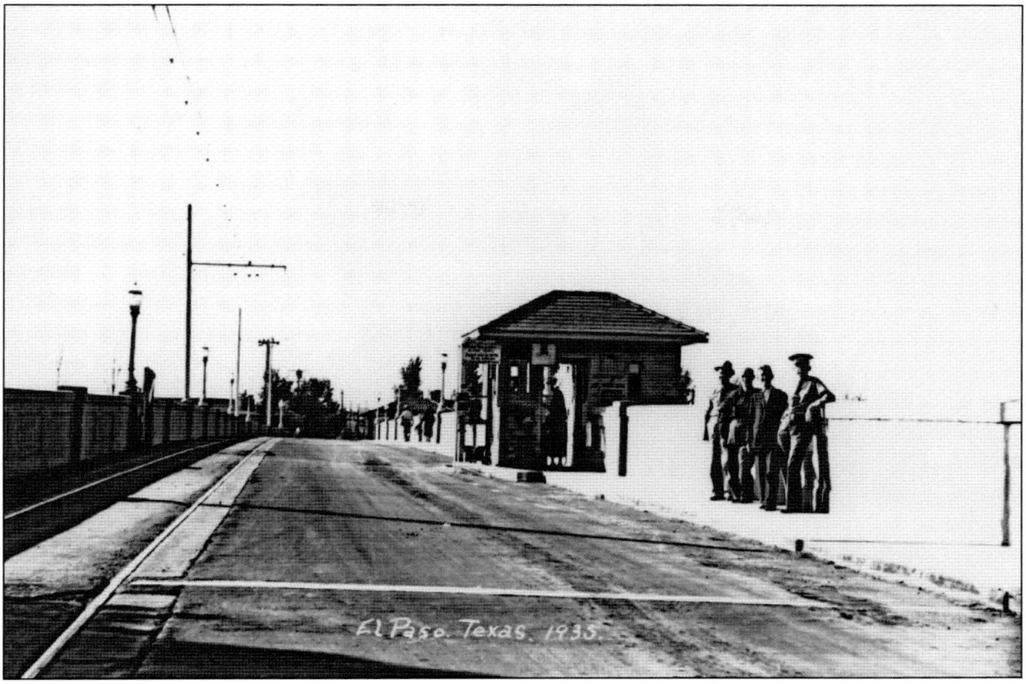


**IN 1935 ON THE STANTON BRIDGE.** This is a clear view of tracks on the Stanton Street Bridge with concrete reinforcing on each side of the rails. Customs officials and civilians are posing for the camera, and traffic is light. This bridge lasted 40 years from the mid-1920s to the mid-1960s.

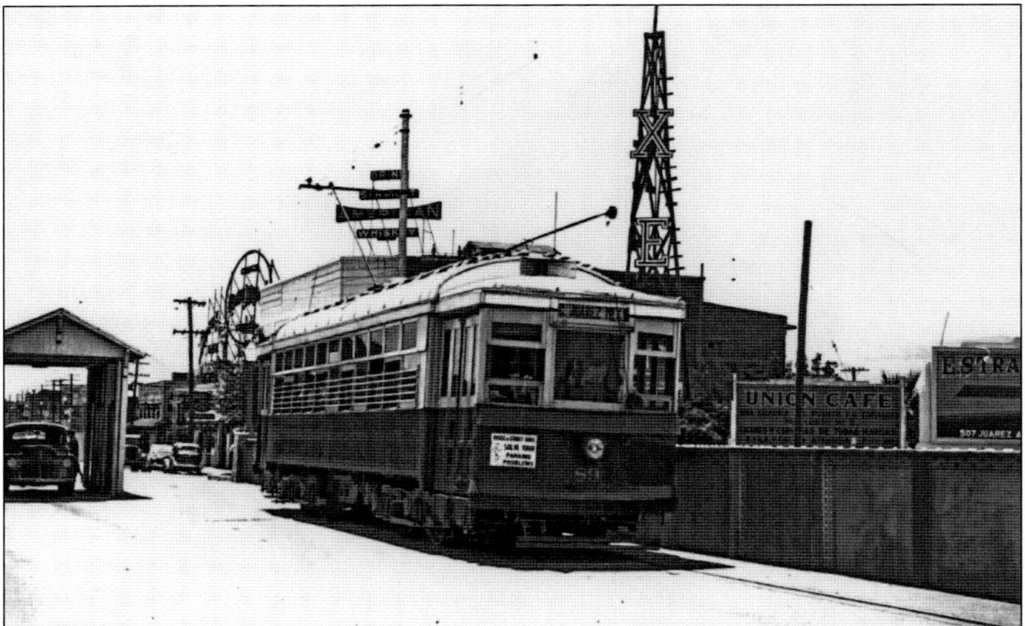


**NO. 89 IN AUGUST 1941.** It is a hot August 14, 1941, four months before Pearl Harbor, when Stone and Webster car No. 89 makes its way across the Santa Fe Street Bridge to return to El Paso from Ciudad Juarez. At this time, the cars still belong to the El Paso Electric Company and are painted white over red.

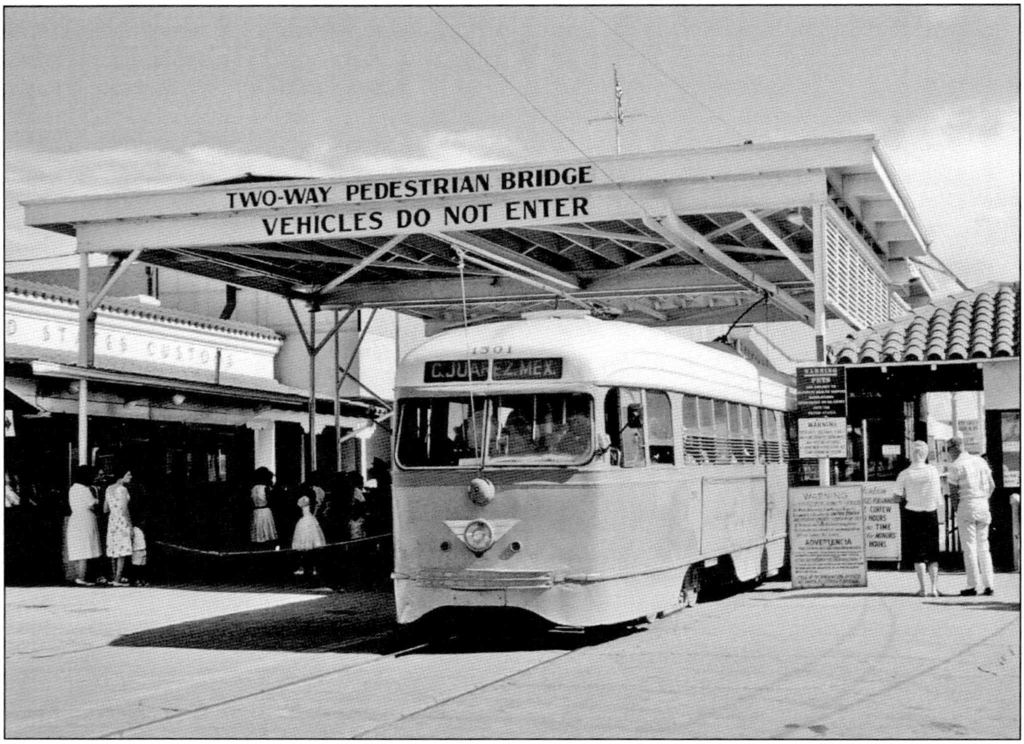


**PCC on the Bridge.** This PCC streetcar came to El Paso in 1950 from San Diego, where it had run from 1937 to 1949. No. 1501 is on the Santa Fe Street Bridge. This is still the 1920s concrete bridge with expanded customs facilities added in the 1940s and 1950s. (Frank S. Novak photograph, courtesy of PDNSPS.)

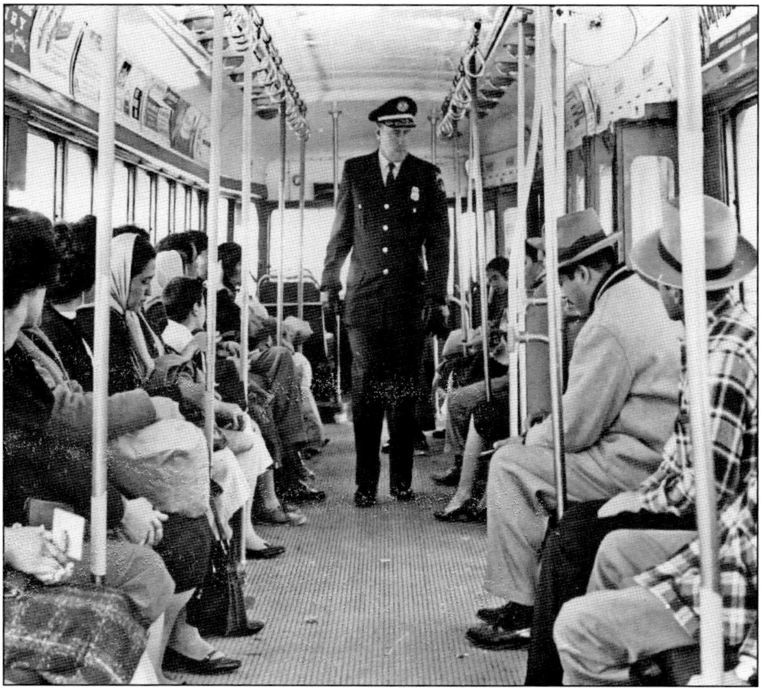

**A Customs Officer Boards.** This somewhat stern-looking customs inspector has boarded a PCC streetcar at the bridge to check passengers and packages. When purchasing the cars, the El Paso City Lines had mandated new longitudinal seating to facilitate inspections. Later passengers simply disembarked, went through customs as the streetcar moved ahead a few feet, then once again boarded the streetcar.

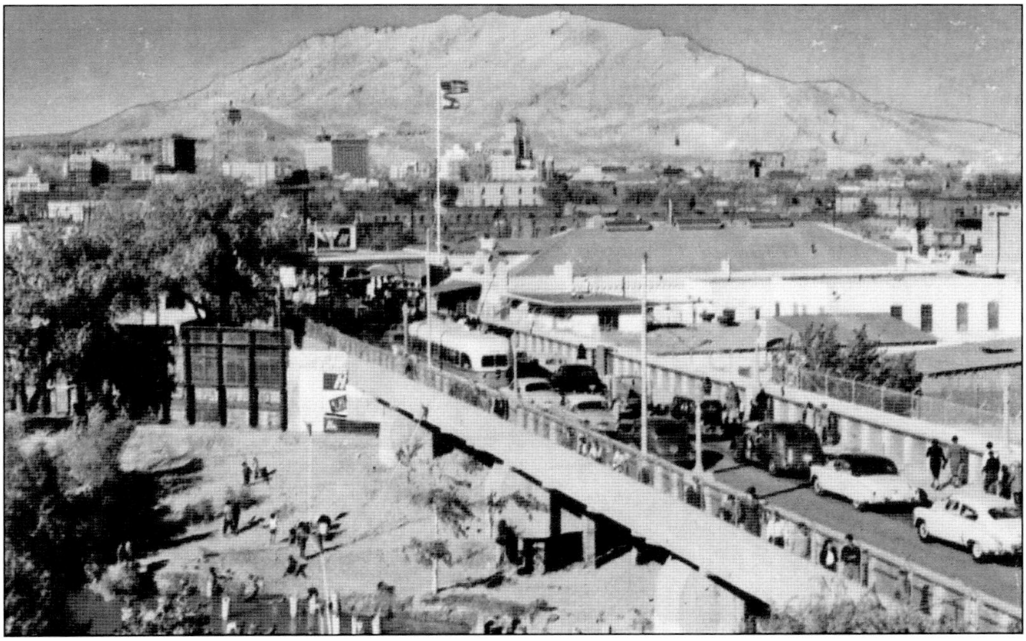

**A 1950s View of the Bridge.** A PCC streetcar mixes with traffic in this 1950s view of the Santa Fe Street Bridge. The original pilings of the old wooden bridge can be seen (left) in the water. The children (left center) are holding up cones on poles to try to catch coins thrown by pedestrians and tourists on the bridge.

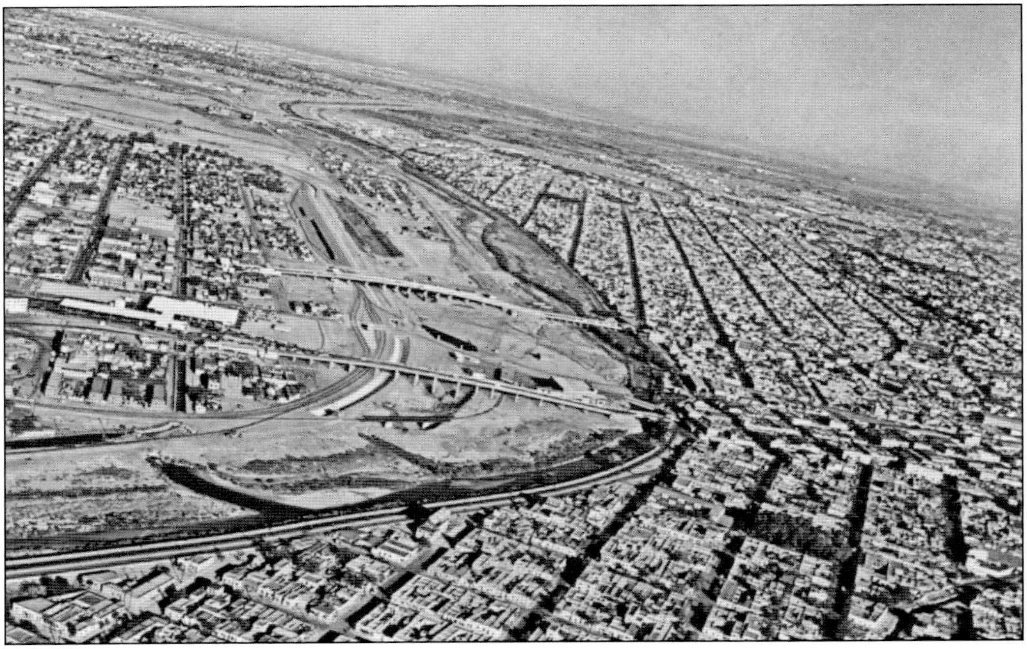

**Aerial View of the New Bridges.** After the Chamizal agreement between the United States and Mexico was signed in 1963, plans were put in place to realign the border, which necessitated building new bridges. Here is an aerial view of the new Paso del Norte Bridge, ex–Santa Fe (lower), and the Good Neighbor Bridge, ex-Stanton (upper). Streetcar tracks were added to the new bridges, and service resumed in 1967.

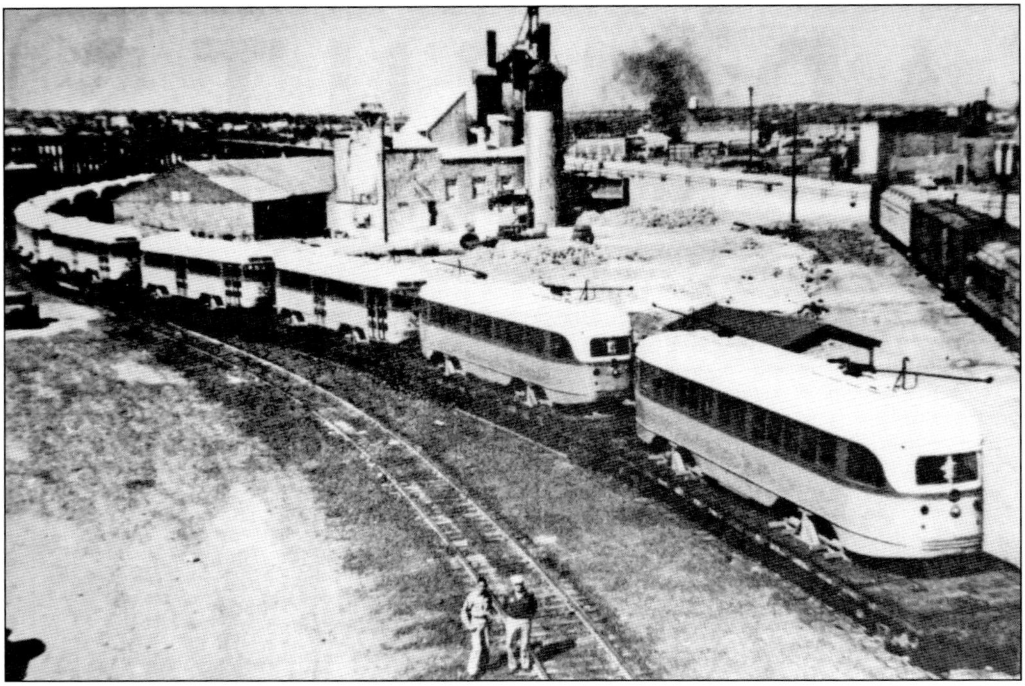

**San Diego to El Paso.** The first 17 PCC streetcars arrived in El Paso on railroad flatcars from San Diego in April 1950. Prior to sending them to El Paso, San Diego repainted them, added a front trolley pole, and changed the interior to longitudinal seating to facilitate inspections at the border.

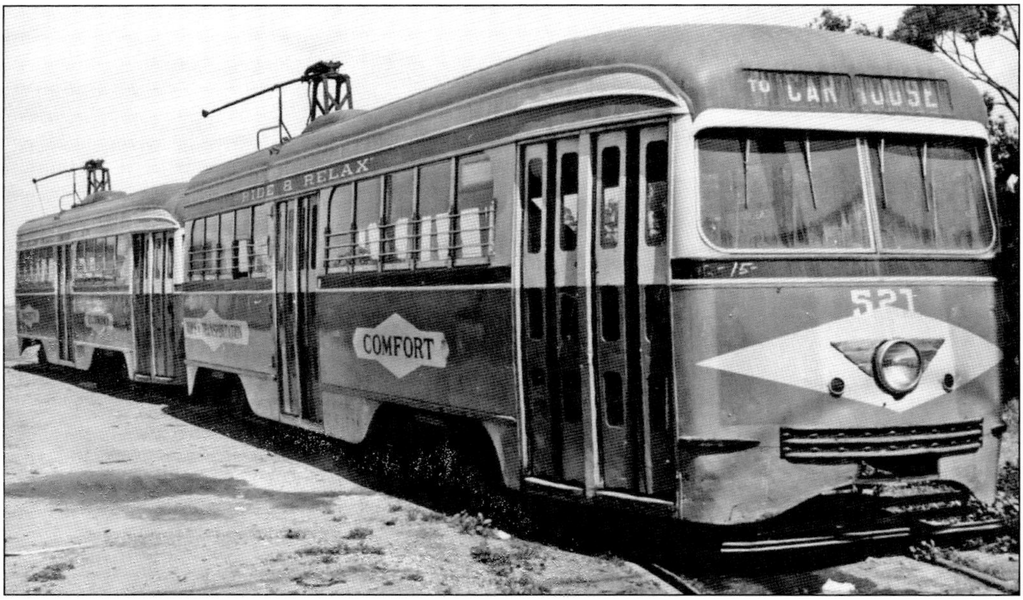


**PCCs Still in San Diego.** This photograph shows car Nos. 521 and 525 in the yard at the West Adams car house awaiting alterations and repainting prior to being sent to El Paso. The PCCs were numbered in the 500s in San Diego but were renumbered in the 1500s in El Paso, possibly to avoid confusion with some of the 1927 500-series still on the property. (Courtesy of John J. Myers Collection.)

# *Ten*

# Modernizing with PCCs

After the Fort Bliss and Park lines were converted to buses on August 17, 1947, only the Juarez line remained in streetcars. By 1950, El Paso City Lines realized it would not be able to convert the Juarez line to buses because of treaty provisions with Mexico that specified a street railway. The decision was made at that time to upgrade the fleet with PCC cars. PCC cars were made from 1937 to 1952 and were named after the Presidents Conference Committee, a group responsible for the design of this second-generation streetcar. The art deco, streamlined design was enormously successful, and thousands were built and used around the globe. El Paso bought 17 used PCCs from the San Diego Electric Railway in 1950 and three more in 1952. After operating successfully in San Diego from 1937 to 1949 and carrying great wartime loads, the cars continued to operate in El Paso and Juarez for 24 more years, from 1950 to 1974. These were first-generation PCCs built by the St. Louis Car Company, ordered in August 1936 and delivered to San Diego in April 1937. They were air-electrics with Westinghouse components. El Paso's PCCs were single-enders intended to operate one way; however, they could be backed if necessary. Since El Paso City Lines had somewhat prematurely taken out track on Myrtle Avenue from Cotton Street to San Antonio Street, it became necessary for operators to back the PCCs down San Antonio Street to Stanton Street to get on the clockwise Juarez loop. To do this, the operator had to take hand controls to the back, kneel on the back seat, insert the controls, and back down the street. Over the years, the PCCs carried millions of passengers back and forth across the border.

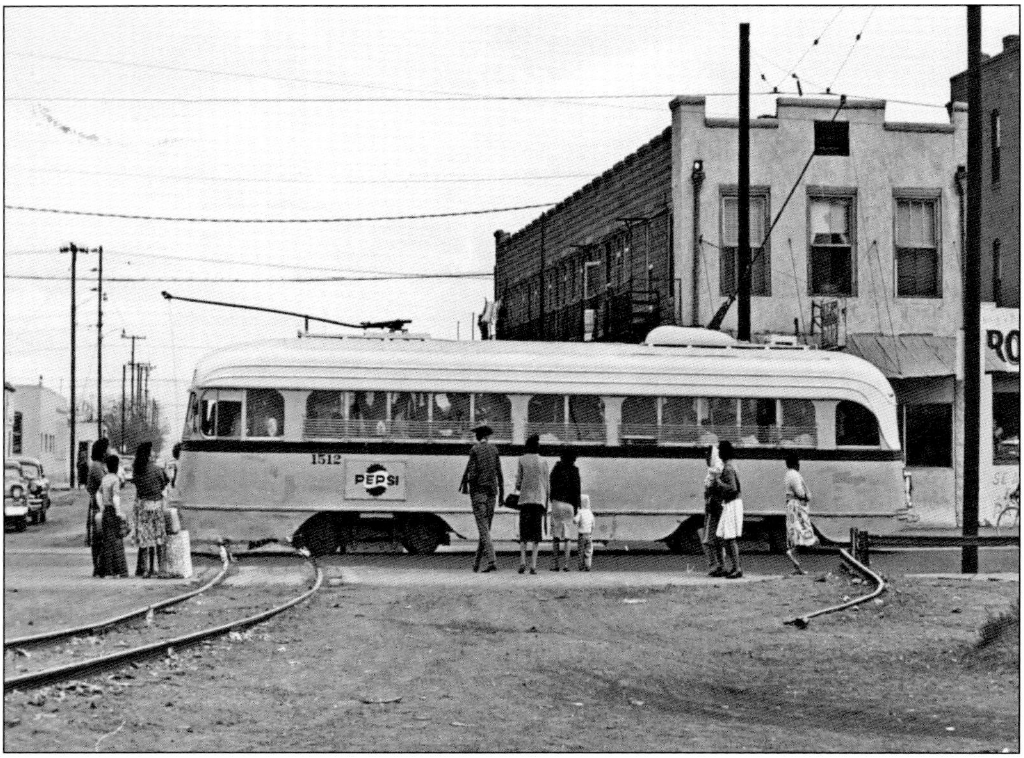


**HEAVY LOADS.** With large crowds of Mexican citizens coming to El Paso to shop or work downtown, the PCCs often carried standing-room-only payloads. The PCCs could accommodate 54 passengers in seats and probably that many more standees. Here No. 1512 is northbound on Chamizal Court crossing the Santa Fe line from the railroad bridge to the Santa Fe yards.

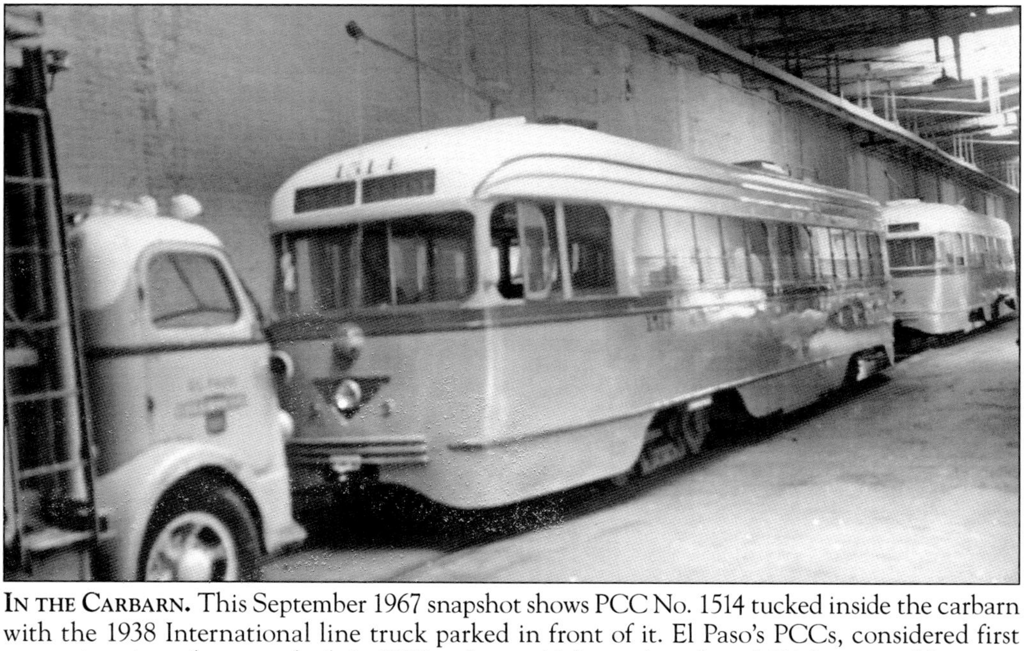

**IN THE CARBARN.** This September 1967 snapshot shows PCC No. 1514 tucked inside the carbarn with the 1938 International line truck parked in front of it. El Paso's PCCs, considered first generation since they were built in 1937 and were 46 feet in length and 8½ feet in width.

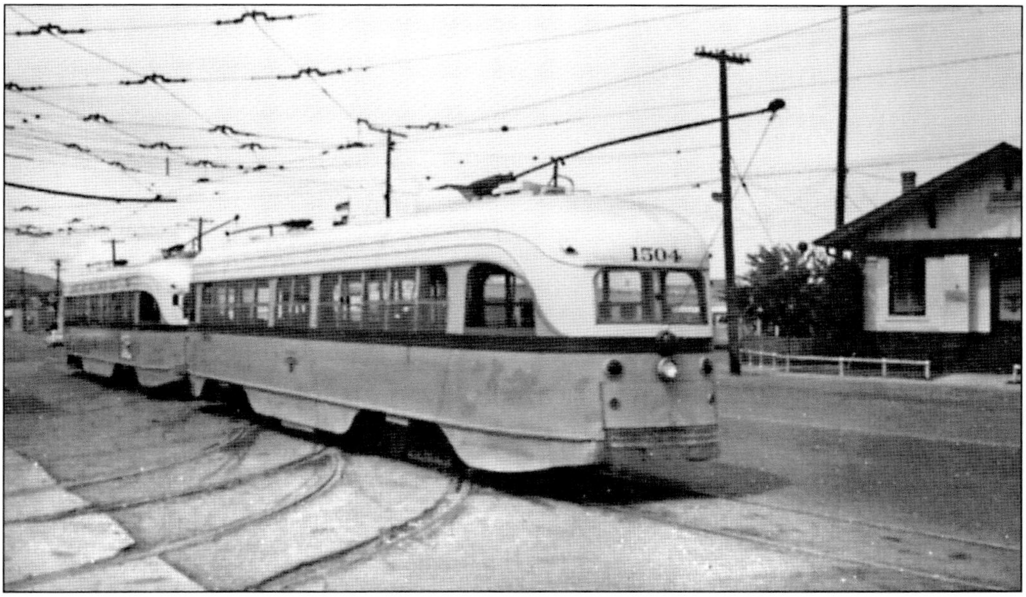


**AN OVERHEAD WIRING MAZE.** This view is looking north on Cotton Street. PCC No. 1504 and one other PCC are parked on the "ladder track" outside the carbarn. El Paso's carbarn had an overlapping turn in switches and somewhat complicated track work. Switches were aligned by using a tool with a socket on the end to throw the ground switch.

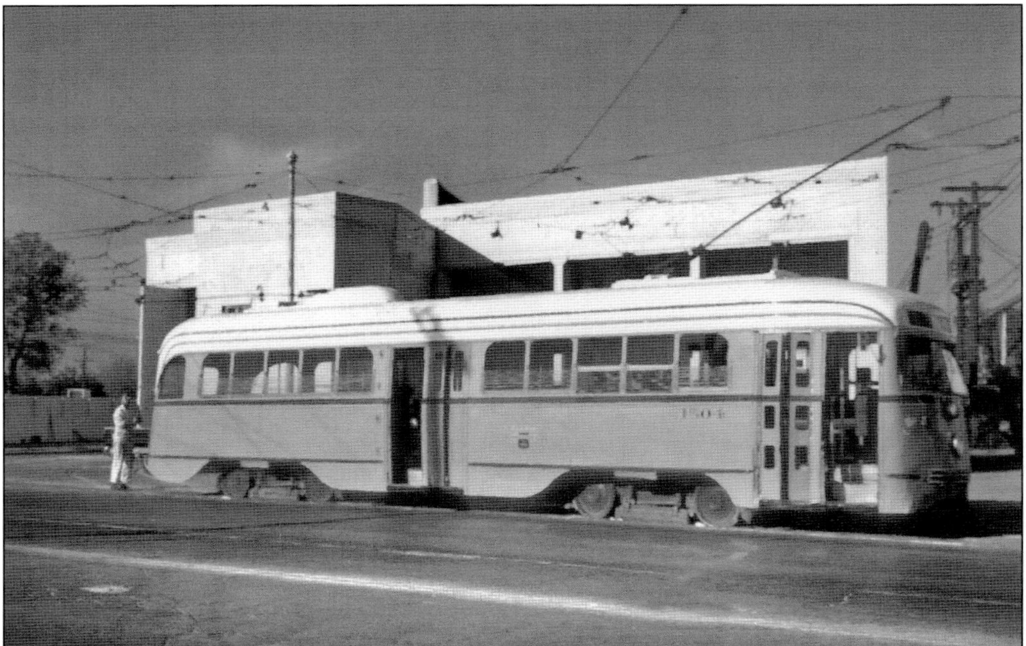

**OUTSIDE THE COTTON STREET BARN.** No. 1514 is outside the carbarn on the ladder track and is preparing to be backed down to San Antonio Street. The rear trolley pole has been lowered, and the front has been raised for the backing movement. The maintenance man in the white coveralls is securing the rear pole.

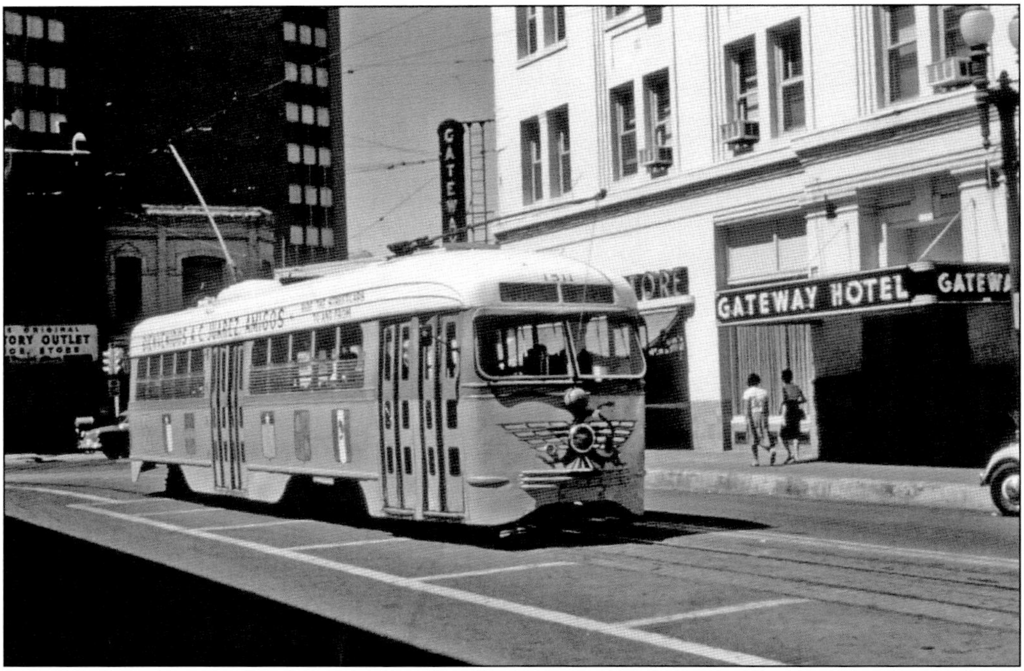


**Queen of the Fleet.** PCC No. 1511 was always the "show" car of the PCC fleet. It was the one that was decorated in various Southwestern designs and advertising to attract tourists to Juarez. The photograph above shows No. 1511 in front of the Gateway Hotel on Stanton Street. The designs and paintings were done by local El Paso artist Jose Cisneros when he worked for City Lines. He was quoted as saying he followed no pattern for the designs—it was simply that he conceived each design from scratch. In the photograph below, No. 1511 is parked on the first outside track at the carbarn and is showing a more sophisticated artwork design, also by Jose Cisneros.

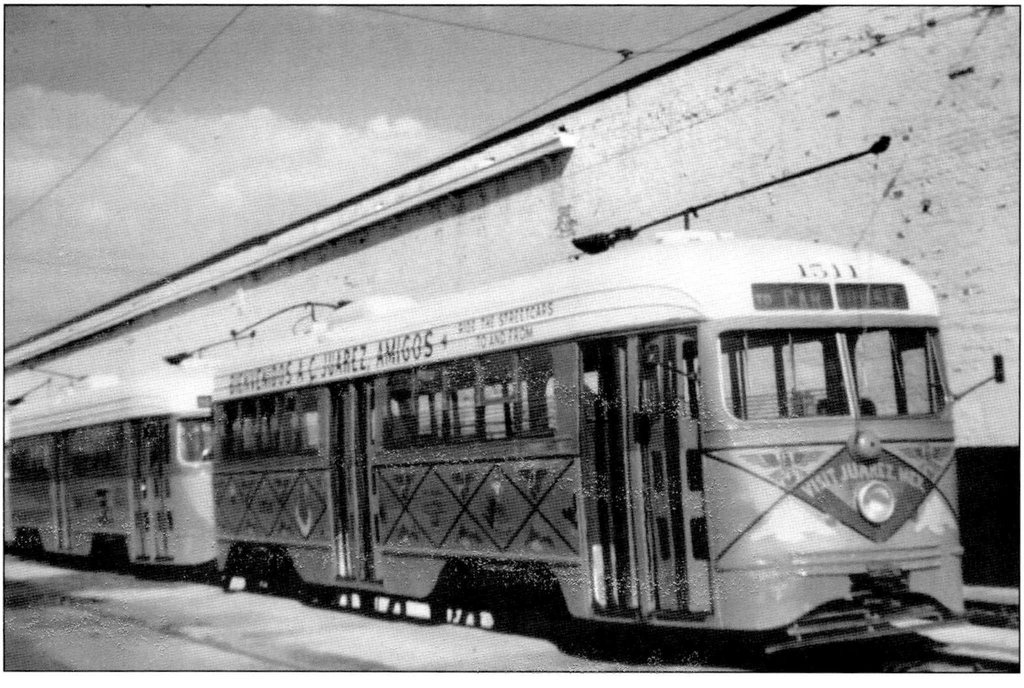

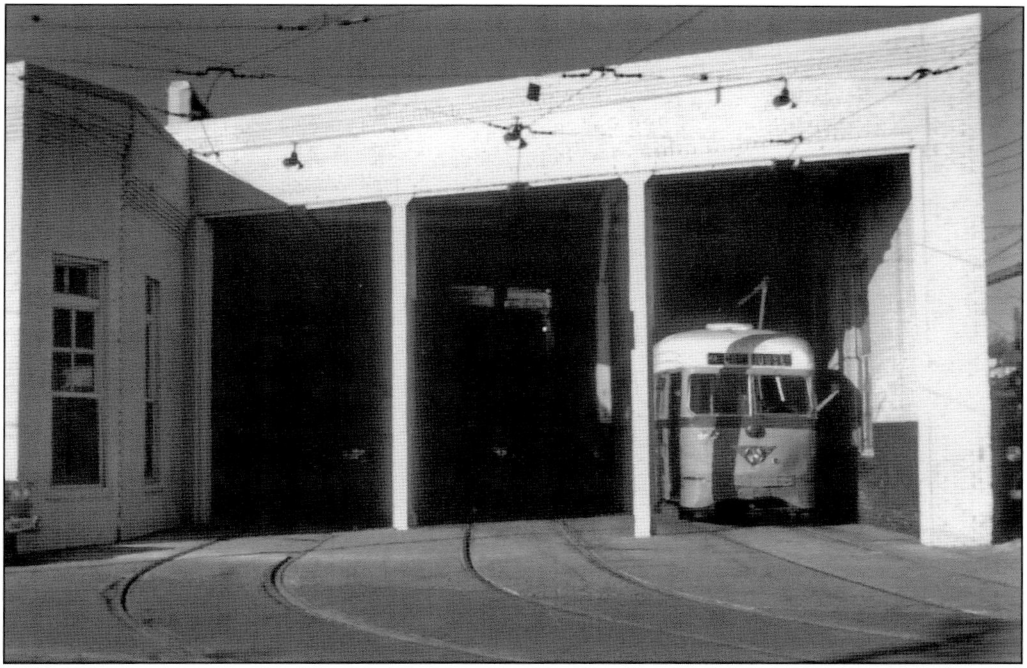

**A Look at the North Bay.** Since the carbarn was built in stages, this image shows the first three tracks on the north side. Offices are located to the left of the scene. Another bay was added to the other side of the office at a date later than 1910. Four outside tracks had been at least partially enclosed before a fire destroyed that addition.

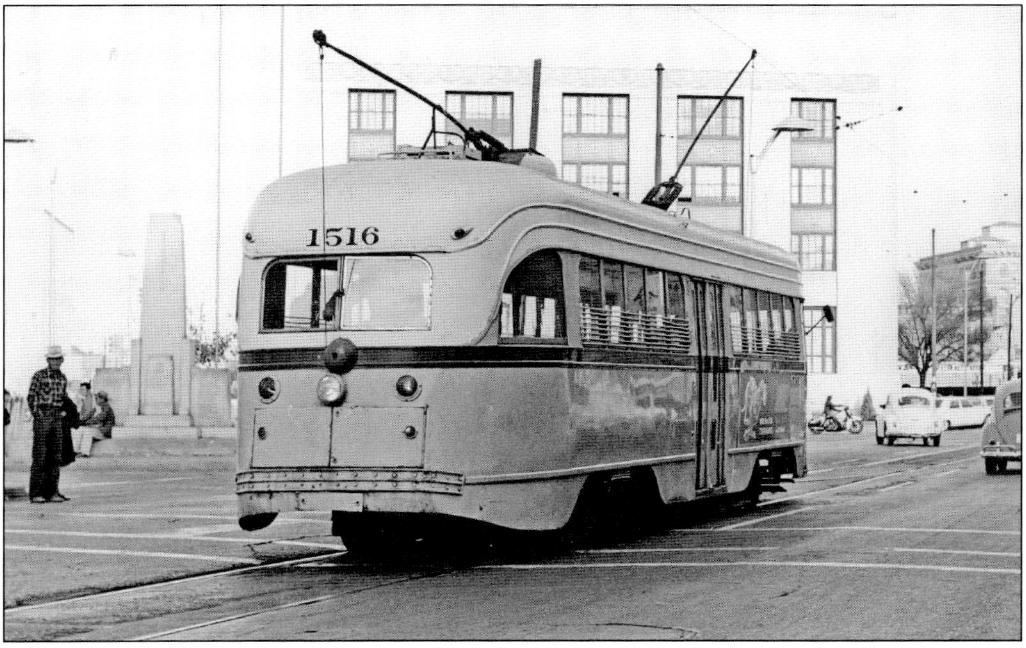


**The Backing Movement.** The motorman can be seen in the back window of No. 1516 as he guides it in reverse down San Antonio Street to get on the Juarez loop. In this 1960s view, VWs seem to be the auto of choice. The U.S. Federal Courthouse is in the background, and to the left is a monument to those killed in World War II and the Korean Conflict.

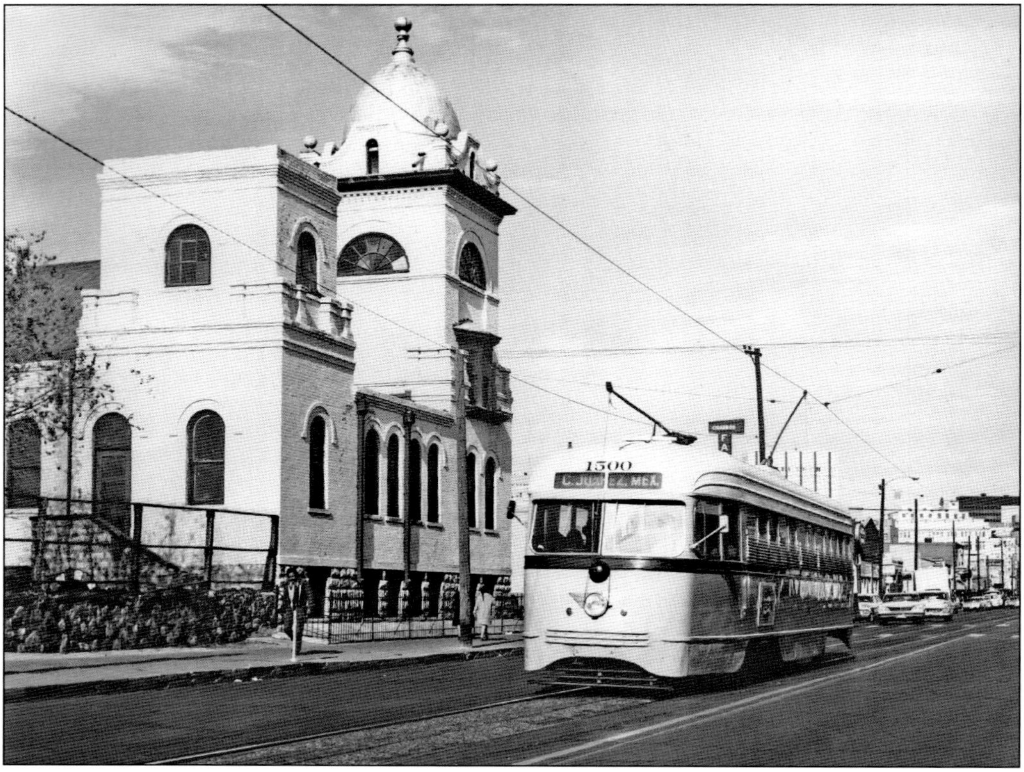


**No. 1500 in the Second Ward District.** Part of central El Paso south of downtown is known as the Second Ward, or *Segundo Barrio*, named for political precincts of earlier days. No. 1500 is southbound on Stanton Street in this 1960s photograph passing a church. Second Ward was, and is, a mixed residential and commercial area with a rich history.

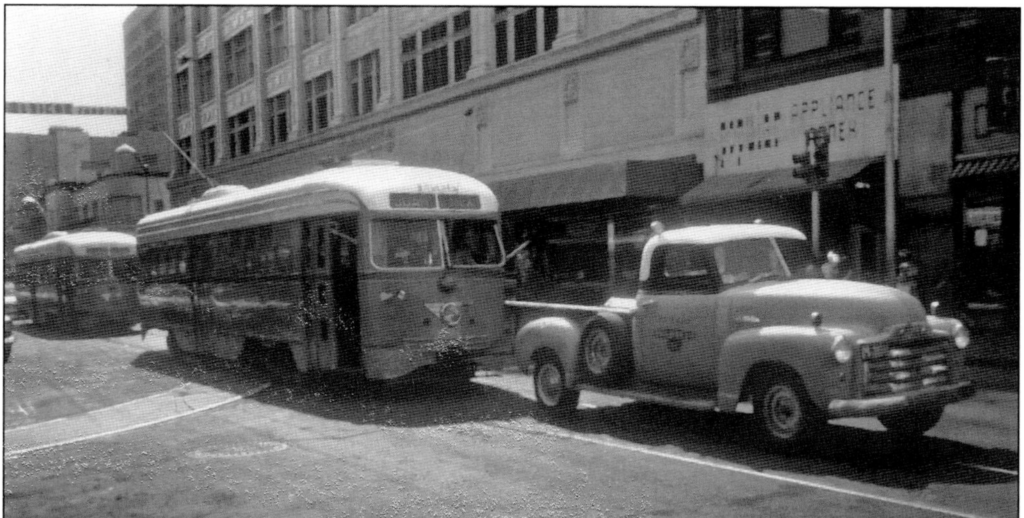

**Getting a Tow.** Although the PCCs generally were extremely reliable, there were occasions when they would have to be towed. Here an El Paso City Lines GMC pickup has a towbar attached to the front of disabled No. 1506 to tow it back to the carbarn. The location is at the intersection of San Antonio and Stanton Streets. Another streetcar is awaiting clearance to proceed.

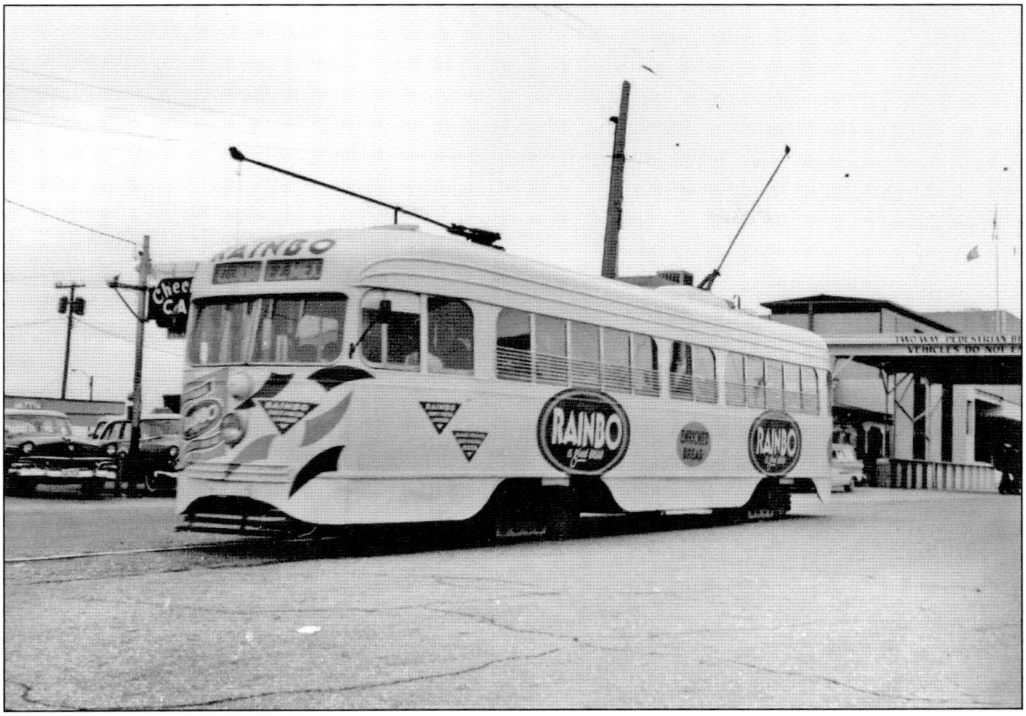


**Advertising Cars.** Long before the advent of graphic-designed wraps, the El Paso City Lines used one or more cars to generate revenue. One PCC (above) is seen in this view painted and decorated for Rainbo Bread. It is entering the United States from the Santa Fe Street Bridge. In the second image (below), No. 1506 is doing the honors for Cruz Blanca Beer, "Mexico's Finest Beer." By this time, No. 1506 is somewhat worse for wear with body dents and dings that have been painted over but not fixed. The windshields of the cars were pivoted and could be pushed out for better ventilation. The cars were not air-conditioned.

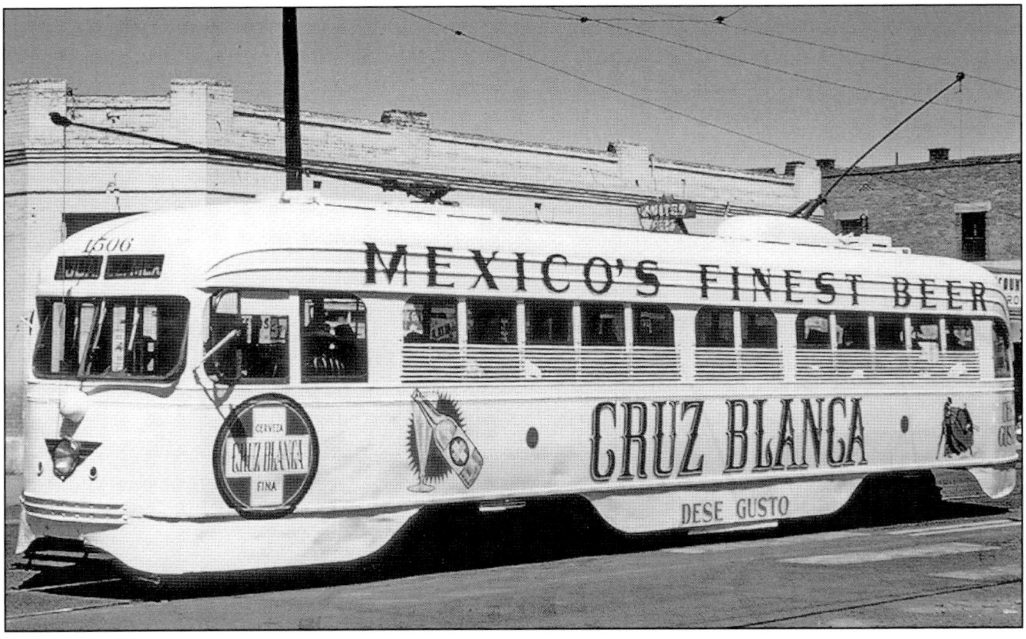

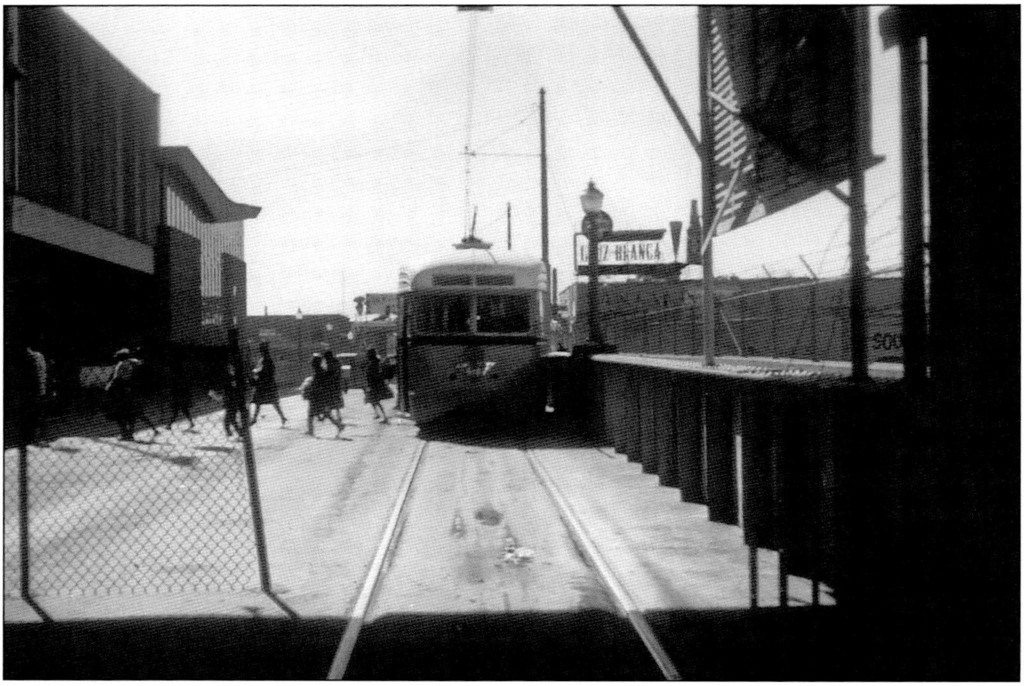

**Customs Inspections.** On the old Santa Fe Street concrete bridge, a temporary fence has been erected. Passengers will disembark from the streetcar and go through customs. The streetcar will then move forward past the fence, and the same passengers will reboard for the remainder of the ride to downtown El Paso.

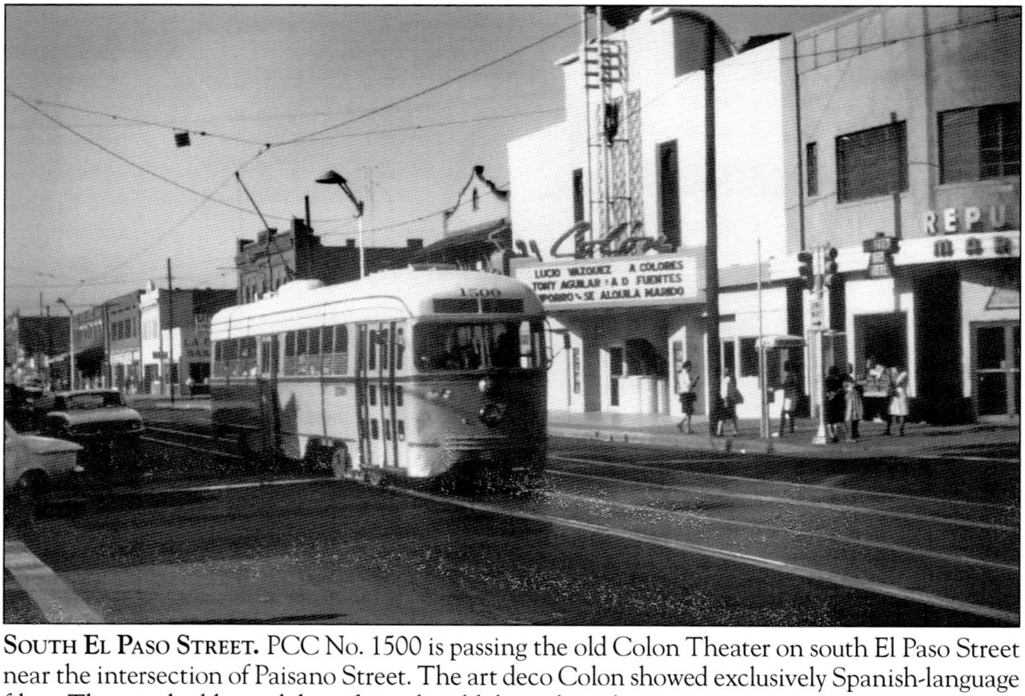


**South El Paso Street.** PCC No. 1500 is passing the old Colon Theater on south El Paso Street near the intersection of Paisano Street. The art deco Colon showed exclusively Spanish-language films. There is double track here from the old days when there was two-way streetcar movement, but now it is one way only, and only one track is being used.

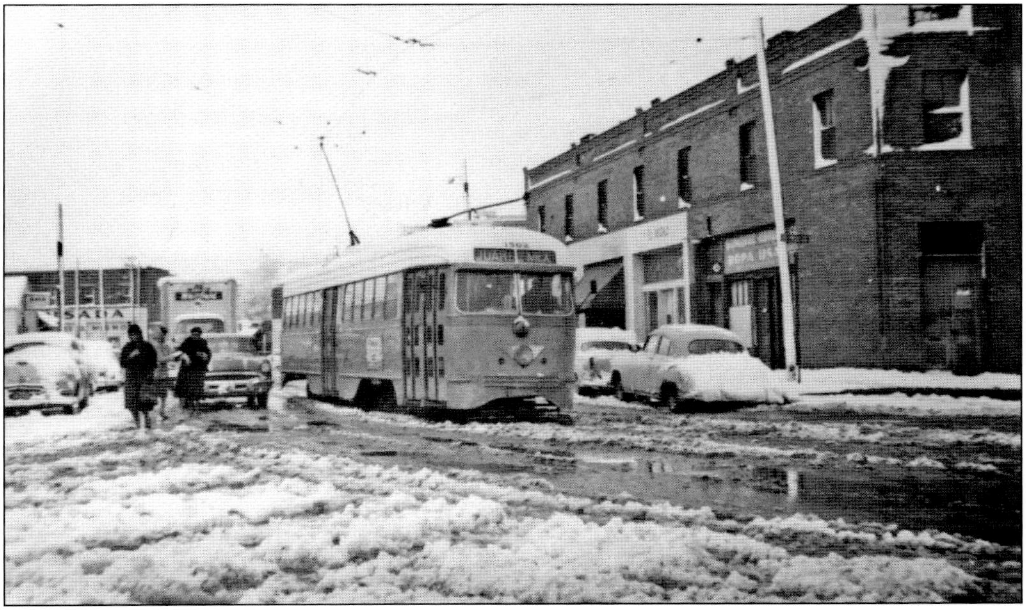

**A PCC in Wintery Weather.** In this 1950s image, No. 1502 is traversing Chamizal Court in the snow and slush. El Paso does have some cold weather from time to time, so the PCCs were equipped with under-seat electric heaters. The braking system consisted of air brakes, dynamic braking, and magnetic track brakes.

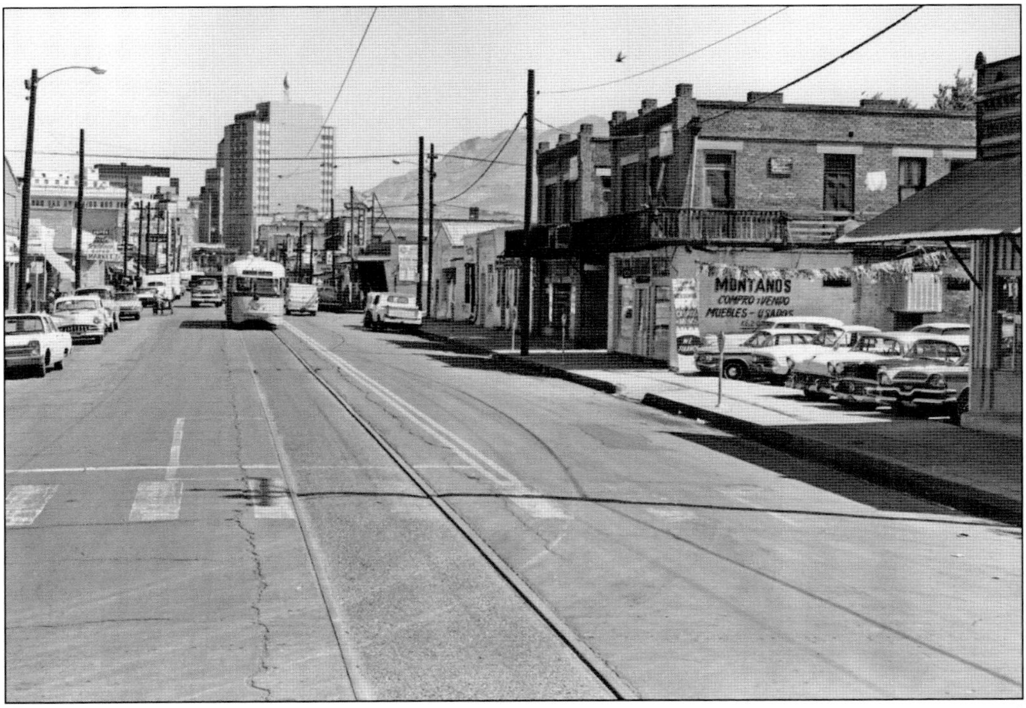


**South Stanton Street.** A PCC streetcar is southbound on Stanton Street toward the international bridge. In the background, the tall building is the "Blue Flame" building, the home of El Paso Natural Gas Company, built in 1954–1955. The flame sculpture on the top of the building changed colors according to predicted weather.

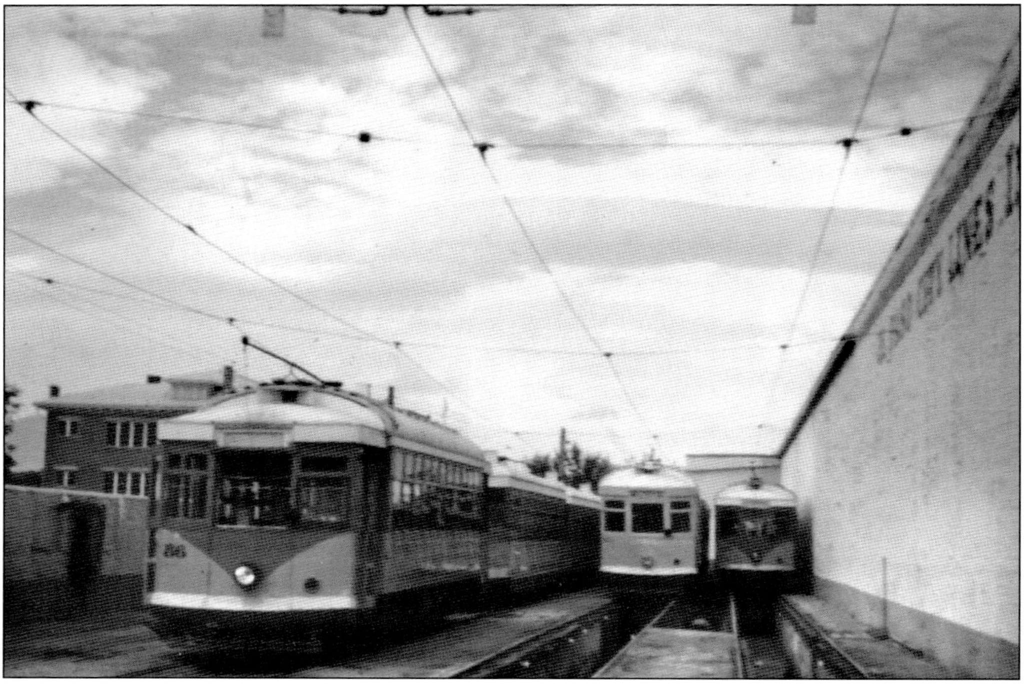

**An Outside View of the Carbarn.** Over the years, the carbarn and the outside storage tracks changed very little: witness the late-1940s view (above) and the 1960s view (below). In the earlier scene, track three has a Stone and Webster car No. 86, followed by two Fort Bliss 500-series cars. Track two is holding a Stone and Webster car painted and prepped for sale to Torreon, Mexico. In the later view, the four outside storage tracks are seen. The far left track was not used after about 1947, and the switch was removed at that time. The brick building (left) is the old San Jacinto School.

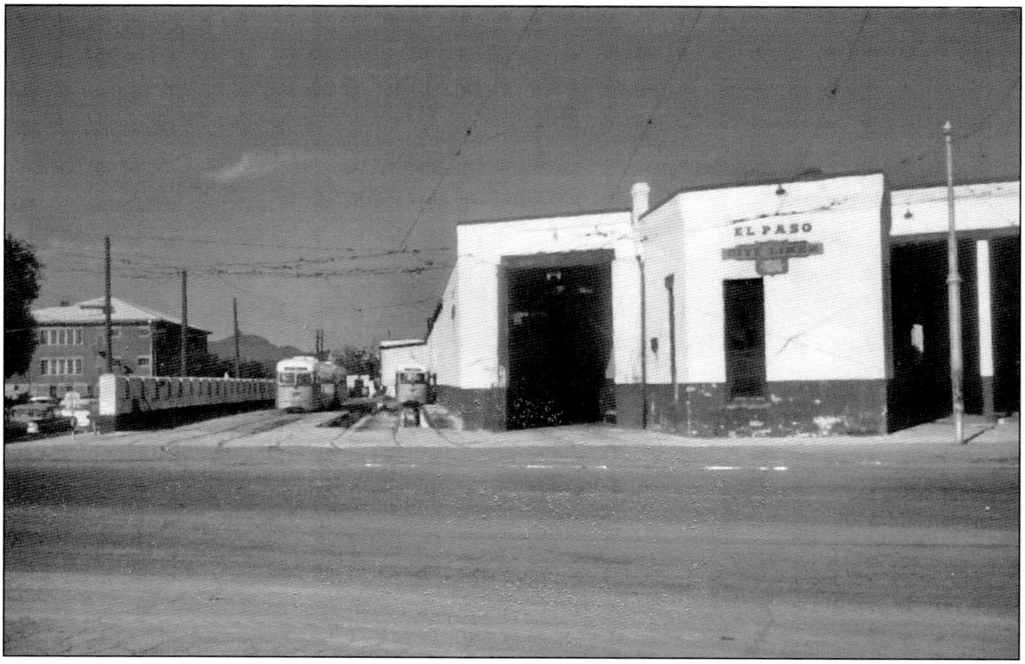

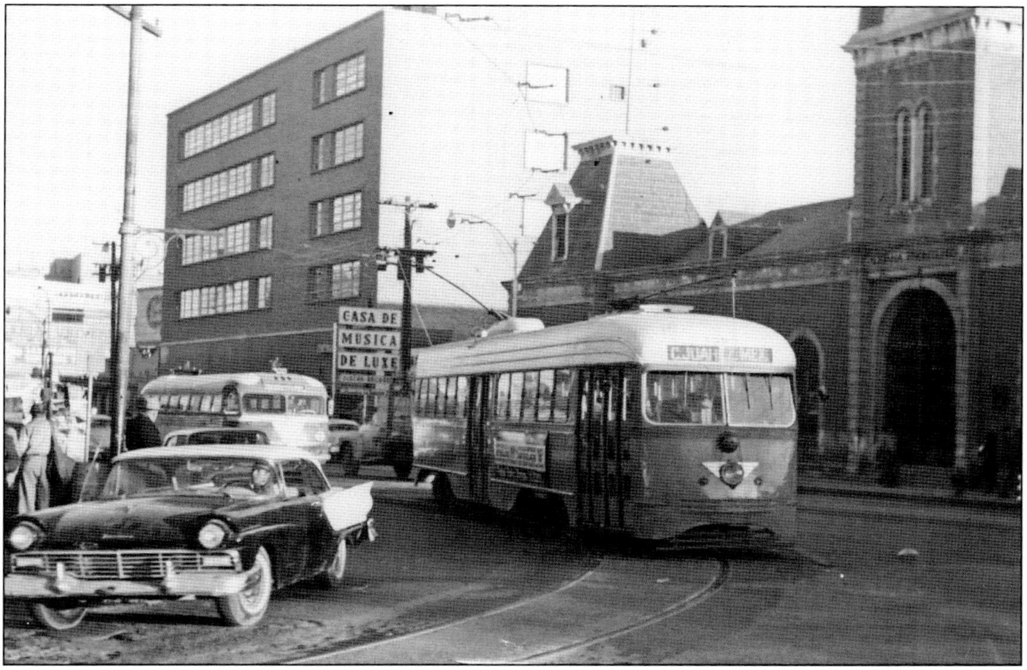


**No. 1505 Passing the Customs House.** No. 1505 is making a left turn following a 1957 Ford and is followed by a Flxible bus in this 1950s view. The old Juarez Customs House has been restored and is in use as a museum. This intersection at Avenida 16 de Septiembre and Avenida Juarez was busy most of the time.

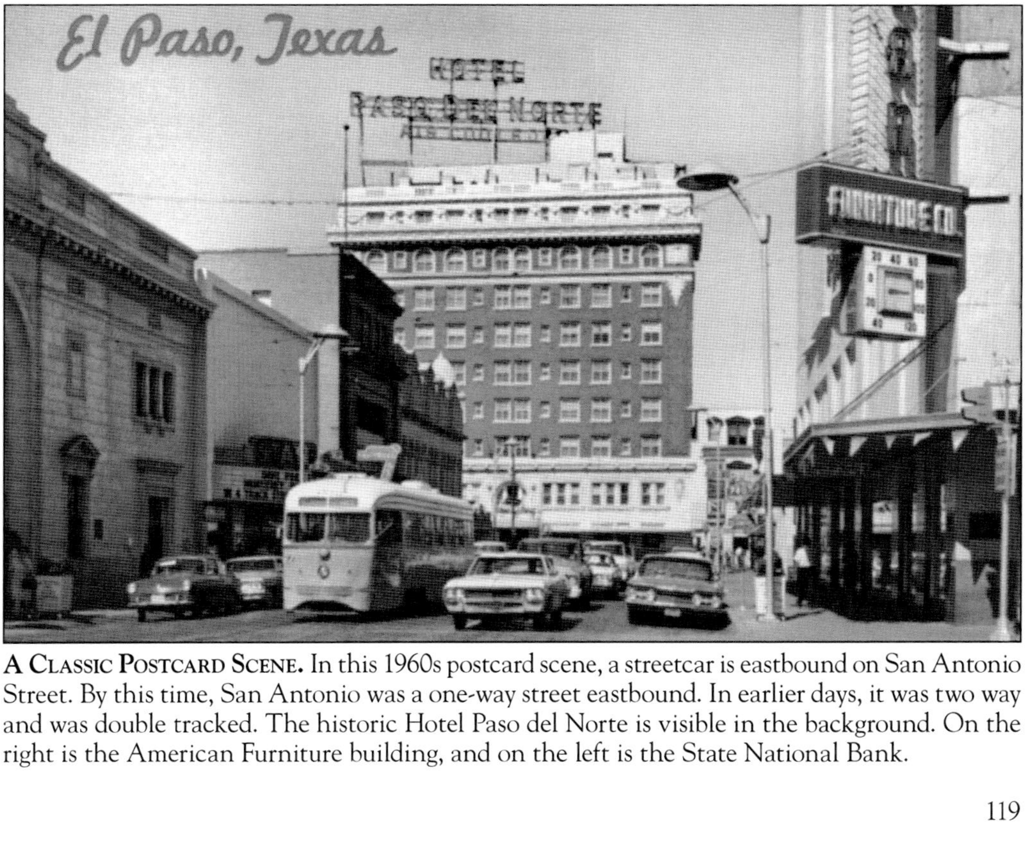


**A Classic Postcard Scene.** In this 1960s postcard scene, a streetcar is eastbound on San Antonio Street. By this time, San Antonio was a one-way street eastbound. In earlier days, it was two way and was double tracked. The historic Hotel Paso del Norte is visible in the background. On the right is the American Furniture building, and on the left is the State National Bank.

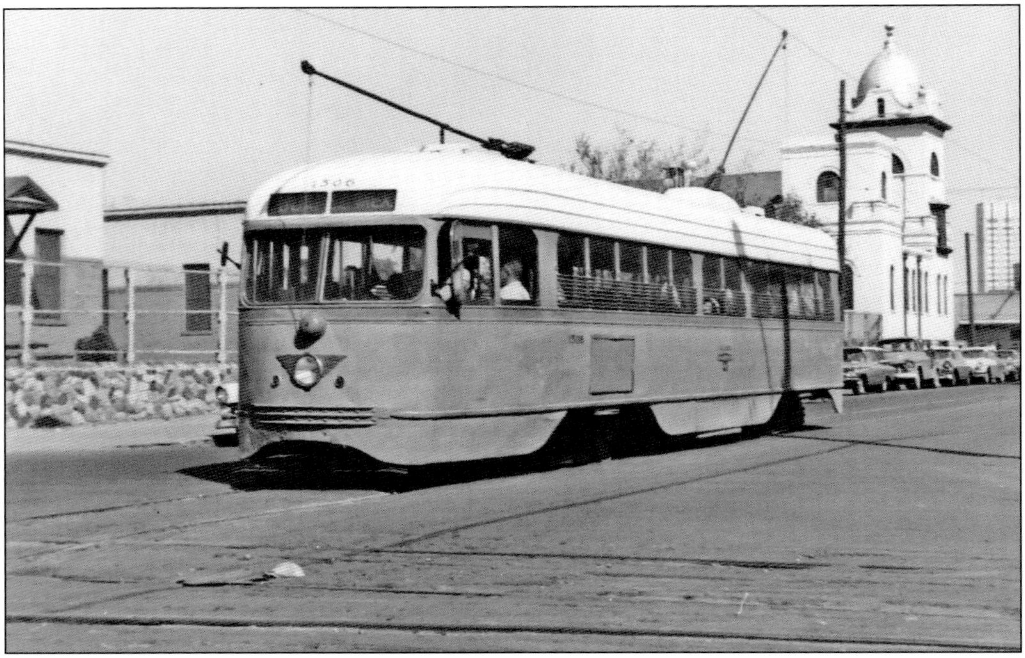

**No. 1506 Undecorated.** Here is No. 1506 without the beer advertisement treatment traveling south on Stanton Street on April 13, 1964. It is approaching a crossover with industrial tracks on Sixth Street, which allowed the Texas and Pacific Railroad to serve a number of industries in the area.

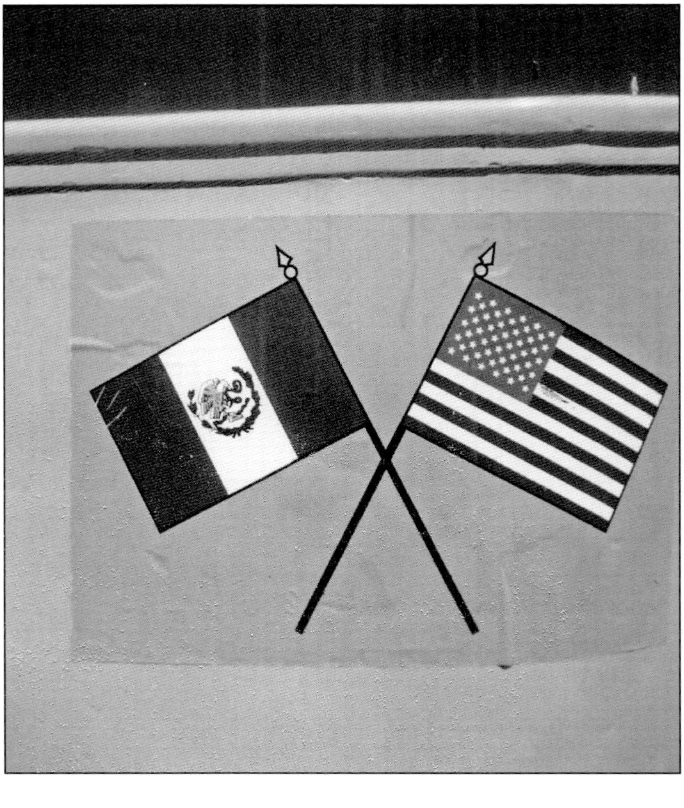

**Flag Insignias.** This graphic of crossed American and Mexican flags was added to the PCC cars in the late 1960s. Although the Juarez line was frequently advertised as the only international trolley line in the world, that was not factual. There was an international line in Europe, and here in Texas, Laredo operated an international line from 1890 to 1920.

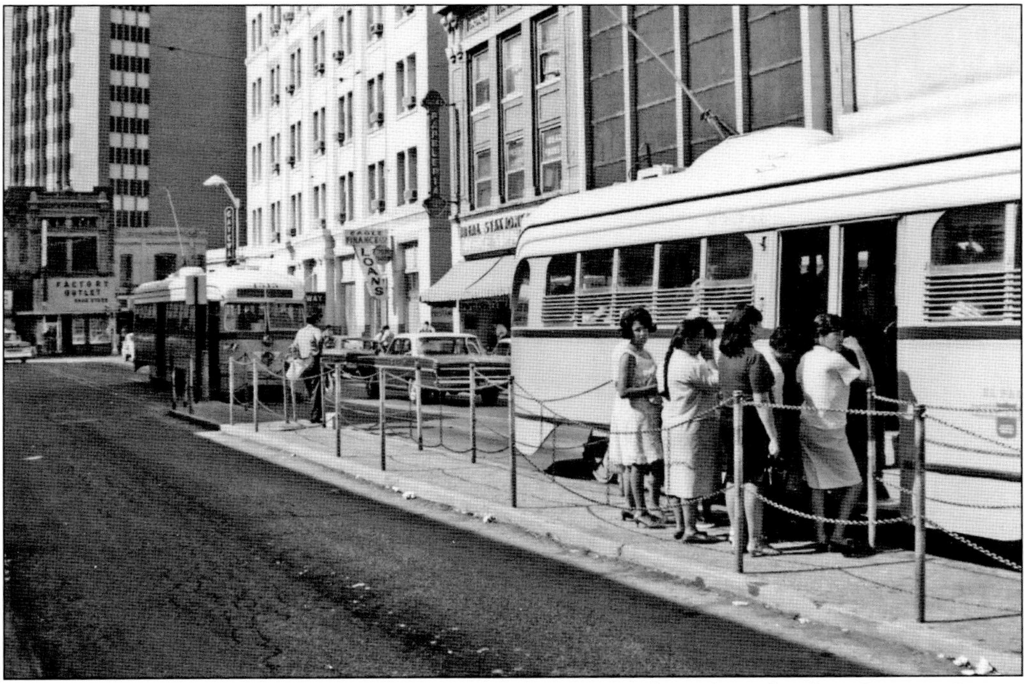


**DOMESTIC WORKERS AND SHOPPERS RETURNING HOME.** At the safety island on Stanton Street, women wait to board a crowded streetcar. If they are not able to get on, they might have to wait for the next car following close behind. The Juarez trolley was known to be a favorite mode of transportation for domestic workers who crossed the border to El Paso, then transferred to buses to their jobs in the suburbs.

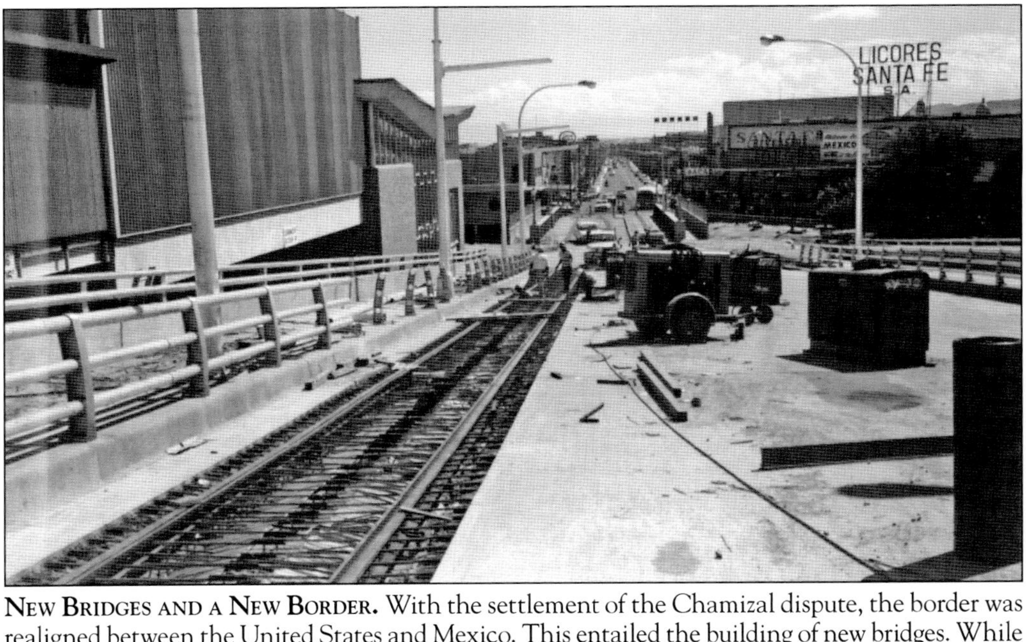


**NEW BRIDGES AND A NEW BORDER.** With the settlement of the Chamizal dispute, the border was realigned between the United States and Mexico. This entailed the building of new bridges. While the construction was going on, bus service was substituted for the streetcars. In this September 1967 photograph, tracks are being laid in one of the new bridges.

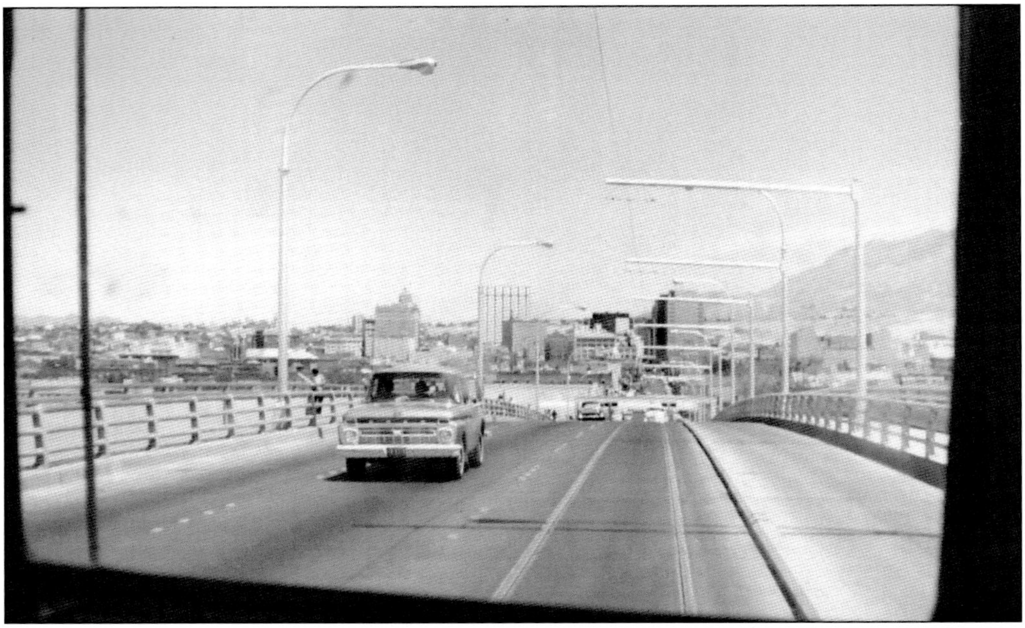

**The New Bridges Open.** In this image, the view is out the rear window of a PCC on the new Stanton Street Bridge with El Paso in the background. One aspect of the new bridges was the steep grades on each side. Operators encountered difficulty stopping when on a down slope and the tracks were wet. To rectify this, City Lines installed sanders on the cars.

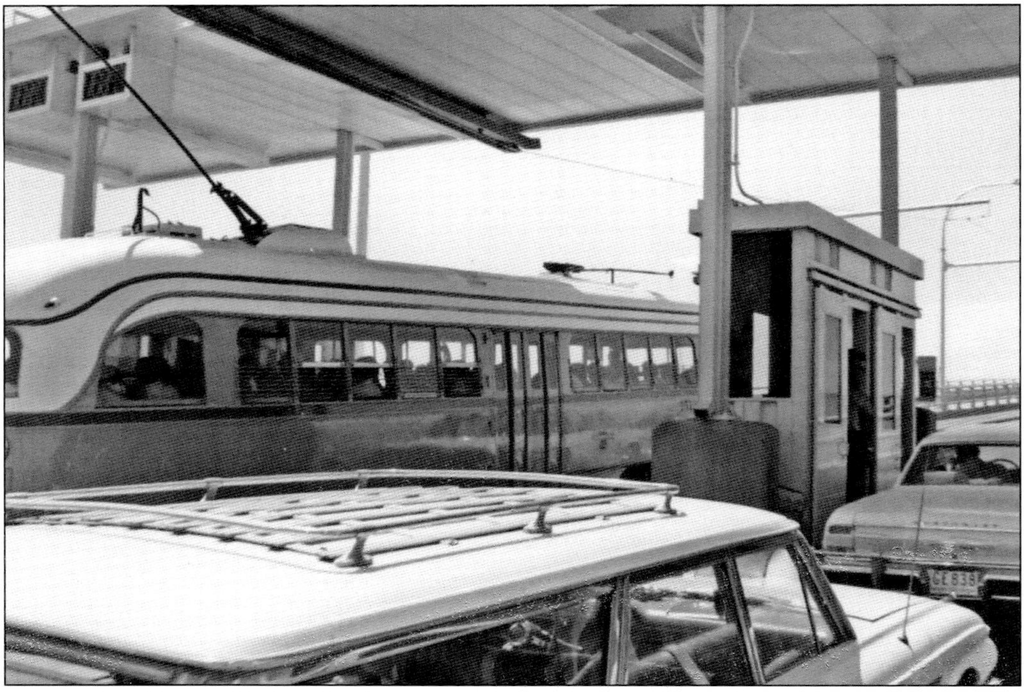

**At the Toll Booth.** El Paso City Lines continued to collect tolls on the bridges that were opened in 1967. The old Santa Fe Street Bridge became the new Paso del Norte Bridge and delivered traffic directly to El Paso Street rather than to Santa Fe Street. When the Stanton Street Bridge was rebuilt, it was known as the Good Neighbor Bridge.

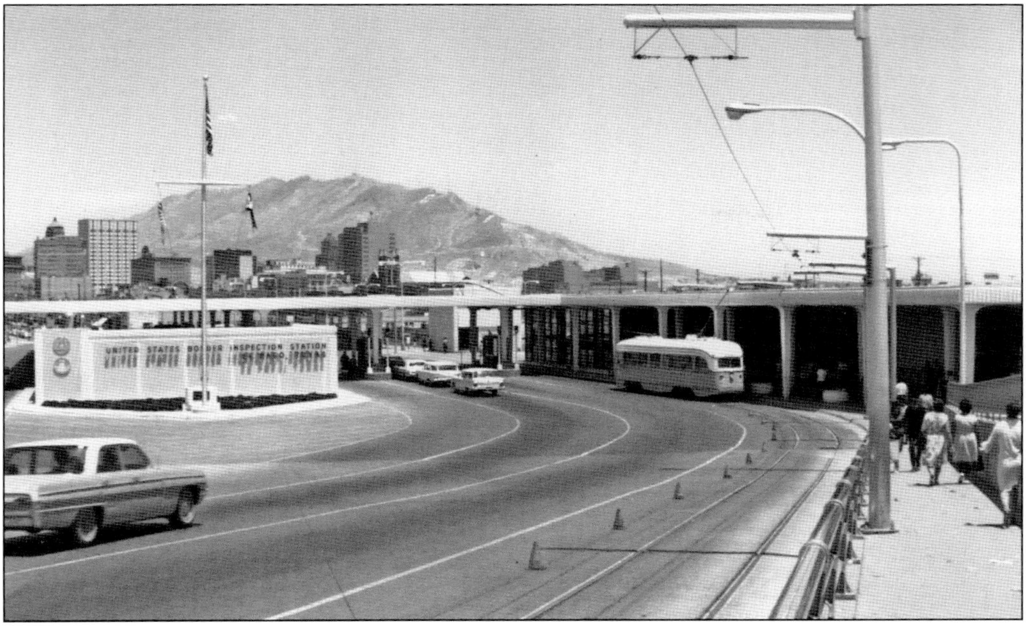

**Paso del Norte Bridge.** Completed in 1967 after the Chamizal agreement between the United States and Mexico resulted in a realignment of the border, the Paso del Norte Bridge continued to handle a large portion of the cross-border traffic. In this view, the Franklin Mountains and the city's skyline are in the background. The streetcar track hugs the right curb, and new catenary is in place.

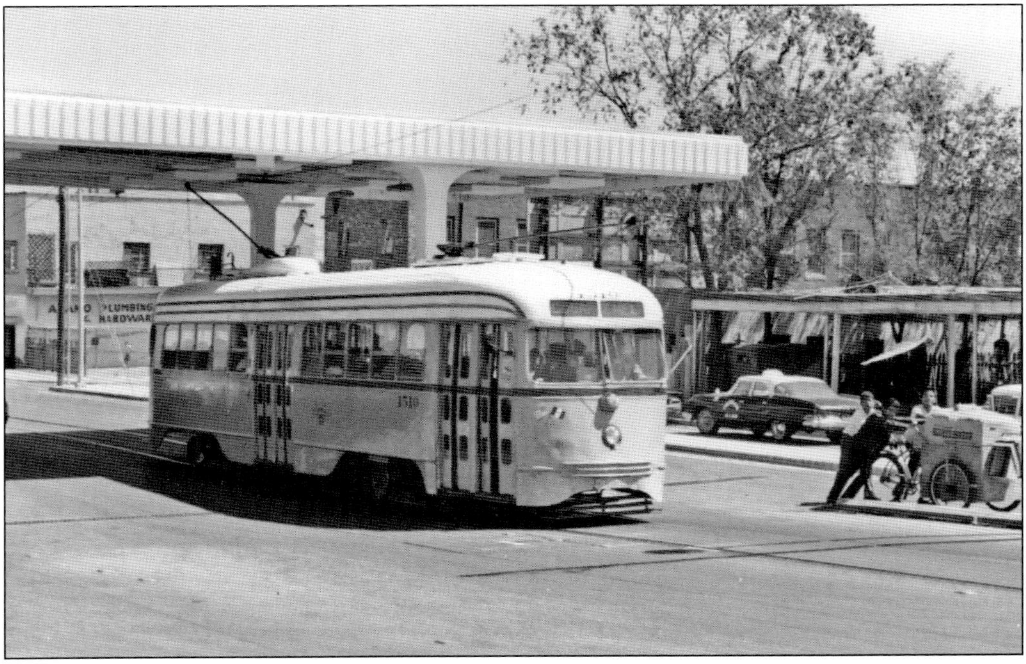

**Entering Mexico.** This El Paso PCC car is coming off the Stanton Street Bridge and entering Mexico on Lerdo Avenue. Pushcart vendors and taxicabs are visible, waiting for potential customers. Vendors did a respectable business, especially in the hot summer months selling *paletas*, ice cream on a stick. If there was traffic, the transaction could occur through the streetcar window.

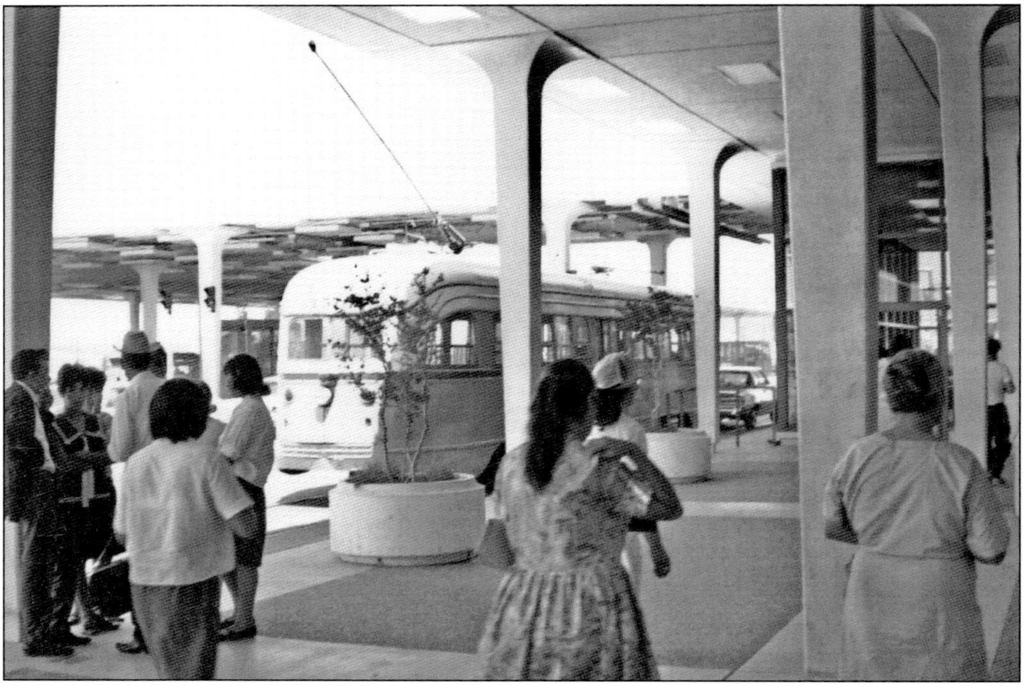

**Shade from the Sun.** With the construction of the new international bridges in the mid-1960s, architects were cognizant of the need for shade, both for vehicles and for pedestrians because the delay at customs could grow long at times. The streetcars had a dedicated lane when passing through customs.

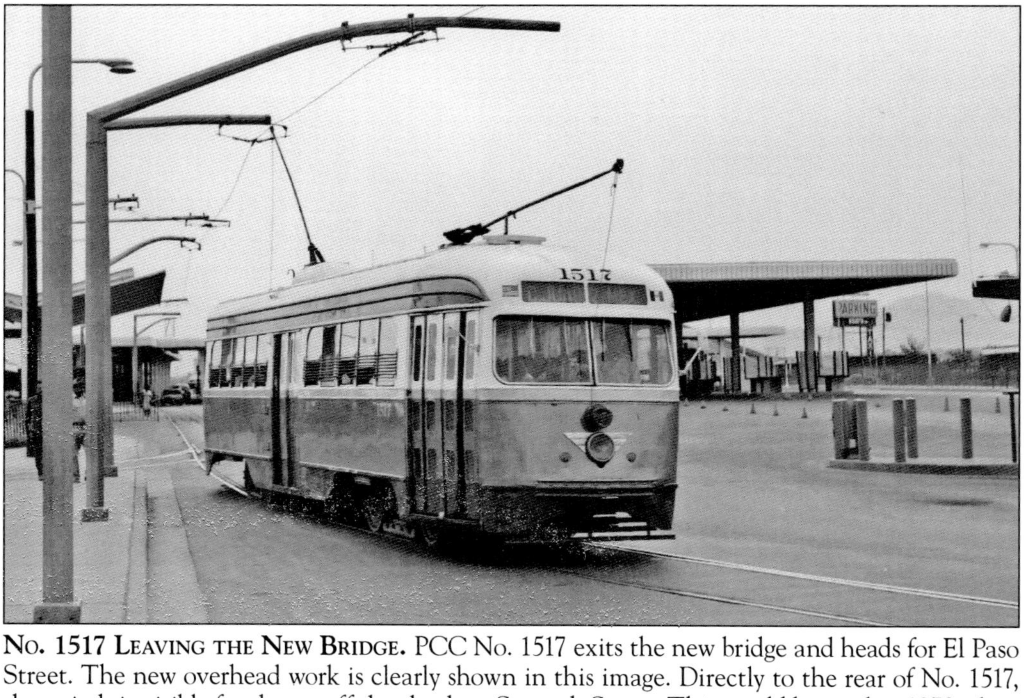


**No. 1517 Leaving the New Bridge.** PCC No. 1517 exits the new bridge and heads for El Paso Street. The new overhead work is clearly shown in this image. Directly to the rear of No. 1517, the switch is visible for the cutoff that leads to Seventh Street. This would be used in 1973 when Mexico blockaded the streetcars and this route was used to run on the United States side only.

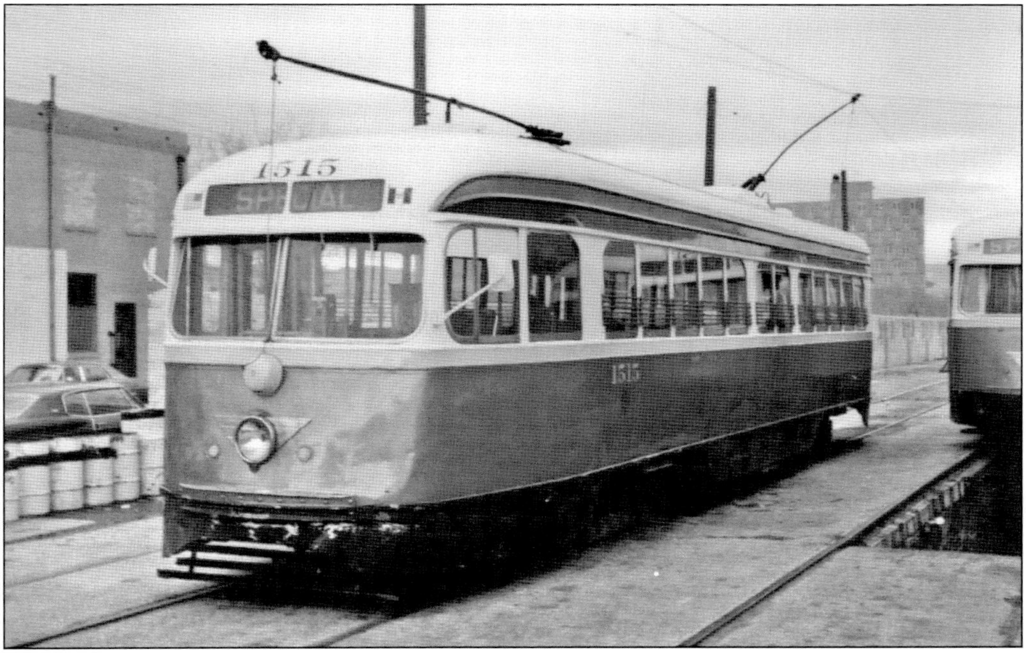


**No. 1515 in the Last Months.** The date is January 1974, and the City of EL Paso is making an effort to run the streetcars on the United States side only after Mexico blockaded the tracks. The city has repainted the cars in a garish green, red, and yellow. No. 1515 is seen here, complete with dents, four months before closure of the line.

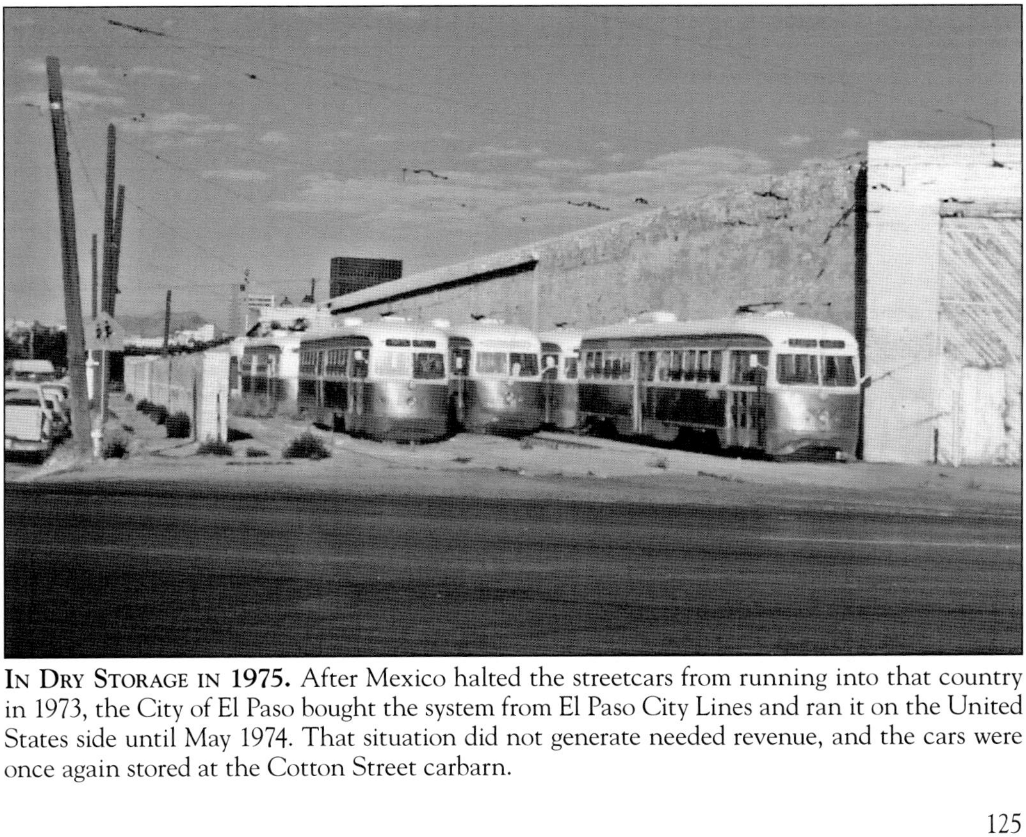

**In Dry Storage in 1975.** After Mexico halted the streetcars from running into that country in 1973, the City of El Paso bought the system from El Paso City Lines and ran it on the United States side until May 1974. That situation did not generate needed revenue, and the cars were once again stored at the Cotton Street carbarn.

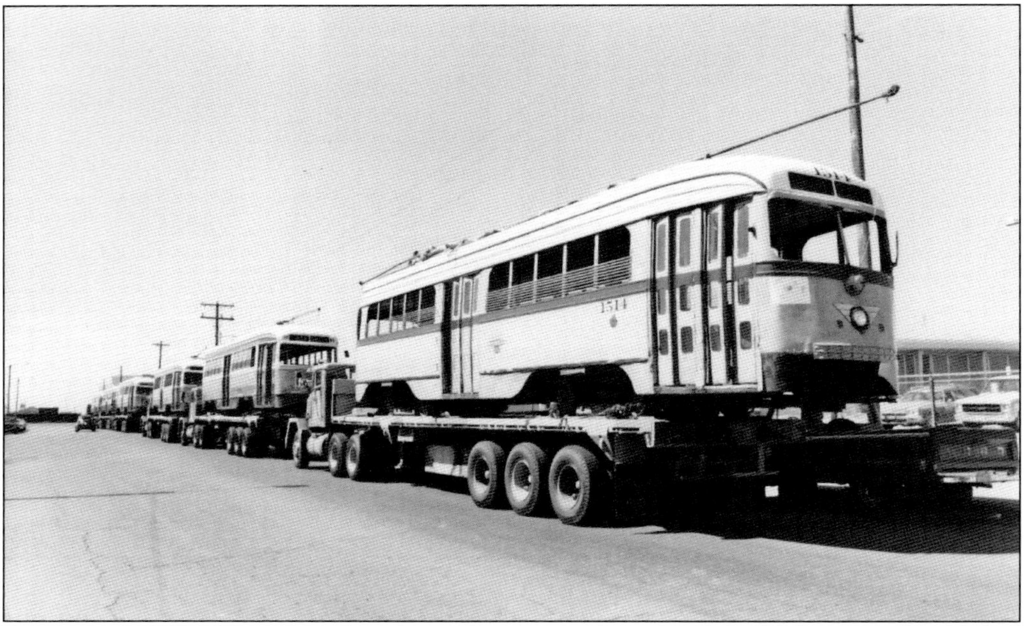

**Paso del Norte Streetcar Preservation Society.** The PDNSPS was formed in 1986 to save the remaining streetcars from the scrap heap. A number were scrapped, three were sold to private individuals, and nine were leased to the PDNSPS. Here the U.S. Army is donating trucks to move the cars to a new location.

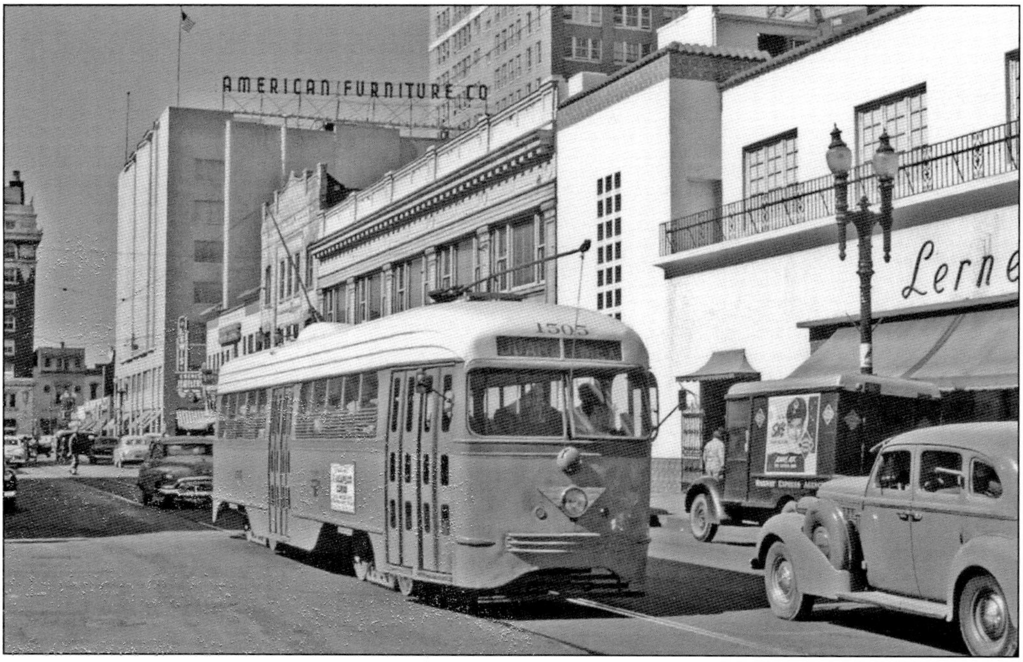


**A 1950s Nostalgia.** It seemed a more genteel time downtown. No. 1505 is on the Juarez loop on June 21, 1952. The Railway Express truck is delivering to Lerner's Dress shop. The 1930s Oldsmobile or Buick is still a daily driver in 1952, while a newer Buick follows No. 1505. In the background, American Furniture has given a modern facade to the old First National Bank Building. (Courtesy of John F. Bromley Collection.)

# Bibliography

Dawson, Ronald E. *Streetcars at the Pass: the Mule Cars of El Paso, the Interurban to Ysleta, and the El Paso Suburban Railway, Vol.1.* New York: iUniverse, 2003.

Leinbach, Henry J. Jr. *The El Paso Electric Company, Transportation Division, A Tentative History.* San Antonio, TX: Texas Division, Electric Railroaders Association, 1975.

Leonard, Edward A. *Rails at the Pass of the North.* El Paso, TX: Texas Western Press, 1981.

Lind, Allen R. *From Horsecars to Streamliners, An Illustrated History of the St. Louis Car Company.* Park Forest, IL: Transport History Press, 1978.

Price, Thomas J. *Standoff at the Border, A Failure of Microdiplomacy.* El Paso, TX: Texas Western Press, 1989.

Consistent with our mission to preserve history on a local level, this book was printed in South Carolina on American-made paper and manufactured entirely in the United States. Products carrying the accredited Forest Stewardship Council (FSC) label are printed on 100 percent FSC-certified paper.

MADE IN THE USA